Gendering the Crusades

Gendering the Crusades

edited by

SUSAN B. EDGINGTON

and

SARAH LAMBERT

COLUMBIA UNIVERSITY PRESS
NEW YORK

Columbia University Press
Publishers Since 1893
New York   Chichester, West Sussex

© The Contributors, 2002

First published in the United Kingdom in 2001
by University of Wales Press

Library of Congress CIP number: LCCN2001097194

ISBN 0–231–12598–4 (cloth)
ISBN 0–231–12599–2 (paper)

∞

Casebound editions of Columbia University Press books are printed on
permanent and durable acid-free paper.

Printed in Great Britain by MPG Books, Bodmin

c 10 9 8 7 6 5 4 3 2 1
p 10 9 8 7 6 5 4 3 2 1

Contents

Preface

JAMES M. POWELL

These essays introduce topics that have captured increasing interest among historians of the crusades in recent decades: gender as a factor in social relationships and the various roles played by women in the crusade movement. In the latter case, the immediate reaction may be to question women's involvement in and impact on what were chiefly military events. These essays quickly lay that view to rest. While several emphasize the military role of women, others reflect the way in which women were integrated into all aspects of the crusades, from preserving the home to participation in business and agriculture, from care of the sick and wounded to logistical support in wars, and from their role in religious life to active political leadership. Can anyone reading the *Alexiad* of Anna Comnena doubt that a person so well informed played a public role? If Philip of Flanders turned to the Abbess Hildegard of Bingen for advice regarding his participation in the crusade, he must have had considerable confidence in her. But what about the ordinary wives and daughters who accompanied fathers and brothers to the East? Their numbers were few. Many men who went to the East married local women, whether Christian or Muslim. Some women from the West became part of the new society that emerged in the twelfth century to ensure the gains made by the crusaders. Others returned to their homes, where they helped to mould local opinion. In both cases, their lives were an essential part of the crusades.

Despite the view that women have been left out of history, and that was largely true in the nineteenth and earlier twentieth centuries, the reality was and is that even the most traditional approach to history had to strain to ignore prominent female historical figures. Unfortunately, what most often resulted was a history of women who acted like their male counterparts. For that, we need only examine the fascinating if tortuous historiography on Joan of Arc, reflecting changing attitudes over the centuries but particularly in the last two hundred years. This approach provided inspiration to young women of the period. The American feminist movement's insight into these issues is found in a volume by Celestia Bloss entitled *Heroines of the Crusades*. Written in the cradle of American feminism, in Auburn, New York, in the 1850s, by a teacher in a women's seminary, this book tries to present 'the true philosophy of female heroism'.[1] Recent research has moved beyond this view, but there are inevitable echoes. Certainly there are examples of women fighting as well as of women in a leading political and military role. The queens of Jerusalem were key political figures, but their political role was tied not merely to their concern for the realm but also for their husbands and their heirs.[2] Putting the matter in terms that better reflect its complexity, the male–female dichotomy alone cannot adequately encompass crusader society.

In the past, too much emphasis has been put on the limitations that confronted women, but that has changed. Now, as we see here, there is more emphasis on what women did. After all, if we are going to present a complete picture of medieval society, we must have a comprehensive picture of the roles that women played.[3] There is no doubt that the crusades tested the limits. Both men and women found themselves in places and relationships very different from those they faced in the West. Our problem is not merely to locate women in the many aspects of crusade history, but to explore the meanings of the relationships revealed in these roles.[4] We should not, for example, be surprised if some contemporaries objected to a military role for women, but we need to get beyond our own time-bound analyses to look more closely at the different perspectives reflected in medieval sources. They no more speak with one voice than do those of our own time, but they are fewer and they are harder to understand. A society that regards certain functions as proper to a particular class has a different view of the role of women than one where gender and class play equal roles. Perhaps the relationship of Philip of Flanders to Hildegard of Bingen or James of Vitry to the mystic, Mary of Oignies, with their implied dependency of male on female offer insights that need to be applied elsewhere in our study of the crusades. Have we fully understood the crusaders' wives? What about the impact of women on decision-making?

The essays printed here are important because they raise questions like these. But they go further. They also show how gender intruded on relations between Latins and Easterners. Cultural differences were given a gender-based interpretation. They alter the terms of research in ways that help us to view human relationships in a broader framework. They give voice to ideas about which we have seldom thought before and provide readers with a further milestone in the study of the history of the crusades.

NOTES

[1] Celestia Angenette Bloss, *Heroines of the Crusades* (Auburn, NY, 1853), 457.

[2] Bernard Hamilton, 'Women in the Crusader States: the Queens of Jerusalem (1100–1190)', in Derek Baker (ed.), *Medieval Women* (Oxford, 1978), 143–74.

[3] James M. Powell, 'The role of women in the Fifth Crusade', in *Horns*, 294–301.

[4] Of course this process is already well under way. See, for example, Sylvia Schein, 'Bridget of Sweden, Margery Kempe, and women's Jerusalem pilgrimages in the Middle Ages', *Mediterranean History Review* 14 (1999), 44–58.

Contributors

MATTHEW BENNETT is a Senior Lecturer at The Royal Military Academy, Sandhurst. He is the co-author of the *Cambridge Atlas of Medieval Warfare* (1996) and a score of scholarly articles on the crusades and chivalric culture. These include: 'Military masculinity in England and Northern France *c*.1050–1225', in D. M. Hadley (ed.), *Masculinity in Medieval Europe* (London, 1999).

KEREN CASPI-REISFELD is a graduate student of the Land of Israel and Computer Science departments at Bar-Ilan University, Israel. She is working on a thesis entitled 'Women warriors during the crusades and the Latin Kingdom of Jerusalem'.

SUSAN B. EDGINGTON, formerly Senior Lecturer at Huntingdonshire Regional College, teaches in further and higher education and works on aspects of the earlier crusades and crusader medicine. Her major project, an edition and English translation of the *Historia* of Albert of Aachen, is forthcoming with Oxford Medieval Texts.

MICHAEL R. EVANS took his BA and MA at Reading University. His Ph.D., 'The crusades and society in the English Midlands *c*.1160–1307', was completed at Nottingham in 1997. He is currently a lecturer at Canterbury Christ Church University College and is researching attitudes to royal death in medieval England, the Robin Hood legend and gender in crusade chronicles.

PETER FRANKOPAN was an undergraduate at Jesus College, Cambridge, where he was Schiff Foundation Scholar. He was Senior Scholar at Corpus Christi College, Oxford, where he wrote his doctoral thesis on the political history of the Mediterranean, Adriatic and the Aegean in the eleventh and twelfth centuries. He is Senior Research Fellow at Worcester College, Oxford.

YVONNE FRIEDMAN is Senior Lecturer in the Department of History and the Martin Zsusz Department of Land of Israel Studies, Bar-Ilan University, Israel. Her chapter is part of a larger research project to be published by E. J. Brill, *Encounter between Enemies: Captivity and Ransom in the Latin Kingdom of Jerusalem.*

NATASHA R. HODGSON is currently a graduate teaching assistant and Ph.D. student at the University of Hull. She is working on a Ph.D. thesis entitled 'Perceptions of women in crusader history'. This examines the way in which women are portrayed in the sources for the crusades in terms of their familial roles, as mothers, wives and daughters.

SARAH LAMBERT is a lecturer at Goldsmiths College, London University. She has published articles on the queens of Jerusalem, and on women in the crusade literature. She is currently working on the life of a female crusader, and a book on gender and politics in the Latin kingdom of Jerusalem.

HELEN J. NICHOLSON is Senior Lecturer in History at Cardiff University. Her published books include: *Templars, Hospitallers and Teutonic Knights: Images of the Military Orders, 1128–1201* (Leicester, 1993); *Chronicle of the Third Crusade: A Translation of the Itinerarium Peregrinorum et Gesta Regis Ricardi* (Aldershot, 1997); and *Love, War and the Grail: Templars, Hospitallers and Teutonic Knights in Medieval Epic and Romance, 1150–1500* (Leiden, 2000). She has also published on women in the Third Crusade and women in the Military Orders.

CONSTANCE M. ROUSSEAU is Professor of History at Providence College, Providence, RI, USA. She is the author of several articles on Pope Innocent III, which include 'The spousal relationship: marital society and sexuality in the letters of Pope Innocent III', *Mediaeval Studies* (1994); 'Gender difference and indifference in the writings of Pope Innocent III', *Studies in Church History* (1998); 'A papal matchmaker: principle and pragmatism during Innocent III's pontificate', *Journal of Medieval History* (1998); 'Pregnant with meaning: Pope Innocent III's construction of motherhood', in *Pope Innocent III and his World* (Aldershot, 1999); 'Pater Urbis et Orbis: Innocent III and his perspectives on fatherhood', *Archivum Historiae Pontificiae* (1999). She is also co-editor with Joel Rosenthal of *Women, Marriage and Family in Medieval Christendom: Essays in*

Memory of Michael M. Sheehan, C.S.B. (Kalamazoo, 1998). She is currently working on a project concerning papal perspectives on gender (1050 to 1300).

SYLVIA SCHEIN is a Senior Lecturer in the Department of General History at the University of Haifa. Her fields of research are the crusades, the Latin Kingdom of Jerusalem and medieval women. Among her publications are: *Fideles Crucis: The Papacy, the West and the Recovery of the Holy Land 1274–1314* (Oxford, 1991); *Cross Cultural Convergences in the Crusader Period: Essays Presented to Aryeh Grabois*, ed. with Michael Goodich and Sophia Menache (New York, 1995); and *Gateway to the Heavenly City: Crusader Jerusalem and the Catholic West, 1099–1187* (Aldershot, 2002).

ELIZABETH SIBERRY, independent scholar, is author of *Criticism of Crusading, 1095–1274* (Oxford, 1985), *The New Crusaders: Images of the Crusades in the Nineteenth and Early Twentieth Centuries* (Aldershot, 2000) and numerous articles.

MIRIAM RITA TESSERA is currently working on her Ph.D. thesis entitled 'The papacy and the Latin kingdom of Jerusalem during the twelfth century' at the Università Cattolica del Sacro Cuore, Milan, Italy. She has published several articles about William of Tyre.

Abbreviations

AHR	*American Historical Review*
AOL	*Archives de l'Orient Latin*
ASS	*Acta Sanctorum quotquot toto urbe coluntur: vel a catholicis scriptoris celebrantur quae ex latinis et greacis, aliarumque gentium antiquis monumentis,* ed. Johannies Bollandus and Godefridus Henschenius, 2nd edn., ed. Joane Carnandet, 70 vols. and supplement (Brussels, Paris and Rome, 1863–75).
Autour	*Autour de la Première Croisade: Actes du colloque de la Society for the Study of the Crusades and the Latin East Clermont-Ferrand, 22–25 juin 1995,* ed. Michel Balard (Paris, 1996).
BIHR	*Bulletin of the Institute of Historical Research*
Cart Hosp	*Cartulaire général de l'Ordre des Hospitaliers de Saint-Jean de Jérusalem, 1100–1310,* ed. J. Delaville Le Roulx (4 vols., Paris, 1884–1906).
CCCM	Corpus Christianorum. Continuatio Mediaevalis
CS	*Crusade and Settlement: Papers read at the First Conference of the Society for the Study of the Crusades and the Latin East and Presented to R. C. Smail,* ed. Peter W. Edbury (Cardiff, 1985).
Crusades Sources	*The Crusades and their Sources: Essays Presented to Bernard Hamilton,* ed. John France and William G. Zajac (Aldershot, 1998).
DNB	*Dictionary of National Biography*
EHR	*English Historical Review*
Gesta regis Henrici	*Benedicti abbatis Gesta regis Henrici II,* ed. W. Stubbs, RS 49, I–II.
Hildegardis Epistolarium	*Hildegardis Bingensis Epistolarium, Pars prima I–XC,* ed. L. van Acker, CCCM 91; *Pars secunda XCL–CCLR,* CCCM 91A.

Hildegardis Opera	*S. Hildegardis abbatissae Epistolae*, in idem, *Opera omnia*, PL 197, 145–382.
Horns	*Proceedings of the Second Conference of the Society for the Study of the Crusades and the Latin East*, ed. B. Z. Kedar (Jerusalem, 1992).
JEH	*Journal of Ecclesiastical History*
JMH	*Journal of Medieval History*
LDO	*Hildegardis Liber divinorum operum*, ed. A. Derolez and P. Dronke, CCCM 92.
LVM	*Hildegardis Liber vitae meritorum*, ed. A. Carlevaris, CCCM 90.
Mansi, *Concilia*	G. D. Mansi, *Sacrorum conciliorum nova et amplissima collectio* (Venice, 1903).
MGH	Monumenta Germaniae Historica
Outremer	B. Z. Kedar, H. E. Mayer and R. C. Smail (eds.), *Studies in the History of the Crusading Kingdom of Jerusalem presented to Joshua Prawer* (Jerusalem, 1982).
PL	*Patrologia Latina*
PPTS	Palestine Pilgrims' Text Society Library
RHC	*Recueil des Historiens des Croisades,* ed. Academie des Inscriptions et Belles Lettres (Paris, 1841–1906)
RHC Lois	*RHC Lois: Les Assises de Jerusalem* (2 vols., Paris, 1841–3).
RHC Oc	*RHC Historiens Occidenteaux* (5 vols., Paris, 1844–95).
RHC Or	*RHC Historiens Orientaux* (5 vols., Paris, 1872–1906).
RHGF	*Recueil des historiens de Gaul et de la France*
ROL	*Revue de l'Orient Latin*
RRH	Reinhold Röhricht (comp.), *Regesta regni hierosolymitani* (Innsbruck, 1894).
RRH Add	Reinhold Röhricht (comp.), *Additamentum* (Innsbruck, 1904).
RS	Rolls Series
Scivias	*Hildegardis Scivias*, ed. A. Führkötter, coll. A. Carlevaris, CCCM 43–43A.
TRHS	*Transactions of the Royal Historical Society*
WT	William of Tyre, *Chronicon*, ed. Robert B. C. Huygens, CCCM 63–63A (Turnhout, 1986).

1

Crusading or Spinning

SARAH LAMBERT

Gender is one of the primary ideas around which medieval society was both structured and imagined, along with other similarly man-made concepts such as status, religion and nationality. This structuring of society according to gender is not a simple question of male and female, of biologically determined natures, but rather a complex system of ideas, values and meanings. The creation of this pair of categories is comparable to the system of 'orders' in which many medieval writers imagined their society, by means of which the intricate and involved lives of medieval peoples were given cultural meaning through the creation of a simplistic triad – those who work, fight and pray.[1]

The literature of the crusades participates in this ordering of its world. For example, in terms of status, its writers engage with the development of the idea of the 'knight' from a merely military description to a highly charged socio-political role.[2] Similarly, by looking at their representations of the 'poor', it becomes clear that this designation is not simply concerned with wealth or even the possession of ready cash, but carries a range of social and religious meanings.[3] This literature is also ordered around concepts of age, especially in the narration of the 'Children's Crusade', a tale which rapidly gained iconic status even though the actual age of the participants is highly debatable.[4] It is ordered in terms of nationality, when the narrative equates 'Franci' with 'Christiani' or makes a dramatic and literary point of listing the many 'nations' comprising each army.[5]

So, in the same way, the narrative is ordered in terms of gender. It is 'gendered' in that its writers use ideas and images which form part of that cultural system to give meaning to the bare structure of events. This is not an anachronistic reading of the texts. As Duby

pointed out, while medieval writers and philosophers sometimes
ignored or concealed the twofold division of gender in their tripartite systems, at other times they directly addressed exactly this issue.[6]
In addition, many of the great scholastic writers of the high Middle
Ages used the language of gender in a deliberately symbolic way to
express ideas and concepts about their society and culture.[7] So we
can expect that such usages in the literature of the crusades were
conscious and recognizable.

The crusade narratives were written within a literary tradition
which tended deliberately to universalize the male experience – to
masculinize the historical world. No one will need reminding of how
sparse are the direct references to women in the vast bulk of
medieval literature. And when women do appear in the texts the references are for the most part episodic and fragmentary. But such a
universalizing tendency, were it to be completely successful, would
embody the seeds of its own failure. If the 'second' gender were to
become completely invisible in the narrative, then the symbolic and
social meanings of masculinity would be neutralized. There cannot
be a singular gender. There can be no idea of male without its opposition in female, no white without black. Consequently we need as
readers to be aware that when medieval writers referred to gender, or
included references to women, they were making a conscious choice
to do so, born out of a desire to reflect the structures of their society. Even when using the apparently simplifying techniques of
parataxis, like the anonymous author of the *Gesta Francorum*,
authors chose what to write, and what to include, with great care.
Each writer created a literary work, choosing elements out of a literal or figurative library of verbal accounts, written models and
traditions, in an ordered way. Their omissions and inclusions can be
used to discover patterns of thought in these writers. I want to look
in this chapter at some of the choices they made, to ask why they
made them, and possibly even to suggest some answers.

A well-known example from outside the area of crusade literature
can be found in the Bayeux Tapestry. Only a handful of female figures appear in this vivid depiction of the events leading up to the
coronation of William I in England. Modern historians have
demonstrated through a close reading of the records how important
women were in this political process, yet they were largely ignored in
this prestigious source.[8] Of those who do appear, one is almost certainly Emma, wife of Canute. She seems to be a figure for sexuality,

and the harm done by the sexually active woman's involvement in politics. Another, a picture of a woman fleeing from a burning house, is used in a symbolic way to indicate domesticity, and the harm done to civilians in warfare. These two elements are in fact common in medieval narratives where women do appear.[9]

Women, often unnamed and unidentified, but evidently not unnoticed, appear now and again in almost all the crusade narratives. My first example is one particularly striking such appearance, taken from an Anglo-Norman Latin account of the response to preaching for the Third Crusade: _ Shaming one another_

> A great many men sent each other wool and distaff, hinting that if anyone failed to join this military undertaking, they were fit only for women's work. Brides urged their husbands and mothers incited their sons to go; their only sorrow being that they were not able to set out with them, because of the fragility of their sex.[10]

This passage is rich in symbolic meanings of all kinds. It reminds the reader of Christ's injunction to his followers that his service will divide families (Matthew 19: 29), and it calls on the classical tag of 'fragilitas sexus' – the weakness of mind and body which supposedly removes women from the active, political, historical sphere.[11] To illustrate his point, the writer uses a very powerful symbol: the distaff. In this passage the men themselves are pictured using this symbol, this representation of a gendered society, to reinforce social organization – to ensure appropriate action, constrained according to a gendered system. The men present non-crusaders with distaffs to imply accusations of inappropriate, womanly conduct, and to represent the crusade as a specifically masculine activity. Mothers and wives apparently concur in this representation, acknowledging their own exclusion, which is justified by the attribution of 'fragilitas'. They also appear to be encouraging men's correctly gendered behaviour. Thus they were able to demonstrate their enthusiastic support for the cause of crusading whilst not crossing prescribed gender boundaries.

Other historians have noticed this passage, and compared it to the practice apparently common during the First World War, of women presenting white feathers to men who did not join the military. However, this comparison is not totally applicable. A white feather might represent cowardice, and could spur the receiver into acts of courage, but courage is merely one aspect of the characteristic 'man', as constructed in this gender system. On the other hand, the distaff is a quintessentially female-ordered object, and makes it clear that the writer has in mind gender, not one of its functions such as valour or skill. The Latin *colus*, or *co(n)lucula*, giving the Old French *quenouille*, designates not just a tool of the cloth trade, but a whole baggage of female symbolism. It was even used in legal texts to define the appropriate way for property to be transmitted through the female line; sisters divided their inheritance 'par conoile'.[12] Spinning was still in the twelfth century a characteristically female activity, even at a time when weaving was becoming more 'industrialized' and performed by a largely male workforce in newly urban settings.[13] The action of spinning continued to have this female connotation into modern times, long after it ceased to be a commonplace female activity, as can be seen by the development in English of the word 'spinster'.

So when the author of the *Itinerarium Peregrinorum* told this touching farewell story, he was trying to establish the crusade as a masculine event – gendering his story. This was not merely representative story-telling; it was setting out the historical stage as male space. This point can be further emphasized by considering the next passage in the text: 'A great number [of men] went from cloister to camp, threw off their cowls, donned mail shirts and became knights of Christ in a new service, replacing alms with arms.'[14] In this passage we can see traditionally prescribed roles being overturned, with monks being stirred by the preaching to abandon their calling and join the crusade. They could not be expected to have the usual masculine attributes of military skill and strength, and indeed the participation of monks in crusades was strongly discouraged by most church authorities because such a journey contradicted the important monastic principle of stability. However, in the view of this author, monks were able to throw off their habits and set out on the journey to Jerusalem without incurring any criticism. The approval with which the author described these monkish crusaders seems to reinforce the previous point – that the crusade was being designated as *male* space, and not simply being reserved for those with military skills. These monks could successfully contest the rules of their chosen lifestyle in the crisis caused by the fall of Jerusalem, whereas the women were contained by the norms of the gender system. On the other hand, women's symbolic possibilities were expanded in this narrative. In the wake of their professed weakness, the women's expressed willingness to be abandoned by husbands and sons reveals a strength of character and an attachment to a virtuous cause which is not generally associated with women *en masse* in medieval texts. It is relatively rare to find women represented collectively as examples of such staunch virtue in medieval narratives. Indeed, later in the same text, this author dismisses women collectively as fickle and weak-minded.[15]

The 'women's farewell' story, in one form or another, appears in a great number of crusade narratives. Brundage has suggested that the rapidity with which this image became popular in accounts of the First Crusade actually reflected Pope Urban's intention that women should not accompany the crusaders in 1095.[16] However, such a conclusion ignores both the retrospective nature of all reports of the pope's sermon at Clermont, and the extent to which crusade preaching deliberately used the existing idea of pilgrimage. The 'male space' of the crusade can be effectively contrasted with contemporary views on more peaceful pilgrimages. It is well established that women formed a substantial portion of the crowds of pilgrims to various European shrines. Despite occasional criticism, there was no wholesale attempt to exclude women from the practice or the image of pilgrimage. Indeed, the relics of some saints were regularly exhibited outside monastic churches, which women were traditionally not allowed to enter.[17] Some early writers described the particular dangers posed for women by long-distance travel, but for the most part their strictures were directed at nuns rather than lay women. Pilgrimage remained open to, and popular with, both men and women throughout the Middle Ages. Since crusade preaching so frequently used the language and imagery of other pilgrimages, it is not surprising that many women considered this new kind of journey to be similarly open to them. The literary reflection of the crusade in the chronicles was quite different, however, and the journey was repeatedly constructed in specifically male terms.

Nevertheless, this simple polar division between male and female can support many different symbolic meanings and it is for the reader to attempt to discover which meanings were being invoked by the use of gendered language in any given context. To demonstrate this, the *Itinerarium* author's use of the word *fragilitas* to account for the non-participation of these women can be usefully explored. This tag from the legal traditions of antiquity was frequently used in medieval texts as a shorthand way of justifying some gendered imbalance in theory or practice, and it appears here to invoke the symbolic gendering of the crusade. However, in narratives of the Baltic crusades, this concept of womanly weakness, and its extraordinary reversal, was used in a quite different way. In this context, it appears on several occasions to symbolize God's power in allowing the crusaders to accomplish otherwise impossible tasks. For example, in the chronicle of Peter von Dusberg, circa 1326: 'The women, laying aside feminine adornment, put on a male frame of mind, girded swords upon the thigh, and ascended the battlements, comporting themselves so manfully (*viriliter*) for their defence, that nowhere was the weakness of their sex apparent.'[18]

Women appeared repeatedly in these chronicles, fighting against the pagans, and winning, to demonstrate that God had apparently turned their physical weakness to strength through their faith. In a study of these narratives, Mazieka has concluded that these writers are using a biblical model, perhaps taken from the story of Judith, after her victorious return from the murder of Holofernes (Judith 15: 11):

> quia fecisti viriliter et confortatum est cor tuum eo quod castitatem amaveris et post virum tuum alterum non scieris ideo et manus Domini confortavit te et ideo eris benedicta in aeternum

> Because you have acted manfully, your heart is strengthened as you have loved chastity, and as you have not known any man other than your husband, the hand of God has comforted you and you will be blessed forever.

Mazieka explains the passage quoted, and others like it, as demonstrating for the Christian propagandists that the Christian God made the weak strong. Death for the pagan at the hands of a supposedly weak woman was all the more shameful for him.[19] This is clearly an ideal image for crusade narratives, which could use femininity as a symbol for weakness, rather than necessarily recording actual female activities. God was perceived to be making the hands of the weak crusaders strong against their pagan enemies. This usage also recalls stories of the Old Testament God sending small battalions of Israelites successfully against the numerically much greater forces of their enemies.[20] In the chronicles of the Baltic crusades, narrators seem to have wanted to emphasize the strengths and dangers presented by the pagan Slavs, and the comparative weakness of the Teutonic Knights and the Christian settlers.

However, this model of weakness personified by women, and turned into strength by God, was not commonly used in the narratives of crusades in the Eastern Mediterranean.[21] Their symbolic language instead used the idea of feminine weakness as a justification for exclusion, reinforcing the gender constraints of the story. Their differing choices from a range of possible symbolic meanings mean that we have to pay careful attention to the varying ways these texts can be read.

We know, because the author of the *Itinerarium*, amongst others, tells us, that some women, possibly quite a lot of women, in fact laid down their distaffs and joined the crusades in the aftermath of the loss of Jerusalem. One of them even returned to tell her own story, which was preserved for us by her brother in Latin verse.[22] Examples of such women can be multiplied extensively, and Helen Nicholson has listed most such references from the Third Crusade sources in a recent article.[23] So, why does our author construct this male space so carefully, and then apparently contradict himself later in the text? This brings us back to the importance of not quite completing the universalization of the male experience. Women have to appear in the text occasionally to reinforce the male qualities which the writer wants to keep in the foreground of his story. The *Itinerarium Peregrinorum* is not alone in this pattern of first masculinizing the crusade and then reintroducing the occasional female reference in apparent contradiction.

One of the most heavy-handed users of this device was Guibert of Nogent. He described how, when the crusaders set out in 1096, women were amongst those nice but worldly things that they had to leave behind. Beautiful women, he said, were treated like worthless pieces of dirt, and abandoned.[24] This idea was repeated many times in the course of Guibert's history. For example, in a speech put into the mouth of Raymond of Saint-Gilles to the crusade troops at Nicaea, he included reminders of the women they had left at home.[25] Guibert's recapitulation of the whole expedition in his book 7 again referred to the tearful farewells of women as the crusaders had left home: and at the siege of Jerusalem, he reminded us that the crusaders' hearts yearned for their wives back at home. Fulcher of Chartres also presented his crusaders leaving behind parents, wives and possessions:

Then husband told wife the time he expected to return, assuring her that if, by God's grace, he survived, he would come home to her. He commended her to the Lord, kissed her lingeringly, and promised as she wept that he would return. She though, fearing that she would never see him again, could not stand but swooned to the ground, mourning her loved one whom she was losing in this life as if he were already dead.[26]

Bernard of Clairvaux, writing of the success of his crusade preaching, constructed a similarly masculine image, saying that women everywhere remained behind 'in a widowed state, while their husbands lived on' – even though he had personally given crosses to a large number of women, including Eleanor of Aquitaine.[27] Ambroise, putting the story of the Third Crusade into verse, described 'Damsels and Dames' weeping at Tours over the departing crusade army.[28] All these writers, like so many others, thus participated in creating the idea of the crusade as a 'gendered' activity, as a male space. They all also revealed later that while some women wept and stayed at home, others tagged along.

As I have suggested, women appear in these tales to remind us periodically of the polarized structure of the society they are depicting – to underline the masculine nature of the event. However, dependent on this are a number of more complex issues. Women remind us of the bipartite, gendered, ordering of society, representing 'difference', or qualities perceived as 'not masculine' in general terms, but they can also be seen to be symbolic of other pairs of difference, other polarities. To return to the First Crusade as narrated by Guibert of Nogent: amongst the handful of references to women participants which he makes are two which stand out distinctly. The first is the story of Christian women supporting 'their' troops in battle by bringing food and water. This is so commonplace as to be regarded as a topos in crusading literature. Guibert placed the story at the battle of Dorylaeum, and he amplified it by saying that: 'God was present in the army, so that the women who had accompanied them stood by their men, bringing water, but more importantly, encouragement and advice.'[29]

Later, when the crusaders were besieged in the city of Antioch, exotic 'Saracen' or Turkish women were seen in the enemy's camp, 'dressed like temples'. They were carrying bags of arrows, but Guibert said they had come 'not to fight but to reproduce'. Of course, the crusaders eventually broke out of the city and routed their besiegers in a dramatic pitched battle. Guibert reported that when the Saracens fled from their encampment, these women abandoned their babies and simply ran away.[30]

These two short episodes use women to symbolize the right and wrong ordering of society. Put bluntly, good (Christian) society has humble and helpful wives whose husbands do not scorn their advice, and who consequently win their battles. Bad (Muslim) society has overdressed nymphets with no 'natural' maternal instincts. This kind of symbolism can be seen in Guibert's other references to women. Women were specifically depicted in his account of Pope Urban's sermon at Clermont as the victims of Turkish violence. They served in this context to point out the wrong ordering of Muslim society, and the threat it posed to the West. The plight of these women was supposed to incite the sympathy of listeners, and encourage them to sign up for the expedition. But this is also a traditional symbolic use of women to signify suffering and victimhood, comparable with the fleeing woman of the Bayeux Tapestry mentioned above. Women and children appear again later as the victims of Peter the Hermit's army, which set out for Jerusalem illicitly and too early. Their sufferings were apparently being used to demonstrate the unlicensed and dangerous status of these 'pre-crusaders' in Hungarian territory.[31]

A similar but more complex pair of associated scenes can be taken from the narrative of Oliver of Paderborn, in his story of the Fifth Crusade. As the crusaders hopefully besieged Damietta, the traditional motif of women fearlessly carrying stones and bringing water, wine and bread to the besiegers was used. Meanwhile, priests prayed and bound up the wounds of the injured.[32] Here, women, warriors and priests represent a tripartite society, but still one in which, as in Guibert's similar passage, each *ordo* performs its allotted role in a proper fashion. By contrast, when the crusaders entered the city after the long siege, they found that: 'Man and wife, father and son, master and slave killed each other by their smell . . . infants at the breasts of their mothers opened their mouths in the embrace of the dead.'[33] Once again, Oliver used a complex multi-focal division of society. The inversion of customary gender patterns and familial and economic relationships was clearly being used to emphasize the disorder caused by the siege and the long resistance by the Egyptians to the crusade army.

In Fulcher of Chartres' account of the First Crusade there are very few references to incidental women after his farewell scenes, and where women do appear they seem to represent either a site of sin or a site of conquest. In the first half of the text, where women appeared they were associated directly with moral problems in the crusade army. At the battle of Dorylaeum, Fulcher presented the view that 'luxury, avarice and other vice' in the crusade army was responsible for their abandonment to the ferocious onslaught of the Turkish army. The sin, and the terror, was associated with the army as a whole, not displaced specifically onto the women.[34] At Antioch, however, the association of women and sexual sin was made clearer:

> Then the Franks, having again consulted together, expelled the women from the army, the married as well as the unmarried, lest perhaps defiled by the sordidness of riotous living they should displease the lord. These women then sought shelter for themselves in neighbouring towns.[35]

Here, the rejection of women symbolized the reordering of the community according to a new morality, from which women, who bore the burden of responsibility for sin, could be excluded. The subsequent sufferings of the army from hunger and battle were represented as trials imposed by God – 'as gold is thrice tried in the fire and seven times purified' – and were followed by victory and the fall of Antioch.[36] This was followed by another encounter with sex and sin. After their conquest of the city, the crusaders were themselves besieged by the forces of the Turkish leader Kerbogha. Fulcher blamed this misfortune on the crusaders themselves, 'for when they had entered the city many of them had commingled with unlawful women'. Because these are virtually the only references Fulcher makes to the presence of women amongst the crusaders, to this point, it seems clear that, for him, the masculinization of the crusade was a necessary part of its representation as a virtuous activity.

After his depiction of the siege of Antioch, crusader women almost disappeared from Fulcher's text, and Saracen women were used to represent the field of conquest, and of total victory. If crusaders captured women and children from the enemy, then they had conclusively triumphed. Towards the end of his tale, in that curious passage where he celebrated the creation of a new 'nation' in the East, those same conquered and captured women seemed to be absorbed peacefully through marriage.[37]

William of Tyre, in his chronicle of the first kingdom of Jerusalem used women in a variety of complex ways. I have discussed elsewhere his treatment of individual elite women in the politics of the kingdoms of Jerusalem and Antioch.[38] But he also made frequent references to ordinary women on the crusades. Although his dependence on Fulcher of Chartres and the *Gesta Francorum*, amongst others, is well established, William used their material in his own idiosyncratic way. Initially he seemed to approve of the involvement of women in the First Crusade. 'No one in the lands of the west paid any attention to age or sex, to status or condition . . . all with one accord took the vow with heart and soul.'[39] But in this passage William was also critical of the mixed motives of those who took the cross, which makes his apparent approval seem a little guarded. However, as his account dealt with the crusaders' progression towards the east, his sympathy became more evident. In Asia Minor, after the crusaders' victory at the battle of Dorylaeum, William described their increasing difficulties:

> Here, overcome by the double distress of intolerable thirst and extreme heat, such as is usual in fiery July, the people began to give way in great numbers. According to report, more than five hundred of both sexes died at that time . . . the pregnant women brought forth their offspring prematurely . . . mothers in agony of spirit cast forth their babies into the camp, some living, some dead . . . other women, moved by feelings of deeper humanity, clasped their babies to their breasts and, regardless of their sex, rolled themselves along the road half nude, concerned rather with the imminent danger of death than with maintaining the respect due to their womanhood.[40]

It is interesting to note that these pregnancies were not criticized, despite the crusaders' supposed status as penitents and pilgrims, and therefore supposedly chaste. William seemed not to share the horror of active sexuality during pilgrimage which Brundage has described as characteristic of the First Crusade chronicles.[41] Instead, he focused on how the dangers of the journey tended to undermine traditional roles and behaviours. This emphasis was repeated later. Whilst William did record the story of the expulsion of women from the camp at Antioch, he restricted this proscription to 'women of ill repute' and placed it in the context of a range of regulations, including prohibitions against games, drink, swearing, theft and 'rapine'.[42] Once the crusaders had entered the city and were themselves besieged there, William continued to focus on women as representative of the social dislocations caused by the war: 'Modesty, a familiar friend, had fled from matrons; reverence no longer attended maidens;

forgetful of their birthright, with worn faces and voices plaintive enough to move hearts of stone, they sought for food everywhere, undeterred by fear of repulse.'[43] This remarkably sympathetic treatment of women's concerns was even extended to the local population. William reported that before the city fell to the army of the crusaders:

> The matrons of Antioch, their daughters and little ones, had gathered on the walls . . . and with groans and tears deplored the slaughter of their friends . . . mothers of many children who had been regarded as fortunate were now considered otherwise, while barren women were thought lucky, and much happier than mothers.[44]

These extracts seem to demonstrate that, at least as far as the First Crusade was concerned, William of Tyre was not constrained by the construction put upon events by his sources. William used basically the same stories as his sources, but, especially in the case of the siege of Antioch, he used them to radically different symbolic effect. He recognized different symbolic possibilities in using the anonymous mass of women in the crusade army to elicit a generalized sympathy from his readership, and an appreciation of the particularly traumatic nature of this first expedition. The drama of the events he described was emphasized by the repeated subversion of the normal order.

So far, I have concentrated on the large numbers of unidentified and undifferentiated women who appear in the sources, but this kind of reading can also be useful in interpreting the accounts some crusade writers give us of known and named individuals. For Joinville, writing of Louis IX's crusade, the many noble French women he named seemed to represent the nuances of domestic power politics. When he referred to women well known to his politically educated audience, it was to demonstrate the social and political positioning of his real subjects. Marriage and the multi-focal relationships it created represented political connections.[45] In an apparently similar way, Villehardouin, in his description of the Fourth Crusade, frequently referred by name to a few politically highly significant women – namely the Byzantine empress and the noble Greek ladies of her court. However, in his very sophisticated account, he used a double-layered system of meanings. He wrote as though to suggest that these rich and influential women were being displayed by the Emperor Isaac as symbols of his power and wealth; but

Villehardouin in his turn used this display to represent the exoticism and degeneracy of the Greek court. The gradual abasement of the empress and her attendants, leading to capture by the Latins, saw them turned into moral as well as financial booty. This reading conforms well to Villehardouin's overwhelming concern for matters of money, its use and display, and the way it influenced policy. These women represented rich exotic prizes, and their cavalier treatment made a stark contrast with the universal grief, which he said greeted news of the death in Acre of Mary, the wife of his hero Baldwin.[46]

I have tried to demonstrate that the representation of women in the crusade chronicles can be read as more than simply representative of the events these writers saw or were told about. A close investigation of these symbolic meanings can reveal a great deal about how the writers carefully constructed their histories. Their representation of the crusade was both based on and contributed to the organization of their culture. It was through narratives such as these that the *idea* of the crusade was created – an idea which then profoundly shaped the subsequent history of Europe.

NOTES

[1] G. Duby, *The Three Orders: Feudal Society Imagined* (Chicago, 1980), *passim*.

[2] See the bibliographical survey by R. Barker, 'When is a knight not a knight?', in S. Church and R. Harvey (eds.), *Medieval Knighthood*, 5, papers from the Sixth Strawberry Hill Conference 1994 (Woodbridge, 1995), 1–17.

[3] B. Bolton, 'Paupertas Christi: old wealth and new poverty in the twelfth century', in D. Baker (ed.), *Renaissance and Renewal in Christian History* (Studies in Church History, 14; Oxford, 1977), 95–103.

[4] See for example the discussion in P. Raedts, 'The Children's Crusade of 1212', *JMH* 3 (1977), 279–324.

[5] A. Murray, 'Ethnic identity in the crusader states: the Franks and the settlement of Outremer', in S. Forde, L. Johnson and A. Murray (eds.), *Concepts of National Identity in the Middle Ages* (Leeds, 1995), 59–73.

[6] Duby, *Three Orders*, 279, 341.

[7] See, for example, C. Walker Bynum, *Jesus as Mother: Studies in the Spirituality of the High Middle Ages* (Berkeley, CA, 1982).

[8] For example, P. Stafford, *Unification and Conquest: A Political and Social History of England in the Tenth and Eleventh Century* (London, 1989) and idem, *Queen Emma and Queen Edith: Queenship and Women's Power in Eleventh Century England* (Oxford, 1997).

[9] K. F. Morrison, *History as Visual Art* (Princeton, 1990), 164–5, 169.

[10] H. Nicholson (trans.), *Chronicle of the Third Crusade: A Translation of the Itinerarium Peregrinorum et Gesta Regis Ricardi* (Aldershot, 1997), 48.

[11] A. Arjava, 'Women and Roman law in Late Antiquity', doctoral thesis (Helsinki, 1994), 147. C. James, 'Women, death and the law', in D. Wood (ed.), *Martyrs and Martyrologies* (Studies in Church History, 30; Oxford, 1993), 25–6.

[12] 'Livre de Philip of Novara', in *RHC Lois* 1: 542.

[13] D. Herlihy, *Opera Muliebra: Women and Work in Medieval Europe* (Philadelphia, 1990), 177 *et passim*.

[14] Nicholson, *Itinerarium*, 48.

[15] Ibid., 124.

[16] J. Brundage, 'Prostitution, miscegenation and sexual purity in the first crusade', *CS* 58.

[17] D. Webb, *Pilgrims and Pilgrimage in the Medieval West*, International Library of Historical Studies 12 (London, 2000), 14, 33.

[18] Peter von Dusberg, *Chronik des Preussenlandes*, ed. Klaus Scholz and Dieter Wojtecki (Darmstadt, 1984), 1: 78. Quoted in Mazieka (n. 19), 229.

[19] R. Mazeika, '"Nowhere was the fragility of their sex apparent": women warriors in the Baltic crusade', in A. V. Murray (ed.), *From Clermont to Jerusalem: The Crusades and Crusader Societies* (Turnhout, 1998), 229–48.

[20] For example, Deuteronomy 32: 30.

[21] One exception is in William of Tyre: WT 403.

[22] P. G. Schmidt, 'Peregrinatio Periculosa: Thomas von Froidmont über die Jerusalem-fahrten seiner Schwester Margareta', in U. Justus Stache, W. Mainz and F. Wagner (eds.), *Kontinuität und Wandel: Lateinische Poesie von Naevius bis Baudelaire* (Hildesheim, 1986), 461–84; *Margaret of Beverley*, trans. S. Lambert (forthcoming).

[23] H. Nicholson, 'Women on the Third Crusade', *JMH* 23 (1997), 335–49.

[24] Guibert of Nogent, *The Deeds of God through the Franks*, trans. R. Levine (Woodbridge, 1997), 29.

[25] Guibert, trans. Levine, 66.

[26] Fulcher of Chartres, *Historia Hierosolymitana (1095–1127)*, ed. H. Hagenmeyer (Heidelberg, 1913), I: vi. Translations are taken from Fulcher of Chartres, *A History of the Expedition to Jerusalem 1095–1127*, ed. H. S. Fink, trans. F. R. Ryan (Knoxville, TN, 1969), here p. 74.

[27] Bernard of Clairvaux, 'Epistola ad Eugenium', *RHGF*, 15, 603.

[28] Ambroise, ll. 303–60.

[29] Guibert, trans. Levine, 66.

[30] Ibid., 103.

[31] Ibid., 48.

[32] Oliver of Paderborn, *The Capture of Damietta*, trans. J. J. Gavigan (New York, 1948), 38.

[33] Ibid., 52–4.

[34] Fulcher, I: xi (trans., p. 85).

[35] Fulcher, I: xv (trans., p. 95).

[36] Fulcher, I: xv (trans., p. 96). For the meaning of *luxuria* see J. Noonan, *Contraception: A History of its Treatment by Catholic Theologians and Canonists* (Cambridge, MA, 1966), 175–7, and J. Flandrin, *Families in Former Times: Kinship, Household and Sexuality*, trans. R. Southern (Cambridge, 1979), 215. According to Brundage, 'Prostitution', p. 281, *luxuria* does mean sex as such.

[37] Fulcher, III: xxxvii (trans., p. 271).

[38] S. Lambert, 'Queen or consort: rulership and politics in the Latin East, 1118–1228', in A. J. Duggan (ed.), *Queens and Queenship in Medieval Europe* (Woodbridge, 1997), 153–69.

[39] P. W. Edbury and J. G. Rowe, *William of Tyre: Historian of the Latin East* (Cambridge, 1988), 45–6; WT 1: 36, p. 93.

[40] WT 3: 17 (16), p. 217.

[41] Brundage, 'Prostitution', 57–8 *et passim*.

[42] WT 4: 22, p. 220.

[43] WT 6: 7, p. 270.

[44] WT 5: 6, p. 233.

[45] *Memoirs of the Crusades by Villehardouin and De Joinville*, trans. F. Marzials (London, 1983), 170, 252, 259.

[46] Ibid., 53, 46, 64–5, 83.

2

Virile Latins, Effeminate Greeks and Strong Women: Gender Definitions on Crusade?

MATTHEW BENNETT

On 1 May 1187, a few hundred brother knights of the Templars and Hospitallers attacked a Muslim force estimated at 7,000 strong.[1] This was an ill-judged assault in which the Christians were heavily defeated, but one man came out of the encounter with credit, 'for he was not afraid to die for Christ'. Jakelin de Mailly, a Templar, 'undertook the battle, one against all' and died 'encircled by the impious people he [had] slain with his victorious right hand'. His Muslim opponents were greatly impressed by his valour:

> In fact, rumour has it that one person was moved with more fervour than the rest. He cut off the man's genitals, and kept them safely for begetting children so that even when dead the man's members – if such a thing were possible – would produce an heir with courage as great as his.'[2]

The issue of the inheritance of martial virtue could scarcely be more clearly outlined than by this dismembering of a brave man, and it was something with which crusaders were concerned from the very first expedition.

According to an apparently eye-witness source:

> What man, however experienced and learned would dare to write of the skill and prowess and courage of the Turks, who thought that they would strike terror into the Arabs and Saracens, Armenians, Syrians and Greeks, by the menace of their arrows? Yet, please God, their men will never be as good as ours. They have a saying that they are of common stock with the Franks, and that no men, except the Franks and themselves, are naturally born to be knights.[3]

These comments, from an anonymous text known as the *Gesta Francorum*, celebrate the First Crusaders' victory over Kilij Arslan's Turks (1 July 1097).[4] The author was at that time in the contingent led by Bohemond of Taranto, the son of a famous warrior father, the Norman adventurer Robert d'Hauteville, who had made himself master of most of southern Italy by the time of his death in 1085. Bohemond, a huge man who had been given the nickname of a legendary giant on his birth (1058), had fought with Robert against the Greeks for the possession of the city of Durres (on the Albanian coast). In 1081, he took part in the battle against the Byzantine emperor Alexius I Comnenus, outside its walls. Anna Comnena, the emperor's historian daughter, attributes Robert's victory to the personal intervention of his wife, the Lombard Sichelgaita. Unfortunately for her ambitious stepson, on Robert's death she pushed forward her own son Roger to inherit the Hauteville territories. Bohemond's title as prince of Taranto was a sop to pride and the main reason that he was on crusade was to win himself a great lordship. We are fortunate to possess a vivid description of Bohemond's manly qualities in the words of Anna Comnena, who wrote the *Alexiad* in celebration of her father a generation after the events she describes:[5]

> His stature was such that he towered almost a full cubit over the tallest men. He was slender of waist and flanks, with broad shoulders and chest, strong in the arms; in general he was neither tapered of form, nor heavily built and fleshy, but perfectly proportioned . . . His hands were large, he had a good firm stance, and his neck and back were compact . . . His eyes were light blue and gave some hint of the man's spirit and dignity. He breathed freely through nostrils that were broad, worthy of his chest and a fine outlet for the breath that came in gusts from his lungs.[6]

In truth, this could be a description of a fine horse, and Anna is quite explicit in calling Bohemond a barbarian – a mere animal with human intelligence: 'Such was his constitution, mental and physical, that in him both courage and love were armed, both ready for combat.'[7] Commentators have noted Anna's feminine appreciation of her father's terrible adversary (and expedient ally); and, because he is human, he possesses intellectual qualities: arrogance, cunning and a way with words, which make him all the more dangerous. Whatever her adolescent frisson at Bohemond's appearance, to Anna, he was not a patch on a real man – her husband, Nicephorus Bryennius:

Everything – strength, agility, physical charm, in fact all the good qualities of mind and body – combined to glorify that man . . . He was a
magnificent soldier, but by no means unmindful of literature; he read all
books and by closely studying every science derived much wisdom from
them . . . a man of learning and his writings gave excellent proof of it.[8]

There can have been few men in Latin Christendom at this time who
could have matched such a range of achievements; not that learning
was unmanly, but even Henry I of England, nicknamed 'Beauclerk'
was not an author. While it was important not to be *miles illiteratus*
by the mid-twelfth century (when Anna was writing), Frederick
Hohenstaufen, almost a century later, is perhaps the first successful
warrior figure to conform to the Byzantine model.

But in the late 1090s there can have been few in the crusader host
who valued learning above more robust virtues required to defeat the
enemy. Knowledge was admired, certainly, and prudence and intelligence, along with bravery and good birth; but bibliophilia was
definitely suspect. The Anonymous and his contemporaries accused
the Greeks of cunning, deception and outright treachery (the mir-
ror-image of Anna's complaints, of course); but above all they were
lacking in military virtues. This was proved by the half-century of
defeats which they had suffered at the hands of the Turks. The First
Crusaders had evidence ready to hand that the emperor expected
them to fight while he and his subjects took the spoils. Following the
siege of Nicaea they complained that they did not receive a penny for
all their efforts. During the long and bitter siege of Antioch, the
Byzantine commander Taticius decamped as soon as the going got
tough, promising aid which never appeared – not in the form of
troops anyway, although food supplies from Cyprus were crucial in
keeping the besiegers going. But logistics never had much appeal as
symbolic of masculine virtue, despite their essential nature (then and
now). As far as the crusaders were concerned, the Greeks and all the
other peoples listed by the Anonymous were weak and cowardly. The
plaintive cry attributed to the suborned Armenian tower commander, Firuz, whose treachery gave up Antioch – 'We have few Franks!
Where is the hero Bohemond? Where is that unconquered soldier?' –
while being blatant propaganda for Bohemond's recruiting mission
in France in order to support his 'crusade' against Alexius in 1106,
also makes the point about self-image.[9]

There is also the fascinating imagined conversation between

Kerbogha and his mother which characterizes the atabeg as super-
stitious and subservient to women, though ultimately disbelieving of
his mother's warnings. Since there is a chapter devoted to the episode
elsewhere in this volume, I shall only comment that the predicted
crusader triumph is attributed not to their fearsome qualities or
those of their leaders, but conventionally and piously to the superior power of the Christian God. If there is a gender divide it is
between the Christian 'Him' and his 'sons' and her (Kerbogha's
mother) because Islam (which is also devoted to a supreme Him) is
not properly represented at all.[10] Yet in twelfth-century Latin
Christendom, which was the reception society for the stories of crusading, the role of women as vehicles for divine inspiration was
reviving. The cult of the Virgin Mary was sponsored by the
Cistercians and their theological mouthpiece St Bernard. Female
saints and mystics were valued as intercessors in a more proactive
form than ever before in the Christian West. How was their gender
defined?

The classic definition of this projection comes from Leander of
Seville, writing just before AD 600. Janet Schulenberg takes the title
of her book from the following quotation: 'Forgetful of her natural
feminine weakness, she [the virgin] lives in manly vigour and has
used virtue to give strength to her weak sex.'[11] An early Christian
martyr who seems to have acted as a model for this kind of interpretation of female spirituality was St Eugenia:

> I have not wanted to be a woman, but preserving a spotless virginity with
> a total effort of the soul, I have acted consistently as a man. I have not put
> on a senseless pretence of respectability so that as a man I might imitate
> a woman, but I, as woman have acted as a man by doing as a man, by
> embracing boldly a virginity which is in Christ.[12]

As the tone of this quotation implies, Eugenia was a transvestite. She
had adopted male dress in order to pursue the holy life, because to
her contemporaries a holy woman was a difficult concept to grasp;
almost a contradiction in terms. Schulenberg identifies this approach
as exemplifying the transgressive nature of sanctity. This enabled
Eugenia to become *femina virilis*. Rasputin-like, she apparently resis-
ted three attempts by her persecutors to kill her, only being finally
despatched by a gladiator. Her virginity was a kind of armour, protecting her from physical assault, but after all she was a martyr and
there would be no point to the story if she did not finally end up

dead. This strange construction of virile femininity is explained by Gillian Clarke: 'Since virtue was construed as masculine (*vir* [man] being said to be the root of the word 'virtue'; the properties of virtue were thus the property of masculinity), women had the potential to achieve virtue only through a "rejecting of her original abject nature".'[13]

There is some debate by commentators – patristic, twelfth-century and modern – as to how much authority, or in simple terms power, the virgin enjoyed in both the spiritual and temporal spheres. When women are defined 'negatively' 'by abstention from heterosexual relations' their chastity can be seen as representing their relative powerlessness: 'Even if they endure as martyrs for the faith, they endure as suffering bodies; rather than as bearers of consciousness or conscience.'[14] Yet they do display their devotion to Christianity verbally; through their own bodies 'suffering but not defeated'; and through their martyrdoms they may defeat dynastic plans, or serve as plaintiffs at a court of law who help to restore justice.[15] These virgins seek their own martyrdom so that, 'in suffering and resisting torture, the virgin body is revealed to be unfeminine, unashamed, impenetrable, and miraculously self-healing'.[16]

The rejection of arranged marriages is something that appears both in classical martyr texts and in twelfth-century ones. Here it seems appropriate to focus on the latter. Christina of Markyate (b. 1096 ×1098) is a famous example of this when she escapes an unwanted match by running away. How is she to do this? By wearing masculine dress and riding off into the distance. 'Why do you respect your feminine sex? Put on manly courage and mount the horse like a man.'[17] Or there is the case of St Oda of Hainault (d. 1158) who refused a husband. In order to ensure that she was unmarriageable she cut off her nose and fled to a nunnery. She later rose to be the prioress of a Premonstratensian house.[18]

Self-mutilation is not a practice employed by people who feel empowered, I suggest, but it is simpler to achieve than the strategy of other determined virgins: to grow a beard. The classic example of this is St Wilgefortis. The derivation of her name has produced some interesting speculation: could it come from the Old French vernacular *Vierge Forte* (strong virgin) or the German *Hilge vatz* (Holy Face)? St Wilgefortis was known as 'Uncumber' (British English: 'disencumber') because apparently she could help women get rid of unwanted husbands. Her own fate was interesting, a spectacular

piece of punishment for her transvestism. Her father had her crucified. Schulenberg includes an illustration of life-size crucifix which
has Wilgefortis bearded, wearing a dress and nailed-up. What an *imi-
tatio Christi*! The saint, like Christ, appears unconquered by death.[19]

Yet, worthy though these female martyrs are and presumably
capable of intercession like all saints, they are scarcely represented as
powerful. For recognizable, hierarchical authority, surely one has to
turn to the Virgin Mary (still known by Catholics as Our Lady, in
what I presume is a memory of the idea of the *domina*, a female with
real power over others). The twelfth century saw the rise of the
Virgin in spiritual and liturgical significance, of course, and she had
some genuinely influential advocates, such as St Bernard of
Clairvaux. In medieval French lyric, she 'appears as a sovereign, willing and able to be personal with her believers as well as to intercede
for them in heaven'.[20]

What enabled less elevated women to achieve the status of virgins?
This might seem rather an obvious question. Yet K. C. Kelly has
examined what it meant to be a virgin in the medieval period. She
quotes a definition which describes virginity as 'a physical technical-
ity' while chastity is 'a quality of the spirit'.[21] Indeed, she invents a
whole new branch of scientific enquiry – which she calls
'Hymenology' – to show how complex the term virginity really is.
Remember that widows were also capable of being seen as virgins.
Chastity was a state of mind, not a state of being. Kelly also presents
a couple of examples of male virginity in her study of martyrologies.
One character, John the Scribe, is tempted by women to turn away
from chastity, so he commits suicide to avoid pollution. As a result,
though, he is described as *vir effeminatus*.[22] Or there is the case of
Pelagius, a beautiful boy who is subject to the lust of a Muslim
caliph (usually identified as 'Abd al-Rahman III, d. 961). The young
Christian defies his persecutor by stripping naked in public, so
apparently demonstrating his rejection of the ruler's advances.
Martyrdom swiftly follows.[23]

Although chastity was virtuous and sex, even within marriage,
could be frowned upon by some theologians, another strand of opinion stressed the importance of sexual intercourse for the
maintenance of good health. That is how the pilgrim poet Ambroise
summarized the losses of the Third Crusade: 100,000 dead through
sexual abstinence and 3,000 from disease![24] It was quite possible
for the same author, along with more clerical types, to condemn

'loitering in taverns' and the fornication with prostitutes which inevitably followed the drinking as being unseemly for crusaders and for both delaying and undermining the expedition.[25] A married man who failed in his duties was seen as culpable, though, as the case of Humphrey of Toron IV shows. He was married to Isabella, heiress to the Latin kingdom of Jerusalem, but he had turned down the opportunity to become its ruler in 1183, and so lost face with the baronage. As a result, in 1190, he was manœuvred into an unwanted divorce by the ambitious crusader Conrad, marquis of Montferrat. The sources are scathing about Humphrey: 'He was more like a woman than a man: he had a gentle manner and a stammer . . . [like] a boy who's almost a girl.'[26] Isabella is also blamed for her feminine weakness and her Greek duplicity (her mother was Maria Comnena, King Almaric's second wife). Even the marriage feast was cursed, some revellers returning at dawn being ambushed by Turks and killed. A bad match was a bad omen for the whole crusade.

The most striking example of a 'failing marriage' was that of Louis VII and his queen. Eleanor of Aquitaine was alleged to have had an affair with her uncle Raymond of Poitiers, prince of Antioch, whilst accompanying her husband in 1148. As Ronald Finucane has pointed out, pilgrimage and crusade actually provided many opportunities for illicit or extra-marital sex, and the clerical chroniclers could do nothing but disapprove.[27] Nothing, that is, except take a prurient interest in such stories. Whether Eleanor was guilty of the adultery of which she was accused is far from certain. John of Salisbury provides the standard account of Louis's suspicions being aroused by his wife spending long periods in discussion with Raymond.[28] It has been suggested that her closeness to her uncle may have been no more than an interest in his cultured conversation, combined with feeling comfortable in a kinsman's company; but the criticisms are more likely to relate to something simpler than intellectual debate. Indeed, the real reason for Louis's discontent may be that Eleanor supported Raymond's plan to attack Nur ed-Din in Aleppo rather than to press on immediately to Jerusalem.

If the clash with her husband had at its root a political and strategic objection then this tells us something about how Eleanor perceived herself: as a maker of policy distinct from her royal husband. If, then, the dispute is represented as being over her infidelity, we also get an insight into how contemporaries constructed such defiance. The story of the relationship being revealed by a courtier (apparently a eunuch!) is a topos found regularly in romances, where a *losengier* (a wicked tale-teller) causes a rift between lovers. By the mid-thirteenth century an anonymous poet – the minstrel of Rheims – could even conflate the 'noble Saracen' genre into the story.[29] Eleanor is apparently so impressed by Saladin's reputation for bravery and courtliness that she writes to him declaring her love, and promising to apostasize and to elope with him if he could manage to spirit her away. The plan almost works, but is revealed to the king by one of her maids, and she is stopped with one foot already on the galley that was to bear her away. I know – wrong crusade! But that is not the point. The poet characterizes Eleanor's actions as being brought about by a desire to highlight Louis's failure in not pursuing the campaign more vigorously. If she is caricatured and vilified (and she is), her husband does not come well out of the situation either, for he is portrayed as weak, foolish and cowardly; hardly an ideal crusader.[30]

Issues of marital and political loyalty could always overlap and become confused in the minds of observers, especially if they had an axe to grind or were benefiting from hindsight following the couple's divorce in 1151. The main reason for this was, of course, dynastic. Eleanor had only produced two daughters and not the son that Louis required. So the issue of consanguinity was conveniently raised to end the union and to allow the king to find a wife who would provide an acceptable heir. Initially the pope, Eugenius III, was reluctant to agree to a divorce and, as the couple made their way back to France, actually put them into bed together in a ceremony of reconciliation at Tusculum.[31] In the end it was to no avail, but the public and openly political nature of the papal intervention shows the critical role of a powerful woman in the dynastic politics of the period.

How great a role could women play in actual warfare at the time, though? This is the most obvious category to which people turn when researching crusader women. In a modern context, where women are actually integrated into the armed forces of many states, the desire to find role-models is understandable; but it is also perhaps the least rewarding exercise. One reason is that the examples are actually extremely rare; another that it is very difficult to find a positive response to the actions of these few amongst our sources; also, there is a frequent tendency to confuse different aspects of military activity, for example the noblewoman acting as a lord in defending fortresses, property, territory and its population, and the individuals who actually performed as warriors, in an essentially transvestite role. Sometimes these last two groups coincided, but more often they did not. While the female rulers operating within the context of lordship can be easily identified, the female warriors are mostly anonymous, and so, unfortunately, become rather suspect as examples.

Eleanor of Aquitaine appears in both categories, of course, in romance at least. A mid-twelfth-century audience was prepared for the idea of women warriors by the popularity of classical stories appearing in vernacular poetry, especially the epic of Troy. This introduced to them Queen Penthesilea and her Amazons, and Benoît de Sainte-Maure describes her in exactly the same terms as he would a Roland or William of Orange.[32] Only later historians have been taken in by this, however, and no twelfth-century source makes the comparison with Eleanor and her court. Even her literary 'courts of love' have been shown to represent a misinterpretation of the consciously Ovidian *De Amore* of Andreas Cappellanus.[33]

There have been studies of women as warriors in the medieval period, but to my knowledge only Helen Nicholson has examined the issue of whether women fought on crusade – specifically the Third Crusade – or not.[34] Drawing on her work on the *Itinerarium Peregrinorum et Gesta Regis Ricardi* she is able to dispel some myths about crusading Amazons. As she properly points out, descriptions of women fighting drawn from Muslim sources are scarcely reliable evidence.[35] This is not because women did not fight at all; but the intent of these authors is to decry Christian mores as uncivilized. The eye-witnesses Baha ad-Din and 'Imad ad-Din claim to have seen the bodies of women dressed in armour on the battlefields around Acre on more than one occasion in 1189–91. The latter goes on to claim that: 'On the day of battle, more than one woman rode out with them like a knight and showed (masculine) endurance in spite of the weakness (of her sex); clothed only a coat of mail they were not recognized as women until they had been stripped of their arms.'[36]

There are many problems with this text – not least the complexities of the translation, which as non-Arabic reader I am not qualified to criticize. For, although there are examples of women serving in disguise in the armies of the modern states over the last couple of centuries, including amongst the cavalry, they would have been recruited and trained to fight like any other soldier.[37] In an age when mounted military combat was learned over years as part of a boy's and young man's life, and jealously guarded as a socially exlusive skill by a military caste, how were women able to acquire the necessary experience in riding and handling weapons that fighting 'like a knight' suggests? It may well be that wearing a mail-coat for protection, especially during a siege, was not that uncommon for women determined to share in the dangers of their menfolk. (Although, even then, such armour was expensive and not available to all soldiers, so how likely is it that a woman would wear it if other active male combatants lacked one?)

The female archer whom both writers describe seems more credible, in that women did exercise with the bow. Also, she was killed defending the crusader encampment around the city and not 'riding out to fight'. Muslim authors did recognize that, in extreme situations, even their own women could be called upon to defend their house and home, or even town walls.[38] Dr Nicholson cites evidence for this and goes on to find Christian equivalents in the *Chronicle* of Ramon Muntaner (although he must be seen as a blatant Catalan propagandist in celebrating the military superiority of his fellow countrymen – and women – over the French). She also describes the happy shot from a trebuchet, operated solely by Toulouse women, which brained Simon de Montfort, the leader of the Albigensian crusade, in 1218.[39] (Sadly, perhaps, for many historians, patriarchy could not be decapitated by a single blow, demonstrated by this example of 'women power'.) What is striking about these last examples, as far as I am concerned, is that women are depicted defending their communities, in what might be considered an extension of their household management role, rather than going on expedition, as did male warriors.

Indeed, the role of women on crusade seems to have been very much as ancillary workers. This is not to demean these activities at all, since they were clearly vital both at moments of crisis and in the general day-to-day management of the expedition. In the first category, the women bringing water to the men fighting at Dorylaeum on 1 June 1099 are praised by the anonymous *Gesta Francorum* author.[40] Both Ambroise and the Latin *Itinerarium* mention that when 'immoral women' were expelled from the crusader camp after the capture of Acre, to encourage the men to set out on the march to Jaffa: 'The only exception was laundresses on foot, who would not be a burden on the army nor a cause of sin.'[41] Ambroise adds that they also performed the role of washing the men's heads and picking lice and fleas from them 'like apes'. Nicholson considers the last remark 'ungracious'; but the poet's intent may be to praise rather than to poke fun at the women (as anyone who has suffered from infestation could tell her).[42] The same sources tell the tale of a praiseworthy woman who died outside the walls of Acre. Apparently she was carrying stones to fill in the ditch surrounding the place, so that siege engines could be brought against the city walls. This does suggest that women could get very closely involved in warfare, if not in fighting hand-to-hand. As a result of this activity, the woman was struck by an arrow and mortally wounded. While she lay dying she asked her husband to use her own body to help fill up the moat. The *Itinerarium* apostrophizes, 'Oh admirable faith of the weaker sex', and Ambroise comments, 'No man ever should forget such a woman.'[43]

Yet, of course, any woman going on crusade was in effect joining an army on the march, with a military objective in view. If it is difficult to find out how many women became involved in combat, it is little less hard to find examples of female leaders in war. They did exist. The civil war of King Stephen's reign in England (1138–54) produced a situation in which his competitor for the throne was the old king's daughter. Although it is far from certain that the Empress Matilda ever played an active role in war, there is no doubt that her namesake, Stephen's queen, did do so. This was due to the king having been taking captive at the battle of Lincoln in 1141. Again, Nicholson teases out the issues involved in this case, for the women involved were supporting the interests of their menfolk rather than their own.[44]

In the specifically crusading context of the *Reconquista*, there is the example of the viscountess of Narbonne, who led a force to the siege of Tortosa (north-eastern Spain) in 1148. This Ermengarde was a remarkable character, widowed as a result of the Christian defeat at Fraga (1134) and renowned for retaining power over her territories, despite being twice remarried, and living until 1197. Just how much generalship she displayed has to be questioned, however, for in the expedition just mentioned she was accompanied by her uncle, the abbot of Lagrasse, equally unsuitable to command in war by virtue of his monastic status. Acting as a leader is not the same as making military decisions, upon which her baronage would expect to be consulted, just as she drew upon their counsel for the management of her viscounty and dynastic policy. She does fall into the category of a woman who went on campaign, however, and, as we have seen, that was in itself quite unusual.[45]

In the Holy Land itself, there is the equally well-known example of Queen Melisende who ruled the Latin kingdom and dominated the political arena despite many challenges for three decades (1131–61). Lois Honeycutt has pointed out that, unlike the Empress Matilda who fought for the rights of her son Henry II to inherit the English throne, it was Melisende's situation as heiress to the kingdom which gave her such status.[46] This is an interpretation based on the chronicler William of Tyre, although the bishop's recent biographers, Edbury and Rowe, urge caution in taking the reading at face value.[47] Honeycutt claims that King Fulk's charters support the view that Melisende kept the upper hand. Following their reconciliation after a split, the documents contain phrases referring to the queen's assent to his actions (which is absent in his acts as prince of Antioch in his own right).[48] The refusal of Melisende to stand down when her son came of age in 1145 is also significant in identifying at least how the queen sought to define her authority. She could not act as an army commander, however, nor did she seek to do so. The words of Bernard of Clairvaux, in a letter written to the queen soon after Fulk's death in 1143, urge her to act as a man by making wise and prudent decisions. Yet he goes on to warn her that this responsibility was actually beyond her as a woman as she should recognize that 'they are great matters which far exceed my strength and knowledge; they are the duties of a man, and I am only a woman, weak in body, changeable of heart, not far-seeing in counsel nor accustomed to business'.[49] Only by relying on the Lord's strength could she hope to prevail. Honeycutt concludes that, like the two Matildas, Melisende needed masculine qualities – 'manly courage ... fortitude and patience' – which women did not naturally possess.[50] Those that could demonstrate these virtues were worthy of respect.

Manly strength, womanly weakness – an unsurprising dichotomy, perhaps. Yet theoretical structures of this nature can never reflect the richness of human experience in any time or culture. Real human beings negotiate the situation in which they find themselves. The essence of a crusade was that it was a journey which left its participants rootless, at least temporarily, and needing to find ways of coping with the difference from living in a settled society. It is difficult to represent accurately the stresses and strains of this experience in gender terms, simply because the narratives we possess were written with the intention of reinforcing the status quo. I do not think that it is accidental that the eye-witness accounts which made up the *Itinerarium* in both Latin and French are most revealing, because they are narrative-descriptive (diary-like) rather than constructed into a history like William of Tyre's, with all that implies. The practical pilgrims were just as much men of their age and did not seek to praise where it was not deserved. But they do recognize the role of women as helpmates in action, just as the anonymous *Gesta* had on the First Crusade. Essentially, gender roles as defined prior to crusade were maintained during the journey. Womanliness was decried, both in women, where it might naturally be deemed to exist, and in men who apparently did not live up to a masculine ideal which required victory as a justification of military virtue. Yet, at the same time, people of the two main genders, and the ungendered, could still demonstrate appropriate behaviour which was worthy of imitation. It was this kind of behaviour about which the audience needed to be told and which both inspired and justified the extraordinary activity of crusading.

NOTES

[1] For an explanation of this encounter, see M. Bennett, '*La Règle du Temple* as a military manual *or* How to deliver a cavalry charge', in C. Harper-Bill, C. J. Holdsworth and J. L. Nelson (eds.), *Studies in Medieval History for R. Allen Brown* (Woodbridge, 1987), 7–19, at 18–19.

[2] *Itinerarium Peregrinorum et Gesta Regis Ricardi*, ed. W. Stubbs (London, 1864) (henceforward cited as *Itinerarium*), bk 1, ch. 2; trans. Helen J. Nicholson, as *Chronicle of the Third Crusade* (Crusades Texts in Translation, 3; Aldershot, 1997), 25–6. This resounding tale appears at the very beginning of the work amidst material emphasizing the role of the Christians' sins and Saladin's military virtues in bringing about the fall of the kingdom of Jerusalem. Ch. 3, p. 27, includes the story that he had 'received the belt of knighthood from [Humphrey II of Toron]' in accordance with the rite of the Franks', so becoming heir to their military traditions rather than a physical inheritance.

[3] *Gesta Francorum et Aliorum Hierosolimitanorum*, ed. and trans. R. Hill (Oxford, 1962), III: ix, p. 21.

[4] This passage also appears, almost verbatim, in Baudri of Bourgueil and further paraphrased in the work of the great historical compiler Orderic Vitalis. The interrelation of the crusader chronicles and the existence of a possible Ur-text is a tricky issue which cannot be addressed here. Suffice it

to say that the representation of warlike 'Saracens' was pretty well diffused through at least northern France by the mid-twelfth century. See M. Bennett, 'First Crusaders' images of Muslims: the influence of vernacular poetry?', *Forum for Modern Language Studies* 22 (1986), 101–22.

[5] Anna Comnena, *The Alexiad*, ed. and trans. E. R. A. Sewter (London, 1969). As will be apparent from the following paragraph, Anna was very interested in matters of gender and virtue. She began writing following the death of her husband Nicephorus Bryennius (1137) and, since he was a historian too, incorporating material from his own work into her story. See J. France, 'Anna Comnena, the Alexiad and the First Crusade', *Reading Medieval Studies* 10 (1984), 20–38, and P. Frankopan, Chapter 5 below.

[6] *Alexiad*, XIII: x, p. 422.

[7] Ibid., XIII: x, pp. 422–3.

[8] Ibid., VII: ii, pp. 220; see also pp. 19–20 and *sub verba* for other references.

[9] *Gesta Francorum*, VIII: xx, p. 46.

[10] Ibid., IX: xxii, pp. 53–6.

[11] J. T. Schulenburg, *Forgetful of their Sex* (Chicago, 1998), 1.

[12] Ibid., 159.

[13] C. L. Carlson and A. J. Weir (eds.), *Constructions of Widowhood and Virginity in the Middle Ages* (Basingstoke, 1999), 3, quoting G. Clarke, '*This Female Man of God': Women and Spiritual Power in the Patristic Age AD 350–450* (London, 1995), 212.

[14] Ibid., 7.

[15] Ibid.

[16] Ibid., 12.

[17] Schulenburg, *Forgetful of their Sex*, 161.

[18] Ibid., 149, noting contemporary mutilation practices, for example, the *Lex Pacis Castrienis* of Frederick Barbarossa against prostitutes (*c*.1150); Orderic Vitalis as vengeance against an enemies' womenfolk in a feud (*c*.1140) and Layamon's in *Brut* (*c*.1200).

[19] Ibid., 152–3, illustration no. 11, between pp. 132 and 133.

[20] Carslon and Weir, *Constructions*, 12.

[21] K. C. Kelly, *Performing Virginity and Testing Chastity in the Middle Ages* (London, 2000), 3.

[22] Ibid., 98–9.

[23] Ibid., 101.

[24] Ambroise, lines 12236–41.

[25] *Itinerarium*, 4: 27 (from where the quotation comes); Ambroise, lines 7058–60.

[26] *Itinerarium*, 1: 63, p. 122 and nn. 256–8.

[27] R. C. F. Finucane, *Soldiers of the Faith: Crusaders and Moslems at War* (London, 1983), 179–81.

[28] D. D. R. Owen, *Eleanor of Aquitaine: Queen and Legend* (Oxford, 1993) summarizes the story, pp. 106–7. This and the following paragraph depend much upon his interpetation.

[29] The co-editor of this volume has worked extensively on this subject. See S. Lambert, 'Heroines and Saracens', *Medieval World* 1 (1991), 3–9.

[30] Owen, *Eleanor of Aquitaine*, 105–7.

[31] Ibid., 28. The royal couple stayed with Eugenius III for two nights: 9–10 October 1149.

[32] Ibid., 148–9.

[33] Ibid., 152–6.

[34] H. Nicholson, 'Women on the Third Crusade', *JMH* 23 (1997), 335–49.

[35] Ibid., 337.

[36] F. Gabrieli, *Arab Historians of the Crusades* (London, 1969), 207.

[37] See, for example, J. Wheelwright, *Amazons and Military Maids: Women who Dressed as Men in Pursuit of Life, Liberty and Happiness* (London, 1989), *passim*.

[38] Nicholson, 'Women', 338; Gabrieli, *Arab Historians*, 218.

[39] Nicholson, 'Women', 344, for both examples.

[40] *Gesta Francorum*, p. 19.

[41] *Itinerarium*, 4: 9, p. 235.

[42] Ibid., n. 18; Ambroise, ll. 5695–8. Some female members of audiences hearing various versions of this chapter have sniffed rather at this example, confining women to domestic chores; but it is the not job of the historian to make the past more like our present, rather to seek to explore the differences.

[43] *Itinerarium*, 1: 50, p. 106; Ambroise, ll. 3625–60 (the quotation is in the last two lines). The incident is described in a series of anecdotes, some rather less salutary in nature; but this should not be read as an attempt to denigrate the woman's role or bravery.

[44] Nicholson, 'Women', 345–6.

[45] See J. Caille, 'Les Seigneurs de Narbonne dans le conflit Toulouse–Barcelone au xiie siècle', *Annales de Midi* 97 (1985), 227–44. I am grateful to Dr Elaine Graham-Leigh for directing me to this article.

[46] L. L. Honeycutt, 'Female succession and the language of power in the writings of twelfth-century churchmen', in J. C. Parsons (ed.), *Medieval Queenship* (Stroud, 1994), 189–201.

[47] P. W. Edbury and J. G. Rowe, *William of Tyre: Historian of the Latin East* (Cambridge, 1988), 81–2.

[48] Honeycutt, 'Female succession', 198–9.

[49] The quotation is from ibid., 199, citing Migne, *PL* 182, col. 557.

[50] Honeycutt, 'Female succession', 200.

3

Home Front and Battlefield:
The Gendering of Papal Crusading Policy
(1095–1221)

CONSTANCE M. ROUSSEAU

In the year 1101, Count Stephen of Blois, after deserting his fellow crusaders at the siege of Antioch in the second wave of the First Crusade, arrived home to suffer much public disapproval. His wife, Adela, concerned with this outcry, often encouraged her husband during their marital caresses to recall the brave deeds of his youth and his present lordly status. Eventually, this 'wise and bold woman' (*mulier sagax et animosa*) as described by the chronicler Orderic Vitalis, persuaded her reluctant spouse to rejoin the crusade and vanquish the Muslims. Thus Stephen, now undaunted, persevered with his comrades until they finally reached the Sepulchre of Christ in Jerusalem.[1]

The preceding anecdote describing Adela of Blois and her husband emphasizes that the attitude of women towards the crusades was highly significant. Similarly, when we examine papal attitudes and policies between the First and Fifth Crusades, we discover a growing acknowledgement that the support of women could promote the church's religio-political goals in the Holy Land and other places where the faith was threatened. Early popes such as Urban II (1088–99) and Eugenius III (1145–53) narrowly defined and gendered crusading as a male military activity and took little notice of women except as inhibitors of the crusade. However, with the loss of Jerusalem to Saladin in 1187, later twelfth- and thirteenth-century popes such as Gregory VIII (1187), Clement III (1187–91), and especially Innocent III (1198–1216), focusing on ultimate Christian victory, gradually broadened their understanding of the crusade to include a spectrum of activities which permitted more female involvement on the home front and even, in very exceptional circumstances, in the field.

The papacy's early theoretical interpretation of the crusade as an 'armed pilgrimage' created a dichotomy between the theory and practice of women's involvement in the crusades. This contradiction arose because of two sets of gender expectations, one governing military, the other devotional activities. Throughout the Middle Ages, warfare was identified as a properly masculine pursuit and prowess on the battlefield was associated with virility and manhood.[2] Yet, Gregory VII (1073–85) regarded the making of war in the service of St Peter as a penitential act[3] and Urban II (1088–99) linked the First Crusade to the ideology of pilgrimage.[4]

This papal emphasis of the crusade as a penitential and devotional pilgrimage resulted in the theoretical possibility that crusading was an activity open to both sexes. Indeed, using language which did not designate the sex of the participants, Urban decreed in 1095 at the Council of Clermont that whoever (*quicumque*) travelled to Jerusalem to liberate the church from Muslim control undertook this journey as a substitute for penance.[5] Women, such as Helena, Paula, Eustochium and Egeria, had long engaged in the religious activities involving penance and pilgrimage.[6] After all, despite the medieval understanding of women's subordination to men in the sphere of social and legal institutions, the sexes enjoyed equality in the sphere of grace.[7] Galatians 3: 28 had established that there was neither male nor female but all were one in Jesus Christ. This economy of salvation meant that, at least in theory, even women could seek communion with Christ's suffering and redemption through holy crusade.

In spite of this theoretical loophole, the early papal encyclicals, with their practical aim of recruiting able-bodied fairly young troops, stressed that males should be engaged in actual military service. The letter of late December 1095 which Urban II sent ostensibly to *all* the faithful (*universis fidelibus, tam principibus quam subditis*) in Flanders, still addressed the recipients as 'brethren' (*fraternitatem*) and assumed that, if God inspired anyone to take the crusading vow, he (*eum*) should meet up with his company on 15 August, the Feast of the Assumption.[8]

A further letter to Bologna, dated 19 September 1096, likewise used gendered language, which suggested that the spiritual benefits of crusade were to accrue only to the male fighter. More narrowly addressed than the previous letter, to the beloved Catholic sons in the clergy and laity (*dilectis filiis catholicis in clero populoque*), it urged that young married men (*iuuenibus etiam coniugatis*) were not to join the crusade thoughtlessly without the agreement of their wives (*sine conniuentia uxorum suarum*).[9] The text thus implies that suitable and effective crusaders would be from the male laity.

For the most part, the chroniclers' accounts of Urban's preaching of the First Crusade at Clermont reaffirmed the narrow definition of crusading in the same masculine gendered language of warfare found in previous letters. One eye-witness at the council, Fulcher of Chartres, reports later in 1100–6 that the pope exhorted the sons of God (*filii Dei*) who had preserved the domestic peace and ecclesiastical rights more manfully (*virilius*) to concern themselves with the difficult situation in the Holy Land.[10] He promised remission of sins to all social orders (*cunctis cuiuslibet ordinis*), both knight and footsoldier (*tam equitibus quam peditibus*), who participated in this endeavour.[11] A second source, Baldric of Bourgueil, writing in *c.*1108, likewise confirmed that the pope used male-gendered language linked to knighthood, a status easily associated with masculine pursuits:

What are we saying, brothers? Hear and understand. You have fastened the belt of knighthood . . . Gird your sword, I say, each man of you . . . and be powerful sons, because it is better that you die in battle than bear the misfortunes of your people and holy places.[12]

Baldric's narrative noted Urban's focus on a male audience by giving his exhortation that the men should not permit the allure of their women or possessions to deter them from going on crusade.[13]

A final account of Urban's sermon at Clermont, written before 1107 by Robert, the Monk of Rheims, however, treats the exclusively male involvement in the crusade more ambiguously. On the one hand, his narrative reiterates Baldric's and suggests that Urban's preaching made a particular recruiting appeal to male listeners, entreating them to remember the brave deeds of their ancestors and not to be dissuaded by love of wives, children or parents.[14] On the other hand, Robert's account indicates that the pope, using inclusive language, addressed the people of France (*gens Francorum*) in his sermon calling for a crusade.[15] When the entire crowd, both men and women, responded very enthusiastically, the pope clarified that neither the elderly, the infirm, nor those most unsuitable for bearing arms should go on crusade. The pope specified that women should not undertake the journey at all without husbands, brothers or official permission. Such individuals, the pope stated, were more detrimental than beneficial to the enterprise.[16] Urban thus discouraged women's direct participation in crusading. According to his perspective, male permission for women to undergo the rigours and dangers of the expedition would probably be quite unlikely. Nevertheless, these papal restrictions still implied that married, unmarried or religious women could assume the cross with proper escort or permission. Perhaps either the notion of crusade as pilgrimage or the papal concerns for the demands of the conjugal debt played a role here.[17] Indeed, Jonathan Riley-Smith listed eight intrepid women, most of them wives, who certainly did accompany the armies of the First Crusade.[18]

Further ambiguities in Robert's narrative result from Urban's exhortation that the wealthy (*ditiores*) should assist the less economically fortunate and lead crusade troops at their own expense, and that lay people (*laicis*) should not travel on pilgrimage without priestly blessing.[19] This gender-neutral language could apply to wealthy laity of both sexes although the preceding evidence certainly suggests a contrary papal intention. Nonetheless, later popes would treat the question of affluent women going on crusade and would create a gender loophole for some very limited female participation on expeditions.

When we turn to papal recruitment of the Second Crusade (1147–9), the sources continue to use gendered language which disregarded women by describing the crusades in terms of patriarchal models of conduct. Eugenius III (1145–53), in his letter of 1 March 1146 to King Louis VII and all the French faithful, noted that his predecessor Urban II had solicited the aid of sons (*filios*) from diverse regions.[20] Invoking the brave deeds of their fathers, Eugenius stressed how his audience's male ancestors had manfully (*viriliter*) expelled the infidel from the land. In granting the remission of their sins, the pope now hoped that the sons would imitate these paternal actions, by strenuously defending those possessions won by their fathers and demonstrating the same courage.[21]

With the destruction of the Christian army and the loss of Jerusalem at the battle of Hattin in 1187, the need for suitable male crusading recruits increased. It is therefore not at all surprising that in 1187 Pope Gregory VIII at first proclaimed the Third Crusade (1189–92) in conventional masculine warrior terms. Addressing the Christian faithful, the pope exhorted:

> And therefore, my sons, . . . accept with an act of thanks this time for penance and doing good deeds, to the extent that it pertains to you, and give yourselves not to destruction but rather to the service of Him, from whom you have received your life and all your possessions, . . . Gird yourselves and be valiant sons . . .[22]

Yet, beginning with the brief pontificate of Gregory VIII, we see a broader understanding of other aspects of the crusade on the home front, particularly that of liturgical support. This twelfth-century papal initiative originated in the intercessory rituals of the past. In the pre-Carolingian and Carolingian periods, popes and emperors had required fasts, masses and litanies at home to gain divine favour for military campaigns in Europe.[23] Since the First Crusade, crusaders in the Holy Land had also been involved in various devotional rituals such as praying, fasting, participating in the mass liturgy, confessing their sins and joining processions with the chanting of psalms before battle.[24] The arduous siege of Antioch in 1098 during the First Crusade even caused its leaders to write to the Christian faithful, requesting fasting, almsgiving, prayers and masses.[25] A similar grave situation arising from the Christian defeat at Hattin now moved Gregory for the first time to call explicitly for intercessory and penitential activities in support of a crusade.[26] Regarding the disaster as divine judgement for the sins of Christians, the pope specified on 18 November 1187 that for the next five years, during Advent, all Christians (*omnes*) would observe a Lenten fast on Fridays and a special mass with intercessory and penitential psalms and prayers would be celebrated on those days. Additionally, all people (*omnes*) who were able would abstain from meat on Wednesdays and Saturdays.[27] According to the chronicler Arnold of Lübeck, Clement III (1187–91), Gregory's successor, continued this practice, ordering all Christians (*omnibus*) to engage in fasting and public prayers.[28] Although not explicitly mentioned, for the first time women at home could participate in these supplicatory activities for the crusade. The success of the crusades had become a collective commitment for all Christians.

Papal recognition of the value of women's contribution to the crusade reached full fruition during the reign of Innocent III

(1198–1216).[29] More than any of his predecessors, Innocent understood crusade participation as a series of gender-indifferent religious activities. His crusade programme also implies his acknowledgement of the role of feminine influence in crusade recruitment.[30]

The feminine role of the crusade recruiter, like that of Adela of Blois, was far from unique in this period. Jonathan Riley-Smith argues that, during the Second Crusade, women's transmission of their crusading enthusiasm to their families could favourably increase the ranks of crusaders.[31] An anecdote provided by Bishop Jacques de Vitry further confirms this suggestion. In the summer of 1216, the bishop, travelling to his new diocese of Acre in the Holy Land, had his horses seized by Genoese men involved in a local raid. Waiting for their return, he preached the crusade to their women and children remaining at home. His sermon inspired these fervent wives, a 'multitude of wealthy and noble Genoese women', not only to take the cross themselves, but also by their example to encourage their husbands to do so. Thus, according to the bishop, the townsmen took his horses and he made their women 'crusaders'.[32]

Innocent's greatest crusade encyclical *Qui maior* (19–29 April 1213), announcing the Fifth Crusade, took both practical crusading goals and feminine enthusiasm into consideration. Following the gender norms of earlier popes, Innocent called for male warriors to participate in military service: 'Therefore, come, most beloved sons, changing your fraternal enmities and disagreements into alliances of peace and affection; gird yourselves to the obedience of the Crucified One'.[33] The decretal also expresses a very comprehensive and gender-inclusive understanding of crusade participation where women are specifically mentioned. The pope ordered that there should be monthly liturgical processions where women and men in separate contingents (*fiat generalis processio seorsum virorum ac seorsum, ubi fieri poterit, mulierum*) should pray for God's liberation of the Holy Land.[34] A procession of this type, stipulating both male and female participants, had already been commanded by the pope a year earlier in Rome as a response to the Muslim incursions in Spain before Alfonso of Castile led the crusade of 1212.[35] Two years later, in the diocese of Liège, according to Innocent's mandate, crusade preachers gave the cross to many individuals of both sexes (*et multis utriusque sexus crucem imponant*) and a procession for all (*omni*) was ordered on the first Friday of the month.[36] During these liturgical activities, the preaching of the cross would take place.[37] An earlier letter of 19 April 1213 to the apostolic legate, Robert Courçon, had decreed that those who heard such sermons would receive a certain degree of remission for their sins.[38] Here was another gender-indifferent devotional activity where women, without travelling to the Holy Land, could gain salvific benefits from the crusade. *Quia maior* further stated that fasting, a penitential activity, would be joined to the prayers of the people.[39] Furthermore, each day during the celebration of the mass, after the kiss of peace, all, both women and men, would prostrate themselves on the ground (*omnes, tam viri quam mulieres humiliter prosternantur in terram*) while the clergy would intone psalms and prayers for the restoration of the East to Christian control.[40]

The penitential and fiscal activity of almsgiving so both sexes could support the crusade was connected to this liturgy on the home front. *Quia maior* stipulated that in each church where the general monthly processions gathered an empty chest would be placed, locked by three keys held by an honest priest, a devout layman and a religious, where not only the clergy but also the laity, specifically men and women (*viri et mulieres*), would place their crusade offerings.[41]

Moreover, in *Quia maior*, Innocent widened the applicability of the crusade indulgence, providing a few outlets where women remaining at home could gain the spiritual advantages of the crusade through their financial sponsorship of male warriors. Using gender-neutral language, the pope designated a sliding scale of indulgences: (1) he would grant full remission of sins to those who personally participated in the crusade at their own or another's expense; (2) he also offered full forgiveness to those who did not personally participate but sent suitable men (*viros idoneos*) at their own expense; (3) the pope further noted that a partial absolution for sins would be granted to those who gave a portion of their goods to aid the crusade – they would share in the remission according to the amount of financial assistance and the intensity of their devotion.[42] In the latter two instances, women on the home front could participate and would certainly benefit.

Most of all, female devotional and fiscal activities merged together in the pope's stipulations concerning the crusading vow. Innocent's predecessors had urged that those who assumed the crusade vow should be carefully examined, advised and approved by the clergy.[43] Presumably, such restrictive procedures would prevent those deemed unsuitable for service, such as women, from taking the vow.

However, in *Quia maior* the pope now broadened the categories of those who could take the crusading vow. The pope decreed that, since examination of personal suitability and capacity to fulfil the vow greatly impeded and delayed assistance to the Holy Land, anyone, with the exception of religious, could take the vow which would be commuted, redeemed or deferred if necessity or expediency required.[44]

Quia maior was therefore highly significant in the gendering of Innocent's crusade policy. A practical man, the pope desired victory. Male warriors were essential; nonetheless, women could also be useful in the attainment of this ecclesiastical goal. Enthusiastic women, like those mentioned by Jacques de Vitry and Orderic Vitalis, partaking in home-front activities, not only might encourage their menfolk to go on crusade, but also by redemption of their crusade vows for gender alone, as allowed by *Quia maior*, could increase the monetary support of the crusade. Moreover, women initially less supportive of the crusade might become more inclined towards it through their home-front involvement. At the very least, both groups of women could provide significant and meaningful assistance by wielding the spiritual and fiscal weapons of holy war, if not weapons on the battlefield.

Not surprisingly, Innocent's conciliar decree *Ad liberandum*, promulgated at the Fourth Lateran Council of 1215, reiterated the need for able-bodied male crusade warriors (*bellatores*) to fight on the battlefield.[45] Yet this canon also contains inclusive language, plural and ungendered, such as *crucesignati, omnes, personas* and *participes*.[46] The decree also refers to individual persons, using the Latin *hominum*, or human,[47] rather than *virum*, or male persons. We can suggest that the Latin usage allowed for the possibility of women's involvement on the crusade expedition itself in exceptional circumstances in order to advance the papacy's defence of the faith.

Evidence to support this comprehensive understanding of crusade participation is found in Innocent's early letter *Quod super his* of 1200, addressed to Hubert Walter, archbishop of Canterbury. Guided by the traditional military standards, the pope stated that, for the most part, women ought to redeem their crusading vows on the basis of their sex. Yet he makes two exceptions. First, if women were unwilling to remain at home, they could follow their husbands on crusade.[48] No doubt recruitment of male warriors would increase if husbands could persuade their reluctant wives to accompany them to the Holy Land. Presumably these women would merely be non-combatants of the camp since the text provides no further information concerning the women's role. The second exception indicated a certain degree of gender flexibility in the norms of military activity. The pope explicitly decreed that wealthy women could lead (*ducere*) warriors to the East at their own expense.[49] We would be going beyond the limits of this source to argue that *ducere* meant actual female participation in the battle; nevertheless, the verb seems to imply active feminine command of troops travelling to Palestine, rather than merely passive women 'accompanied' by male warriors as translated by one scholar.[50] Innocent never recanted this inclusion of prosperous women leading crusade armies as stated in *Quod super his*, a decree which would later enter the Decretals of Gregory IX (X. 3. 34. 8).

After the death of Innocent III, the crusade policy of his successor Honorius III (1216–27), who actually directed the Fifth Crusade, continued to implement the home-front activities which permitted female fiscal and liturgical participation. A letter of 22 April 1216 specifically authorized the dispensation of vows of female crusaders (*mulieribus crucesignatis*) deemed unsuitable so that those noblewomen who were wealthy could send other male warriors (*bellatores*) subsidized at the women's expense.[51] On 24 November 1217, the pope further noted that the Roman clergy and the people (*populo*), whom he did not differentiate by sex, had joined in a procession to gain divine favour for the crusading expeditions of Duke Leopold of Austria and King Andrew of Hungary travelling to the Holy Land.[52] Therefore, during the thirteenth century, liturgical, penitential and financial support which involved both sexes became an established feature in the crusade movement.[53]

Medieval women could serve as catalysts for advancing papal goals. Pre-1187 crusading policies of the papacy did not appreciate this fact and marginalized women since, for the most part, participation in the crusade was narrowly defined as masculine military service. Conventional gender expectations governing religious devotion and warfare operated so that the theory and practice of crusade as holy war and pilgrimage were in opposition. Women were deprived of the remission of sins which the crusade offered. Popes Gregory VIII, Clement III and especially Innocent III, despite evident limitations in their policies, brought women more into the centre of the crusade movement by designating liturgical, devotional, penitential and fiscal activities which could foster women's ownership of the crusade on the home front and, in very exceptional circumstances, on the march. These policies also ultimately attempted to reconcile theory and practice. Most women would not travel with or lead crusading armies; but now these women waiting at home could still enjoy some if not all of the salvific benefits of the crusade as if they had undertaken the journey themselves. Clearly, women's prayers and alms on the home front must be viewed according to traditional gender norms where female activity is ancillary to male endeavours. Nevertheless, these popes tried to galvanize feminine influence to promote their religio-political agenda in the East. Crusade was an enterprise for all Christians, regardless of sex.

NOTES

[1] Marjorie Chibnall (ed. and trans.), *The Ecclesiastical History of Orderic Vitalis*, 5 (Oxford, 1975), bk X, p. 324.

[2] Megan McLaughlin, 'The woman warrior: gender, warfare, and society in medieval Europe', *Women's Studies* 17 (1990), 194.

[3] Erich Caspar (ed.), *Das Register Gregors VII*, 1 (Berlin, 1967), 2. 49, p. 190; 3. 11, pp. 271–2; H. E. J. Cowdrey, *Pope Gregory VII* (Oxford, 1998), 654–8.

[4] Jonathan Riley-Smith, *The Crusades: A Short History* (London, 1987), 37.

[5] Robert Somerville (ed.), *The Councils of Urban II*. 1: *Decreta Claromontensia* (Annuarium Historiae Conciliorum Supplementum, 1; Amsterdam, 1972), 74. 'Quicumque pro sola devotione, non pro honoris vel pecunie adeptione, ad liberandam ecclesiam Dei Hierusalem profectus fuerit, iter illud pro omni penitentia ei reputetur.'

[6] Maureen Purcell, 'Women crusaders: a temporary canonical aberration?', in L. O. Frappell (ed.), *Principalities, Powers and Estates: Studies in Medieval and Early Modern Government and Society* (Adelaide, 1979), 57.

[7] Renée Metz, 'Le Statut de la femme en droit canonique médiéval', in *La Femme et l'enfant dans le droit canonique médiéval* (London, 1985), 59–113, at 112.

[8] Heinrich Hagenmeyer, *Die Kreuzzugsbriefe aus den Jahren 1088–1100* (Innsbruck, 1901), 136–7, no. 2. 'Fraternitatem uestram iam pridem multorum relatione didicisse credimus barbaricam rabiem ecclesias Dei in Orientis partibus miserabili infestatione deuastasse, . . . si quibus autem uestram

Deus hoc uotum inspirauerit, sciant eum in Beatae Mariae Adsumptione
cum Dei adiutorio profecturum eiusque comitatui tunc se adhaerere posse.'

⁹ Ibid., pp. 137–8, no. 3. '. . . iuuenibus etiam coniugatis prouidendum est,
ne temere tantum iter sine conniuentia uxorum suarum adgrediantur.'

¹⁰ *Fulcheri Carnotensis, Historia Hierosolymitana (1095–1127)*, ed. H.
Hagenmeyer (Heidelberg, 1913), 130–8, at 132–3.

¹¹ Ibid., 134–5.

¹² Baldric of Bourgueil, 'Historia Jerosolimitana', *RHC Oc* 4:. 12–16, at
14–15.

¹³ Ibid., 15.

¹⁴ Robert of Rheims, 'Historia Iherosolimitana', *RHC Oc* 3: 728. 'O for-
tissimi milites et invictorum propago parentum, nolite degenerari, sed
virtutis priorum vestrorum reminiscimini. Quod si vos carus liberorum et
parentum et conjugum detinet affectus . . .'

¹⁵ Ibid., 727.

¹⁶ Ibid., 729.

¹⁷ For a discussion of the conjugal debt and the crusade, see James A.
Brundage, 'The crusader's wife: a canonistic quandary', *Studia Gratiana* 12
(1967), 425–41.

¹⁸ Jonathan Riley-Smith, *The First Crusaders (1095–1131)* (Cambridge,
1997), 196–226.

¹⁹ Robert of Rheims, 'Historia', 729.

²⁰ Peter Rassow, 'Der Text der Kreuzzugsbulle Eugens III, vom 1. März
1146, Trastevere', *Neues Archiv* 45 (1924), 300–5, at 302. 'Predecessor eten-
im noster felicis memorie Urbanus papa tamquam tuba celestis intonuit et
ad ipsius deliberationem sancte Romane ecclesie filios de diversis mundi
partibus sollicitare curavit.'

²¹ Ibid., 303. 'Que per gratiam Dei et patrum vestrorum studium, qui per
intervalla temporum eas defendere et Christianum nomen in partibus illis
dilatare pro viribus studuerunt, . . . et alie urbes infidelium ab ipsis viriliter
expugnate . . . Verumtamen si, quod absit, secus contigerit, patrum fortitu-
do in filiis imminuta esse probatur.'

²² A. Chroust (ed.), 'Historia de expeditione Friderici imperatoris', *MGH
Scriptores rerum Germanicarum*, NS 5 (Berlin, 1928), 6–10, at 9. 'Cogitate
itaque, filii, . . . vos, et penitendi ac bene agendi tempus, quantum spectat ad
vos, cum gratiarum actione recipite et date vos ipsos non in exterminium, sed
in observationem ei, a quo et vos et vestra omnia accepistis, . . . accingimini
et estote filii potentes . . .'

²³ Christoph T. Maier, 'Crisis, liturgy and the crusade in the twelfth and
thirteenth centuries', *JEH* 48 (1997), 628–57, at 629.

²⁴ Ibid., 628.

²⁵ Ibid., 630; Hagenmeyer, *Die Kreuzzugsbriefe*, 153–5, at 155.

²⁶ Maier, 'Crisis', 632.

²⁷ Johannes Ramackers (ed.), *Papsturkunden in Frankreich,* 2: *Normandie*

(Göttingen, 1937), 385–6, no. 290: 'nos de communi fratrum nostrorum consilio multis episcopis approbantibus constituimus, ut omnes usque ad quinquennium saltem per omnes sextas ferias in cibo quadragesimali ieiunent et missa, ubi cantanda fuerit, in hora nona cantetur, quod etiam a prima dominica de aduentuusque ad natale domini statuimus obseruandum. Feria uero quarta et sabbato indifferenter omnes, qui bene ualent, a carnibus abstinebunt.'

[28] Georg Pertz (ed.), 'Arnoldi Chronica Slavorum', in *MGH SS* 21 (Hanover, 1859), 170.

[29] For a discussion of Innocent III and crusading, see James M. Powell, *Anatomy of a Crusade, 1213–1221* (Philadelphia, 1986) and Helmut Roscher, *Papst Innocenz III und die Kreuzzüge* (Göttingen, 1969).

[30] He certainly recognized female influence over husbands' virtuous behaviour. See *PL* 216: 753 where he cites 1 Cor. 7: 14 – a faithful wife could save an infidel husband. For a discussion of ecclesiastical writers' acknowledgement of women's influence in moral suasion, spiritual development, religious conversion and monastic patronage, see Sharon Farmer, 'Persuasive voices: clerical images of medieval wives', *Speculum* 61 (1986), 517–43.

[31] Jonathan Riley-Smith, 'Family traditions and participation in the Second Crusade', in Michael Gervers (ed.), *The Second Crusade and the Cistercians* (New York, 1992), 101–8.

[32] R. B. C. Huygens (ed.), *Lettres de Jacques de Vitry* (Leiden, 1960), 71–8, at 77; James M. Powell, 'The role of women in the Fifth Crusade', in *Horns*, 294.

[33] G. Tangl (ed.), *Studien zum Register Innocenz' III* (Weimar, 1929), 88–97, at 91. 'Eya igitur, dilectissimi filii, dissensiones et emulationes fraternas in pacis et dilectionis federa commutatantes, accingimini ad obsequium crucifixi . . .'

[34] Ibid., 95. 'Ideoque statuimus et mandamus, ut singulis mensibus semel fiat generalis processio seorsum virorum ac seorsum, ubi fieri poterit, mulierum in humilitate mentis et corporis cum devota orationum instantia postulantium . . .'

[35] *PL* 216: 698–9; Maier, 'Crisis', 633. For a detailed description of this procession see Christoph T. Maier, 'Mass, the Eucharist and the cross: Innocent III and the relocation of the crusade', in John C. Moore (ed.), *Pope Innocent III and his World* (Aldershot, 1999), 351–4.

[36] G. Pertz (ed.), 'Reineri annales 1066–1230', in *MGH SS* 26 (Hanover, 1859), 671.

[37] Tangl, *Studien*, 95: 'proviso prudenter, ut semper in ipsa processione verbum salutifere crucis cum diligenti exhortatione populo proponatur'.

[38] *PL* 216: 827: 'concedimus ut qui ad tuam vocationem devote convenerint ad audiendum verbum salutiferae crucis, de injunctis sibi poenitentiis vice nostra certam valeas indulgentiam impertiri'.

[39] Tangl, *Studien*, 95. 'Orationi vero ieiunium et helemosina coniungantur, ut hiis quasi alis facilius et celerius ipsa volet oratio ad piissimas aures Dei . . .'

[40] Ibid., 95–6. 'Singulis quoque diebus intra missarum solennia, post pacis osculum, . . . omnes, tam viri quam mulieres, humiliter prosternantur in terram, et a clericis psalmus iste: "Deus, venerunt gentes in hereditatem tuam" alta voce cantetur . . .'

[41] Tangl, *Studien*, 96. 'In illis autem ecclesiis, in quibus conveniet processio generalis, truncus concavus statuatur, tribus clavibus consignatus, una penes honestum presbyterum, alia penes devotum laicum at tertia penes aliquem regularem fideliter conservandis, in quo clerici et laici, viri et mulieres helemosinas suas ponant in terre sancte subsidium convertendis secundum dispositionem eorum, quibus hec fuerit sollicitudo commissa.'

[42] Tangl, *Studien*, 91–2. '. . . omnibus qui laborem istum in propriis personis subierint et expensis, plenam suorum peccaminum, . . . veniam indulgemus et in retributione iustorum salutis eterne pollicemur augmentum. Eis autem, qui non in personis propriis illuc accesserint, sed in suis dumtaxat expensis iuxta facultatem et qualitatem suam viros idoneos destinarint, et illis similiter, qui licet in alienis expensis, in propriis tamen personis accesserint, plenam suorum concedimus veniam peccatorum. Huius quoque remissionis volumus et concedimus esse participes iuxta quantitatem subsidii et devotionis affectum omnes qui ad subventionem ipsius terre de bonis suius congrue ministrabunt.'

[43] James A. Brundage, 'The votive obligations of crusaders: the development of a canonistic doctrine', in *The Crusades, Holy War and Canon Law* (Aldershot, 1991), 77–118, at 94.

[44] Tangl, *Studien*, 93–4. 'Quia vero subsidium terre sancte multum impediri vel retardari contingeret, si ante susceptionem crucis examinari quemlibet oporteret, an esset idoneus et sufficiens ad huiusmodi votum personaliter prosequendum, concedimus, ut regularibus personis exceptis suscipiant quicumque voluerint signum crucis, ita quod, cum urgens necessitas aut evidens utilitas postulaverit, votum ipsum de apostolico possit mandato commutari aut redimi vel differri.'

[45] G. Alberigo and N. P. Tanner (eds.), *Decrees of the Ecumenical Councils I Nicea to Lateran V* (Georgetown, VA, 1990), Lateran IV, 267–71, at 268.

[46] Ibid., 267, 268.

[47] Ibid., 268.

[48] *PL* 216: 1261–2, at 1262. 'De mulieribus autem hoc credimus observandum, ut quae remanere noluerint, viros suos sequantur euntes; caeterae vero, nisi forte sint divites, quae secum in suis expensis possint ducere bellatores, votum redimant quod voverunt, aliis terrae sanctae subsidium singulis secundum proprias facultates diligenter inductis.'

[49] Ibid.

[50] James A. Brundage, *Medieval Canon Law and the Crusader* (Madison, WI, 1969), 77.

[51] Petrus Pressutti (ed.), *Regesta Honorii Papae III*, 1 (Rome, 1888), 93, no. 529. 'Concedit facultatem dispensandi . . . cum mulieribus crucesignatis, ita videlicet quod ipsi crucesignati ac specialiter mulieres nobiles atque divites aliquos bellatores per se mittant in ipsius Terre succursum aut pecuniam in subsidium conferant iuxta proprias facultates . . .'

[52] Ibid., 149–50, no. 885. 'Iniungit, ut . . . preces ad Deum fundant pro felici eventu Andreae regis Hungariae, qui cum Leopoldo Austriae et Octone Maraviae ducibus ingenti cum exercitu Babiloniam intraverant: se quoque processionem fecisse cum clero et populo Vrbis.'

[53] Maier, 'Crisis', 634–5.

4

'Unfit to Bear Arms': The Gendering of Arms and Armour in Accounts of Women on Crusade

MICHAEL R. EVANS

When Pope Urban II preached the First Crusade at Clermont in 1095, he included women among those who were to be excluded as 'unfit for arms'. In so doing, he was stating a commonplace of medieval ideas on gender roles, namely that arms were 'male' and women were therefore unsuited to bear them. As Megan McLaughlin has observed, medieval warfare 'was generally viewed as the quintessential masculine activity . . . descriptions of warfare in medieval texts were peppered with references to gender, references which equated fighting ability with virility'.[1] Nevertheless, stories of women donning armour or taking up arms to fight for the faith abound.

Sources for warrior women are highly problematic. In the words of Helen Nicholson, 'Our problem is that in both the European Christian and the Muslim culture, it was expected that good, virtuous women would not normally fight . . . Therefore Christian writers would not record women fighting in the crusading army, because this would discredit the crusaders . . .'[2] Conversely, Arab historians made the most of such accounts in order to do just that. Women are usually described by crusade chroniclers in stereotypical female roles, notably those of washerwoman or prostitute;[3] when they take on the supposedly 'male' role of warrior, they are presented as 'honorary men', fighting 'manfully' in spite of the disadvantage of their sex. William of Tyre, describing the fall of Jerusalem to the armies of the First Crusade (an event to which he was not an eye-witness), wrote that 'even women, regardless of sex and natural weakness, dared to

assume arms and fought manfully, far beyond their strength'.[4]
Wives and mothers who urged their menfolk to go on the Third
Crusade regretted 'that they were not able to set out with them
because of the weakness of their sex'.[5] The valiant Margaret of
Beverley fought 'like a man' in defence of Jerusalem against the army
of Saladin.[6]

This chapter addresses the question of descriptions of women
wearing armour and bearing arms, in order to examine the implications for perceived gender roles of women taking on such archetypal
masculine attributes. It will look at some well-known accounts of
women in the crusades to demonstrate this point, and examine these
in the light of literary and moral attitudes to the bearing of arms and
the wearing of armour by women.

In a famous and controversial passage, the Muslim chronicler
'Imad ad-Din recorded that Frankish women went into battle at the
time of the Third Crusade dressed in men's clothes and wearing
armour and helmets. Because of this, they were not recognized as
men until killed and stripped of their armour.[7] We should perhaps
be wary of 'Imad ad-Din's account, as he was given to verbosity and
rhetoric, and the idea of the enemy employing female warriors may
be a literary topos to demonstrate the 'unnatural practices' – military
and, by implication, sexual or social – of the opponent. His description of Christian warrior women is immediately followed by, and
should be viewed in context with, a description of the appalling
immorality of Christian prostitutes, told with great rhetorical flour-
ishes and gleeful outrage.[8] His chronicle displays an appalled
fascination with sexual matters; for example, he dwells at length and
almost with relish on the rape of captured women.[9] Equally, however, he is 'recycling' an old story. Compare 'Imad ad-Din's account
above with the description of third-century Persian soldiers by the
Byzantine historian John Zonaras: 'It is said that when the Persian
dead were being stripped, among them were found women equipped
and armed as men.'[10]

An interesting comparison can be made with Muslim sources on
the arming of their own women in the crusade period. Usamah ibn-
Munqidh's famous *Kitab al-I'tibar* (written *c*.1185) relates accounts
of Christian women in the Latin East, whom Usamah saw as being
without shame – telling, for example, how Frankish women accompanied their husbands or fathers into the traditionally male domain
of the bath-house, openly conversed with strange men in the streets,

and even shared their beds with male visitors.[11] These stories, like 'Imad ad-Din's of Christian warrior women, are intended to emphasize the enemy's barbarism. Usamah was quite capable of regarding individual Franks as his friends, while seeing them as a race as less than human, 'as animals possessing the virtues of courage and fighting, but nothing else'.[12] His stories are entertaining, but deal in stereotypes. For example, the story of the Frank who finds his wife in bed with another man, and accepts her tortuous excuses that she is merely being hospitable to the visitor, is a *fabliau* trope, of the foolish (usually old) man who is unable to see the evidence of his wife's adultery before his very eyes, and accepts unlikely excuses. This trope is known in later Western literature, for example, in Chaucer's *Merchant's Tale*. Usamah treats his accounts of Frankish customs humorously: for example, he tells the story of a Frankish woman who not only appears at the bath-house, but does not demur when Usamah's servant looks up her dress to see if she is really a woman. He follows that with a story of a Frankish priest who performed euthanasia on a dying man by blocking his nostrils with wax, before concluding, 'we shall now leave the discussion of their treatment of the orifices of the body'.[13] Despite his first-hand knowledge of the Franks, Usamah's work should therefore be treated with care as a source for the conduct of Frankish women.

What then of his stories of warlike Muslim women? Usamah groups a number of stories of fighting women together, namely: a cousin, Shabib, whose cousin's mother dons armour; Usamah's own mother's role in organizing the defence of the castle of Shayzar; a slave of Usamah's grandfather, who picks up a sword and goes into battle; a Frankish woman who inflicts wounds on an Egyptian amir by hitting him with a pot, and a woman of Shayzar who captures three Frankish men.[14]

On the face of it, we have a reliable source of information on Muslim warrior women, as Usamah was writing about his own, Muslim, side, and even knew or was related to some of the participants. However, we should be wary, not least because of Usamah's anecdotal style, relating as he does stories that were invariably told him by a friend or relative, and which he was writing down some sixty or more years after the event. As Hitti, one of Usamah's translators, puts it, 'amiably rambling in his talk and reminiscences, our nonagenarian spins one anecdote after another'.[15] More pertinently, Usamah's work, like that of Christian chroniclers, had an instructive

purpose; the title *al-I'tibar* translates roughly as 'learning by example'. It is not an autobiography as such, and its author 'leaps from
anecdote to anecdote'.[16] As it is both anecdotal and didactic, the
work is doubly problematic as a source.

In this light, the story of Shabib's cousin's mother dressing in
armour is seen as a moral exemplar. The woman does not actually
fight; she dons armour and wears a sword to encourage her hesitant
male kinsman. The stereotypical nature of the passage is shown by
the repetition of the topos of the warrior not recognized as female
until her armour is removed; in this case, the woman warrior is alive,
but at first Shabib takes her to be a man, and is terrified until she
removes her helmet and 'behold! it was none other than the mother
of his cousin, Layth-al-Dawlah Yahya'. The moral of the story is
that Shabib needed a woman's example to restore his courage; she
rebukes him when he recommends flight: 'What a wretched thing
thou doest! Thou leavest thy uncle's daughters and the women of thy
family to the ravishers . . .' Layth-al-Dawlah's mother's 'manly'
action serves to point up Shabib's unmanly abandonment of his
female cousins, and her taunts become the spur for him to regain his
manhood, as we are told that he took up arms and subsequently
'became one of our noteworthy cavaliers'.[17] Al-Dawlah's mother
plays the role, on behalf of her daughters, of the German women of
Tacitus, who spur on their menfolk by reminding them that they (the
women) will be enslaved if the battle is lost.[18] Another example of a
spirited woman is Usamah's own mother, who, fearing her son was
dead, distributed swords and armour to the defenders of Shaysar,
and placed her daughter on the wall of the castle, so that she could
be the more easily thrown to her death rather than be dishonoured if
the battle were lost. Despite Hitti's heading, 'Usamah's mother as a
warrior', she did not take up arms or don armour herself.[19]

These examples notwithstanding, Usamah shares with our other
authors a sense of the unnaturalness of women fighting. The two
above examples occurred in emergency situations – sieges or battles
lost or feared lost. Two other examples of bellicose women cited by
Usamah were a slave and a Frank, both members of groups who
were alien to the Muslim aristocracy to which Usamah belonged.
Furthermore, the anecdotes of warlike women are preceded by the
tale of Buraykah, a sorceress and former slave.[20] This is no coincidence, but a deliberate segue, as Usamah remarks: 'The undaunted
spirit of this bitch [Buraykah] brought to my mind the memory of

events which happened to our women in the battle that took place between the Isma'ilites and ourselves, although the two categories of women are quite different.'[21]

The topos of armoured women revealed as men when stripped of their armour is an extremely venerable one. Herodotus employed it in describing that archetype of female martial activity, the Amazon. He describes how the Scythians, 'thinking that they [the Amazons] were young men . . . fought in defense of their property, and discovered from the bodies which came into their possession after the battle that they were women'.[22]

It is significant that this topos should originate in a tale of the Amazons, as these female warriors were in Western literature the epitome of unnatural conduct in women. Amazons were well-known to medieval writers, and, at least until Christine de Pisan 'rehabilitated' the Amazon queens in her *Cité des Dames*, were usually synonymous with barbarism and an overturning of the natural order in which war was a male preserve and women were subject to men. The Amazon had surrendered her femininity in a number of ways, not only by becoming a warrior and a holder of political authority. She had rejected the 'natural' role of woman as mother (the Amazons were supposed to kill all male offspring), and had even physically mutilated the symbol of womanhood and motherhood, by cutting off one of her breasts. The word Amazon was explained in post-classical accounts as meaning 'breastless', creating the tradition that they severed their right breasts in order to use a bow more effectively. We may note the way in which the 'unnatural' role of woman as warrior is directly related to her unnatural rejection of motherhood and of the very physical evidence of her motherhood and womanhood. They were also unfeminine in their sexual practices; at best, they were often represented as devoted to virginity, at worst as cynically selecting mates for their breeding potential. In either case, they rejected the woman's assigned role as nurturing wife and mother.

Amazons were not always viewed in a negative light, however, in medieval literature. The twelfth-century Norman author Benoît de Sainte-Maure's *Roman de Troie* shows the Amazons as paragons of chivalry and an amalgam of the ideal virtues of both knight and lady. Their homeland, *Amazoine* or *Feminie* is presented in paradisial terms. They are presented as having risen above womanhood; Penthesilea's response to Pyrrhus's taunt that it is 'tedious and disagreeable' to bear arms against women is that Amazons are not 'weak and feeble' like ordinary women.[23]

The Amazons were associated with barbarism, with the untamed regions outside (male) civilization. They were traditionally identified with Scythia, on the edge of the Greek world, and in mythology were 'tamed' through defeat by Greek princes. The Amazons were, in effect, 'orientalized', becoming part of the exotic eastern Other. This could accommodate both positive and negative conceptions of them; Benoît's idealized *Feminie* fits an orientalizing view of the Edenic East, seen in works such as the Alexander romances. His Penthesilea is still the Other, no matter how admiringly she is painted. In a story that was to become a source for Boccaccio and Chaucer, Theseus defeats the Amazons and marries their queen Hippolyta. The Queen is tamed by being brought into Greek civilized society, but also by returning to the 'natural' order of subjection to her husband. In Chaucer, 'Hippolyta is just the woman whom Theseus happened to marry, and she is hardly noticeable. Her Amazon past is far behind her, and she is a dutiful and obedient helpmeet.'[24]

A 'real' parallel to this orientalizing of warrior women can be seen in the claim by Franciscan Jordan of Giano, writing in the mid-thirteenth century, that the Mongols employed women warriors, and his remark that 'she who fights best is regarded as the most desirable, just as in our society she who weaves and sews best is more desired than the one who is beautiful'.[25] Jordan's opinion is revealing of Western Christian attitudes to gender and labour in its equation of weaving as woman's work and warfare as man's. As we shall see, this gendering of labour is important in Western accounts of crusader women.

With some exceptions, Amazons are horribly punished for transgressing the laws of nature in medieval accounts of the Trojan Wars. In most such accounts, the Amazon Queen Penthesilea is defeated and killed in combat by Pyrrhus, son of Achilles, and her body is dismembered (in some versions, while she is still alive) and cast into the river. In the pseudo-history of Dictys of Crete, the Greeks say that this is because she 'transgressed the bounds of nature and her sex'.[26] It is clear that Penthesilea has made herself unfeminine by donning armour, and only regains her femininity when dead. In some classical versions of the legend, reminiscent of the topos of the warrior only revealed as female when stripped of her armour, she is killed by Achilles, who posthumously falls in love with her when her helm is removed to reveal the face of a beautiful woman.[27] However, medieval renditions deny her even this element of womanhood.

An interesting example of the assumed contradiction between warfare and motherhood occurs in Guibert of Nogent's chronicle of the First Crusade, the *Dei Gesta per Francos*. Guibert (who was not an eye-witness) refers to Saracen women among the army of Kerbogha, in order to heighten the sense of its exoticism. Following a description of the great wealth and ample supplies of the Muslim army, Guibert recounts how women, looking like a new version of the goddess Diana of old, arrived carrying bows and quivers. These women were evidently pregnant, as they were there not to fight, but apparently to bear children. However, when the battle was over, the women, fleeing in fear of the Franks, were found to have abandoned their new-born babies on the grass.[28] This passage combines the Amazonian attributes of fighting with bows and unnatural attitudes to reproduction and motherhood. The figure of Diana is a suitable one, as she combined seemingly contradictory elements; she was a huntress, yet also a protectress of children; a virgin, yet the goddess of childbirth. Guibert describes the young women as *virgines*, which they could clearly not have been (at least in the sense of 'virgins') given that they bear children. Nowhere, incidentally, does Guibert state explicitly that they fought with the bows and arrows that they bore. The incident is an insertion into the story by Guibert, and does not appear in his principal source, the anonymous *Gesta Francorum*.

Lorraine Stock has described how medieval romance was unable to depict a woman as both armoured *and* feminine. She has demonstrated how, in the mid-twelfth-century *Roman d'Eneas*, the warrior woman Camille is denied the 'arming' passage traditional for knights in romance, and her clothing is presented as decorative and 'feminine', in contrast to the male Eneas, who possesses armour studded with precious stones. Conversely, in the thirteenth-century *Roman de Silence*, the heroine Silence is allowed to don armour and engage in warfare, but is gendered male.[29] In other words, armour makes the man.

Before moving on from the subject of Amazons, we should address the famous story of how Eleanor of Aquitaine and her ladies on the Second Crusade dressed as Penthesilea and the Amazons, and how their scandalous behaviour was blamed for the failure of the crusade. This is a later myth, although grounded in contemporary reports of Eleanor's supposedly scandalous behaviour, and a reference by the Byzantine writer Niketas Choniates to a 'German' woman as 'another Penthesilea' and her companions as 'more mannish than the Amazons'.[30] Magoulis cites Stephen Runciman for the identification of Eleanor with Penthesilea, but adds that 'Runciman, however, does not cite his source.'[31] It is therefore another example of martial qualities being attributed to the women of the barbarous Other, in this instance the Franks as viewed by the Greeks, with the story being given extra life by the assumptions of modern historians. The full version of the tale did not appear until Agnes Strickland's nineteenth-century history of the queens of England.[32]

We have seen how accounts of armoured women fighting in the Frankish ranks must be read with a great deal of caution. This is not to say, however, that the presence of fighting women among the crusaders was entirely a figment of 'Imad ad-Din's imagination. He and Baha ad-Din both recorded the presence of a woman archer at Acre, and the discovery of a dead woman killed in the fighting. Both of these are more 'realistic' accounts, more laconic and less rhetorical than the 'armoured women' stories. Interestingly, in neither of these accounts is there a reference to armour. It is specified that the woman archer employed a wooden bow, perhaps implying the use of a relatively unmartial weapon, in contrast to the crossbow or composite bow that might be wielded by a seasoned warrior. We are left with the impression of women who were drawn into the fighting by necessity in the emergency of a siege. This was apparently the situation in which women were most often involved in medieval warfare.[33] Fully fledged mounted, armoured warfare remained the preserve of the (by definition, male) knight. The Frankish woman witnessed by 'Imad ad-Din and Baha ad-Din was using an unknightly weapon, the bow, as did the Amazons.

Similarly, Christian accounts of women fighting in 'emergency' situations show a gendered approach to weaponry. To take one example from the *Itinerarium*, women are recorded defending the crusader camp from attack by Saladin's army, but they do not take up knightly arms: 'Our women pulled the Turks by the hair, treated them dishonourably, humiliatingly cutting their throats; and finally beheaded them. The women's physical weakness prolonged the pain of death, because they cut their heads off with knives instead of swords.'[34] A few points can be made about this passage. Once again, it is not just to be taken as a literal description of events; the killing by Christian women is described precisely to emphasize the shame of the Muslims who are killed so 'humiliatingly'. It is the very unnaturalness of women as killers that makes this so shameful, another variation on the theme that women are not supposed to fight, because of their 'weakness'. In a sense, this passage is a variation on the use of the fighting-women motif to cast shame on the enemy. Importantly, we again meet the gendering of weaponry, as the women do not use swords, the weapon of the knight, but knives, a civilian weapon.

The crusades by their nature may have been exceptional wars, in which women camp-followers were more likely to become involved in the fighting. However, we can see the gendering of weaponry in examples of women fighting in non-crusading contexts. To use another twelfth-century example, Juliana, daughter of Henry I, fired on her father with a crossbow at the siege of Breteuil in 1119. As well as using an 'unknightly' weapon, Juliana's action was in the context of an ambush rather than open warfare, and earned the thorough disapproval of the chronicler Orderic Vitalis. He regarded Juliana's ruse as a 'woman's trick' and an example of 'treacherous intent', proving that 'there is nothing so bad as a bad woman'. The fact that Henry had connived in the blinding and mutilation of her daughters (his own grand-daughters) did nothing to soften the chronicler's harsh verdict. Juliana received her just deserts for so usurping a man's role; trapped in the besieged castle 'the unlucky Amazon got out of the predicament shamefully as best she could' by leaping from the battlements 'shamefully, with bare buttocks, into the depths of the moat'.[35] Again we see the association of shame with women fighting, although in this case the shame is with the woman who takes up arms, not her male victims.

Orderic does, however, provide us with a more sympathetic portrait of a warrior woman elsewhere in his *Ecclesiastical History*. He relates the story of the conflict between two Norman women, Helwise, countess of Evreux, and Isabel of Conches in 1090. Isabel is portrayed in very positive terms:

> [She] was generous, daring and gay, and therefore loveable and estimable to those around her. In war she rode armed as a knight among the knights; and she showed no less courage among the knights in hauberks and sergeants-at-arms than did the maid Camilla, the pride of Italy, among the troops of Turnus. She deserved comparison with Lampeto and

Marpesia, Hippolyta and Penthesilea and other warlike Amazon queens
. . .[36]

So Orderic was capable of placing a warrior woman among the
Amazons in a 'positive' sense. But, again, the overall context is one
where a woman bearing arms was unnatural. Although Isabel is
praised and Helwise condemned as 'cruel and grasping' both are
seen as transgressing their position as women by the fact that they
'dominated their husbands and oppressed their vassals'. The war
was supposedly 'fomented by the malignant rivalry of two proud
women', when Helwise insulted Isabel, and 'so the hearts of brave
men were moved to anger through the suspicions and quarrels of
women'.[37] Orderic perhaps is alluding to Isabel's Amazonian
exploits when he tells us that in her old age she repented the sins of
her youth and became a nun, a course of action also taken by the
bellatrix Juliana.[38]

The presence of fighting women on the Third Crusade is also supported by Frankish sources, of which one of the most interesting is
the story of Margaret of Beverley. Her experience was recorded by
her brother Thomas, a monk at Froidmont, so it is filtered through
a male cleric's pen.[39] In Jerusalem, while under siege from Saladin,
she took to the defence of the city 'like a man', wearing a cooking
pot for a helmet and carrying water to men on the walls, and was
wounded in action by Saladin's siege-engines.[40] The reference to the
cooking pot is interesting. In the dire circumstances facing the
Franks following the defeat at Hattin in 1187, it is not surprising that
all kind of household implements might have been employed as
weapons, but the reference occurring in the context of a woman
fighting introduces a slight note of gender-stereotyping, and of
strangeness. We are reminded of common satirical images of fighting women, such as that of the woman jousting with a distaff, that
occur in manuscripts of the time.[41] A sense of the strangeness of this
motif can be perceived in the other contexts in which Randall lists a
distaff appearing:

Ape with; Apes tilting astride birds; Beast with; Boar and dog with; Hare
with; Hybrid Franciscan; Hybrid man with; man and hybrid man, seated;
Man with; Mermaid with; Merman and hybrid woman with; Nun,
Dominican; Pig with; St Margaret; Squirrel with; Stork as woman;
Woman with . . .[42]

Men who were reluctant to take part in the Third Crusade were sent wool and distaffs by their detractors, to demonstrate that if they lacked the courage to fight, then they would be better engaged in woman's work.[43] This practice has been compared to the giving of white feathers to men who did not volunteer to fight in the First World War,[44] but there is a significant difference: whereas white feathers were usually given by women, the *Itinerarium* author tells us that 'men sent each other wool and distaff'. In this manner, crusade participation was maintained as a male preserve, even while female imagery was being employed. To return to an Amazonian theme, in Joseph of Exeter's late twelfth-century *Bellum Troianum*, the Greeks are scornful about fighting against the Amazons, whom they describe as 'girls lobbing their distaffs'.[45] In the association of the distaff with woman, and womanly labour, we see a recurrence of the idea of gendered labour seen in Jordan of Giano's comments on Mongol women.

William of Tyre, in his description of the siege of Jerusalem that was the culmination of the First Crusade, describes women in a secondary military role, offering support to male fighters: 'Women also, that they might have their share of the work, cheered the fighters to renewed courage by their words and brought them water in small vessels that they might not faint upon the field of battle.'[46] As in the account of Margaret of Beverley's actions, the motif of women carrying water appears. Like the woman armed with a cooking pot, it is easy to imagine such an event occurring in battle, but it also carries strong overtones of gender-stereotyping; women, unfitted to warfare, are relegated to carrying water and cheering on the men. Helen Solterer, in a study of the literature of the *Tournoiment des Dames* (entirely fictional women's jousts) commented that the role of spectator was usually assigned to women in the literature of the (male) tournament, 'an exhibitionist display before an admiring female crowd'.[47]

In conclusion, while we have seen some of the varied ways in which women were involved in the crusades, an examination of the sources has probably told us more about male attitudes to women on crusade than the actual role of women in the fighting. Gender roles were defined by the donning of armour and wielding of weapons, so armoured women ceased to be women, while fighting women employed 'female' weaponry. Women could on occasion fight in their own right, but this seems to have occurred only in unusual or

desperate circumstances, and when it did occur it was viewed as
unusual or unnatural by Christian and Muslim writers alike, and
their arms and armour were often represented in such a way as to
reflect the supposed unmartial nature of women. The Christians saw
the martial qualities of Frankish women as admirable, but remarkable coming from the 'weaker' sex; the Muslims viewed them as
further proof of the immorality and barbarism of the infidel.

NOTES

[1] M. McLaughlin, 'The woman warrior: gender, warfare and society in
medieval Europe', *Women's Studies* 17 (1990), 194.

[2] H. J. Nicholson, 'Women on the Third Crusade', *JMH* 23 (1997), 340–1.

[3] G. Paris (ed.), *Ambroise, L'Estoire de la Guerre Sainte* (Paris, 1897), ll.
5695–8; H. J. Nicholson (ed. and trans.), *Chronicle of the Third Crusade: A
Translation of the* Itinerarium Peregrinorum et Gesta Regis Ricardi
(Aldershot, 1997), 235, 264–5.

[4] '. . . et mulieres, oblite sexus et inolite fragilitatis immerores, tractantes
virilia, supra vires, armorum usum apprehendere presumebant'; WT 403.
English trans. from E. A. Babcock and A. C. Krey (eds. and trans.), *A
History of Deeds Done Beyond the Sea* (2 vols., New York, 1941), 1: 362.
This incident is not described in any other written source, and William's
source for it appears to be oral tradition or possibly a *chanson de geste.*
William tells us that he relied for events before his own lifetime on 'traditions'; WT 100; P. W. Edbury and J. G. Rowe, *William of Tyre, Historian of
the Latin East* (Cambridge, 1988), 44–5.

[5] *Itinerarium*, 48.

[6] P. G. Schmidt, '*Peregrinatio Periculosa*: Thomas von Froidmont über
die Jerusalem-Fahrten seiner Schwester Margareta', in *Sonderdruck aus
Kontinuität und Wandel: Lateinische Poesie von Naevius bis Baudelaire*
(Hildesheim, 1986), 461–85; R. Finucane, *Soldiers of the Faith: Crusaders
and Moslems at War* (London, 1977), 178–9.

[7] F. Gabrieli (ed. and Italian trans.), *Arab Historians of the Crusades,*
English trans. E. J. Costello (London, 1969), 207.

[8] Ibid., 205–6.

[9] H. Massé (ed. and trans.), 'Imad-ad-Din al-Isfahani, *Conquête de la
Syrie et de la Palestine par Saladin* (Paris, 1972), 34, 50.

[10] B. G. Nieburg (ed.), *Corpus Scriptorum Historiae Byzantinae: Ioannes
Zonaras* (2 vols., Bonn, 1841–5), 2: 595; my thanks to Professor John
Drinkwater for pointing out this reference to me, and for providing his
English translation (unpublished).

[11] P. K. Hitti (ed. and trans.), *Usamah ibn-Munqidh, Memoirs of an Arab-Syrian Gentleman* (New York, 1929), 165–7.

[12] Ibid., 161.

[13] Ibid., 167.

[14] Ibid., 153–9.

[15] Ibid., 15.

[16] R. Irwin, 'Usamah ibn Munqidh: an Arab-Syrian gentleman at the time of the crusades reconsidered', in *Crusades Sources*, 73.

[17] *Usamah*, 153.

[18] H. Mattingley (ed. and trans.), *Tacitus: On Britain and Germany* (Harmondsworth, 1948), 107.

[19] *Usamah*, 154.

[20] Ibid., 152.

[21] Ibid., 153.

[22] Quoted in A. W. Kleinbaum, *The War against the Amazons* (New York, 1983), 6.

[23] Ibid., 51–8.

[24] Ibid., 61.

[25] Robert Marshall, *Storm from the East: From Genghis Khan to Khubilai Khan* (London, 1995), 136.

[26] Kleinbaum, *Amazons*, 46.

[27] Ibid., 25.

[28] '. . . pharetratae cum arcubus advenere virgines, ut veteris in eis Dianae nova cerneretur species, ut non causa bellandi sed potius sub obtentu putarentur convenisse gestandi. Prelio plane maiori exactos ab his qui interfuere asseritur quod etiam recens nati infantuli, quos in ipso procinctu expeditionis enixae mulieres fuerant, dum pro urgentium Francorum insecutione preproperant seque morarum ac oneris impatientes exoccupant, medio proiecti repperirentur in gramine, uti eos, dum sibi quam illis plus metuunt, negligenter effuderant.' R. B. C. Huygens (ed.), *Guibert de Nogent: Dei Gesta per Francos et cinq autres textes* (Turnhout, 1996), 225.

[29] L. K. Stock, '"Arms and the (wo)man" in medieval romance: the gendered arming of female warriors in the *Roman d'Eneas* and Heldris's *Roman de Silence*', *Arthuriana*, 5 (1995), 56–83.

[30] H. J. Magoulis (ed. and trans.), *'O City of Byzantium', Annals of Niketas Choniates* (Detroit, 1984), 35.

[31] Ibid., 376, n.153.

[32] D. Townsend, 'Sex and the single Amazon in twelfth-century Latin epic', in D. Townsend and A. Taylor (eds.), *Tongue of the Fathers: Gender and Ideology in Twelfth-Century Latin* (Philadelphia, 1998), 136; A. Strickland, *Lives of the Queens of England* (12 vols, London, 1840–7), 1: 297–8.

[33] McLaughlin, 'Woman warrior', 196.

[34] *Itinerarium*, 89.

[35] M. Chibnall (ed. and trans.), *The Ecclesiastical History of Orderic Vitalis,* 6 vols. (Oxford, 1972–80), 6: 212–14. The word 'Amazon' is Chibnall's translation; Orderic did not in fact use this word, but *bellatrix*, warrior woman.

[36] Ibid., 4: 212–14

[37] Ibid., 4: 212.

[38] Ibid., 3: 128; 6: 278.

[39] Schmidt, 'Peregrinatio periculosa', 461–85; Finucane, *Soldiers*, 178–9.

[40] Schmidt, 'Peregrinatio periculosa', 478.

[41] See, for example, L. M. C. Randall, *Images in the Margins of Gothic Manuscripts* (Berkeley and Los Angeles, 1966), figs. 708, 709, 719.

[42] Ibid., 91.

[43] *Itinerarium*, 48. Interestingly, this image makes it into Strickland's highly coloured description of Eleanor of Aquitaine and her ladies on the Second Crusade: 'this band of madwomen sent their useless distaffs as presents to all the knights and nobles who had the good sense to keep out of this insane expedition'. Strickland, *Queens*, 298.

[44] *Itinerarium*, 48 n. 64.

[45] Kleinbaum, *Amazons*, 59.

[46] '. . . sed et mulieres, ne tanti expertes laboris esse viderentur, viris in agone desudantibus potum, ne deficerent, ministrabant in vasculis et verbis efficacibus eos ad certamen animabant'; WT 407–8. English translation, Babcock and Krey, 1: 367.

[47] H. Solterer, 'Figures of female militancy in medieval France', *Signs* 16 (1991), 529.

5

Perception and Projection of Prejudice: Anna Comnena, the *Alexiad* and the First Crusade

PETER FRANKOPAN

The *Alexiad* of Anna Comnena is not an easy source with which to deal. There are several occasions in the text where the author makes mistakes, either in terms of the omission of important events (which we know about from elsewhere), of the duplication and even triplication of episodes, or of a chronology which, on close examination, often proves to be suspect and defective.[1]

If commentators have not always identified the full extent of the difficulties posed by the content of the text – in particular tending to take Anna's sequence of events at face value – they have also been quick to highlight specific passages to argue that the author's account is heavily biased in favour of the emperor Alexius I Comnenus. It is regularly stated that Anna Comnena offers a prejudiced, distorted and one-sided view of her father's reign, and of the First Crusade specifically.[2]

But implicit here is also the idea that the *Alexiad* is somehow more slanted than the other sources for the First Crusade. Certainly it would only be right to note that, if we are to admit that Anna is 'ignorant' of the causes of the First Crusade, then we should say the same about all the Western chroniclers;[3] if Anna is to be criticized for praising 'what is, in the end, duplicity towards [Alexius'] rivals and friends', then the authors of sources like the *Gesta Francorum* should be censured in similar terms for their own obvious biases and shortcomings.[4] In short, it is essential that any commentary on the *Alexiad*'s coverage of the First Crusade must be set in the context of, if not directly compared with, the accounts of the Western chroniclers who wrote about the same events.[5]

It is not hard to understand why Anna Comnena's account has been singled out in this way, and why it has been approached by modern scholars in a different manner from the other sources of this period. In the first place, although the *Alexiad* does cover the arrival of all the various crusade leaders in Byzantium in 1096–7, the focus of the text's coverage of the First Crusade – at least from Constantinople onwards – rests squarely on Bohemund and above all on his betrayal of Alexius at Antioch, continuing a major theme of Anna's work that seeks to establish the Norman as the emperor's nemesis.[6] Of course, Anna's intentions here may also run deeper and extend to providing a context, and perhaps even a negative parallel, for the events of the 1140s, when Antioch and the Normans were, once again, key problems facing Byzantium.[7]

In other words, the fact that the author's intentions appear so clear – if not for the *Alexiad* as a whole then at least for the chapters on the First Crusade – means that the starting-point for analysis of Anna Comnena's account is that the author is working to a specific agenda, and that the text is therefore of dubious quality. Again, though, it is worth stressing that in this respect there is limited difference between the *Alexiad* and the Western sources for the crusade, whose intentions and motivations are no less easy to detect – focusing as they do not only on the capture of Jerusalem, but also on another important theme, namely that the Byzantines, and Alexius in particular, had deceived the soldiers of Christ.

The issue of Anna's motivations is, of course, exacerbated by the fact that the *Alexiad* is the only Byzantine text which covers the crusade in any detail (John Zonaras gives it less than twenty lines), which means that there is no natural literary counter-balance to the author's interpretation of events.[8] This is, of course, in sharp contrast to the varied Latin sources which, when taken together, appear to allow us a more rounded view of the crusade from a Western perspective, as we see the crusade leaders (and their historians) jostling with each other for position. This means that the *Alexiad*'s flaws and the author's opinions and biases are inevitably and considerably more exposed than those of her (Western) peers.

Nor does the author's proximity to her subject help matters, and it is worth stressing that Anna is not only aware of this, but repeatedly goes out of her way during the course of the text to stress the extent to which she has tried to be impartial: indeed she goes so far as to say that she wishes that she were not related to the emperor, in her attempt to diminish her readers' suspicions that the account of Alexius' reign as a whole may be biased.[9] While the author's candour is easy to dismiss as disengenuous, it is in obvious dissonance with the unquestioning and unapologetic Latin chroniclers who followed their lords on crusade, and seem unaware of their own subjectivity, let alone make any excuses for it.[10]

Ironically, of course, Anna's protestations about her desire and efforts to be unbiased serve to draw attention to this issue, and require the reader to confront the question of impartiality. The author's claims, then, predicate a response from commentators, and this is an important factor in understanding analyses, and above all criticism, of the *Alexiad* – as Stendhal puts it, 'qui s'excuse, s'accuse'.[11] Certainly, it seems to have been precisely Anna Comnena's interjections which elicited such an acute response from Edward Gibbon in *The History of the Decline and Fall of the Roman Empire*: stating that the text is no more than an unreliable and prejudicial account written by a loving daughter, rather than by an objective observer, Gibbon dismisses the text, concluding that the *Alexiad* 'betrays in every page the vanity of a female author'.[12] It is worth noting here that Gibbon is by no means the only commentator to have reacted in this way to either the text or to its author.[13]

However, even the most cursory reading of the *Alexiad* shows us how much easier it is to make such criticisms than to back them up. In fact, for all the comments by Gibbon (and by more recent commentators) about Anna Comnena's style and her deliberate attempts to eulogize her father, there are only a handful of places in the text where any such bias can truly be identified. Indeed, if anything, the opposite is true: for example, Anna makes it clear that Alexius was lucky to escape with his life when a campaign against the Pechenegs went horribly wrong after a show of misplaced confidence on the part of the emperor.[14] Similarly, the author leaves little doubt as to her feelings about the atrocities committed by Comnenian troops during their entry to Constantinople in the spring of 1081.[15] But perhaps the most telling feature which reveals the extent to which accusations that the text is replete with prejudice and bias are misplaced comes from the numerous and extraordinarily frank accounts of the various attempts to overthrow the emperor during the course of his reign: the fact that Anna faithfully records the many (failed) coups to depose her father – and that she provides so much detail about them – is of crucial importance here, since it points clearly to the conclusion that, for one reason or another, Alexius neither enjoyed extensive popularity during the course of his reign, nor was he particularly successful in satisfying the demands of the aristocracy in Byzantium in this period.[16] That the author was prepared to include and develop so negative a theme to run through the course of the text should go some way to countering claims that the text is simply a panegyric to the emperor Alexius Comnenus by a loving daughter, determined to show him only in a favourable light.

Naturally, the issue of Anna's honesty and of the reliability of the *Alexiad* as a whole is of considerable significance to any analysis of the chapters which deal with the First Crusade. The text does pose problems. For example, Anna Comnena fails to discuss the origins of the crusade, simply stating that no sooner had the emperor completed an engineering project by Nicomedia than he 'found himself unable to relax, hearing a rumour that countless Frankish armies were approaching'.[17] As we have seen, this is often seized on as being a clear case of the author favouring her father by omitting to mention the role he played in the genesis of the First Crusade.[18] There may, however, be another, simpler, explanation here, namely that Anna, writing in her convent some fifty years after the events she describes, genuinely did not know of her father's involvement in attracting armed pilgrims to Constantinople and beyond in the 1090s.[19] At least some weight can be given to this hypothesis by pointing out that Anna not only fails to mention the role played by her father, but also fails to mention that played by the pope, Urban II: the author is quick elsewhere in the text to attack the papacy in general, and Gregory VII in particular, for meddling and interfering in Byzantium's affairs.[20] If Anna had been fully versed in the context for, and the causes of the crusade, we might have expected her to use the opportunity to criticize the pope for his leadership and patronage of what was to prove such a disastrous episode for the Byzantine Empire.[21]

Of course, the fact that Anna omits crucial information about the origins of the First Crusade strikes a chord with her coverage elsewhere in this section of the text. The best analogy here is the *Alexiad*'s threadbare, mistaken and misleading account of the events which followed the departure of Taticius from Antioch at the start of 1098.[22] Careful comparison of the *Alexiad* with the Western sources shows that Anna's chronology for the period which followed is seriously defective and utterly unreliable.[23] Key events, such as the

capture of Jerusalem by the crusaders, are mentioned only in passing, while the fall of Edessa is not noted at all.[24] Anna's account of
the period after Antioch also contains factual errors. For example,
the author reports that Godfrey of Bouillon not only fought at but
was captured during the course of the battle of Ramleh in 1102, even
though it is known that he had died two years earlier.[25] Other
episodes are also surprisingly omitted, such as the capture of
Bohemund by the Danishmenids – which Anna would surely have
included in her account had she known about it, given the constant
hostility shown towards this individual in the course of the text.[26]

The mistakes, errors and omissions in Anna's coverage of events
after early 1098 presumably reflect the problems of her source material – and above all the lack of evidence which the author had at her
disposal here. In this way, the obvious explanation for the dramatic
fall-off in the quality of information is that Anna had found it difficult to gather material that was relevant – a hypothesis which backs
up the view which has been frequently expressed that the author
obtained at least some of her information about the crusade and
about the crusaders from Taticius: in other words, it is no coincidence that the departure of the Byzantine general from Antioch in
1098 corresponds so neatly with a marked decline in the quality of
Anna's information. Put simply, the author had been deprived of a
key source of information.[27]

But while Taticius appears to have been a very important source
for Anna Comnena – and particularly for her coverage of the events
which took place from the fall of Nicaea up to Antioch – he was certainly not the only source on which the author was able to draw for
her account of the crusade as a whole. For if we can nominate
Taticius as the supplier of at least some information, then we can
also suggest other figures who may have provided Anna with reliable
and accurate evidence elsewhere in this section of the text. And, of
course, the close analysis of the *Alexiad* which enables us to do this
has a crucial by-product, for it enables us not only to draw some conclusions about the reliability and accuracy of Anna's coverage of the
crusade, but also to understand how and why the text was put
together.

The author herself is not enormously helpful when it comes to
revealing her own sources – either for the crusade, or for her father's
reign in general. Towards the end of the *Alexiad*, Anna states that she
had been able to rely on an unspecified number of accounts written

by veterans who had served with the emperor on at least one campaign.[28] This raises more questions than it solves.[29] Anna also says that she was an eye-witness for some of the events which she describes – a statement which can only apply to a handful of the episodes which appear in the text. In the first place, Anna was born at the end of 1083, and consequently is not a credible source of information for at least the first decade of her father's reign.[30] Furthermore, the fact that there is no evidence to support the view that the author ventured far from Constantinople, coupled with the fact that her sense of geography is so obviously suspect, suggests that, as we would expect of a *porphyrogenita* princess, Anna's personal experiences were limited to what she saw at the imperial court.[31]

It is possible, however, to identify a more credible series of sources on which Anna Comnena was able to draw in the composition of her account of the First Crusade. And even the briefest analysis here reveals that the author's coverage was not only drawn from a rich tapestry of witnesses to the events which appear in the text, but also explains why it is that, in spite of the problems posed by the *Alexiad* in terms of omissions and mistakes, Anna Comnena was able to provide us with so much high-grade information about the First Crusade.

The author may well have been able to rely, at least in part, on the evidence of her uncle, George Palaeologus, who was also one of the emperor's most trusted friends and advisers. Of course, it is significant that Anna names George at the end of the text as her single most important source for the material which appears in the *Alexiad*.[32] It is therefore no coincidence that Palaeologus plays a prominent role in several lengthy and detailed episodes in the text.[33] In the chapters on the crusade, however, he enjoys limited visibility, appearing only when he delivers a stern rebuke to Tancred shortly after the capture of Nicaea.[34]

There are, however, other individuals who appear to have provided Anna with material here – even though neither they nor their contribution are acknowledged by the author. John Comnenus, Anna's cousin, who was governor of the key town of Dyrrachium at the end of the eleventh century, is the obvious and logical source for the excellent and detailed information about the arrival of the various crusaders in Byzantium in 1096–7.[35] The fact that the text contains a long account of the Byzantine reconquest of western Asia Minor suggests that John Doucas, the general who led the expedition and who was another of Anna's uncles, may have provided the author with a substantial amount of the material which appears in the *Alexiad*.[36] Meanwhile, Anna's husband, Nicephorus Bryennius, whom some suspect of having drafted the *Alexiad* if not of having actually written it, was involved in negotiating with and supervising the crusaders when they were camped by Constantinople in 1097, and was therefore well placed to provide the author with information about some if not all these matters.[37]

If these three individuals are the most obvious sources for snatches of information or for larger slabs of evidence which appear in the text, then they are by no means the only ones to whom we should look for the material which Anna used in her account of the First Crusade. For in addition to the episodes where Taticius, George Palaeologus, John Comnenus, John Doucas and Nicephorus Bryennius feature prominently, there are also a clutch of incidents which are reported at varying length and detail which centre on figures such as Constantine Euphorbenus Catacalon, Nicholas Maurocatacalon and his son Marianus, Constantine Opos and, above all, Manuel Butumites.[38] While it would perhaps be an oversimplification to assume that the central character of each episode was the source of its transmission into the text, one point is clear: that Anna Comnena's coverage of the crusade contains a large number of accounts which must have been drawn, one way or another, from eye-witnesses.

The fact that the author of the *Alexiad* had access to a wide range of source material goes some way towards explaining the extraordinarily high quality of the information which appears in this section of the text. As we have seen, Anna's account of the First Crusade has two obvious shortcomings, namely that the author's knowledge of the build-up to the crusade is poor, and that the coverage of the events which followed Antioch is sketchy and erratically arranged. In both cases, however, the natural conclusion is that this is a reflection of either the paucity or the outright failure of Anna's sources – or perhaps of both. The remainder of the account of the crusade, however, is of very high quality indeed.

There are obvious clues to the fact that the section of the text which deals with events between the arrival of Peter the Hermit in Byzantium and the departure of Taticius had received a considerable amount of editorial attention. In the first place, there are none of the chronological errors which characterize so much of the *Alexiad*, and the sequence of events is sound. The narrative flow is also smooth, and there are few gaps in the chapters concerned.[39] Of the four lacunae which have been identified by Reifferscheid, Leib and Liubarskii, one appears to represent a single word which is missing from the earliest manuscripts.[40] Another appears at the very end of the report of Alexius' activities in western Asia Minor.[41] The other two represent gaps which the author had left for a specific piece of information to be inserted once further research had been completed. While it is not known why Anna was unable to find the relevant details – an indiction number and a measurement of distance respectively – the fact that these are the only occasions where the narrative is interrupted provides a clear indication that the author has spent a good deal of time gathering and arranging her material here.[42]

The sheer volume and the obvious quality of evidence which Anna had managed to get hold of is also impressive. The author is able to tell us, for example, not only that Hugh of Vermandois had been shipwrecked, but also where he had been washed ashore.[43] She is also able to reveal that both Bohemund and another crusader, most probably Richard of Brabant, did not land at Avlona or even at Dyrrachium, but made for different landing spots entirely.[44] We are given precise details about the encampment of the crusader armies by Constantinople, as well as specific information about how the emperor sought to keep the various forces apart from each other in an attempt to minimize the danger which they posed to Byzantium and to his own position.[45] We are told of his dealings with the crusade leaders, and of his efforts to encourage them to make an oath of loyalty to him personally.[46] We are provided with an intimate and highly credible account of Alexius' careful treatment of Bohemund which rings true on all counts – including, memorably, not only the Norman's refusal to eat the meat which had been left in his quarters, but also the emperor's understanding that this would be the case.[47] We learn a great deal of information about the siege of Nicaea in 1097, ranging from the name of the tower which was the focus of the crusader onslaught to the treatment of the Turks who were captured when the town fell, to the reception which the emperor held for the crusade leaders at Pelekanum afterwards.[48]

While it is true that the crusader chronicles generally have little to say about Byzantium, about Constantinople and Nicaea, or about the emperor himself, it is of crucial importance to stress that there is little in any of these accounts which contradicts what Anna tells us about the crusade before Antioch. Certainly, the interpretation of events differs substantially; however, there should be little doubt about the quality of the material contained in the *Alexiad* for the period between the arrival of Peter the Hermit in Byzantium and the departure of Taticius at the start of 1098. In fact, comparison with the Latin sources shows that there are perhaps as few as three factual errors in this section of the text.[49] Moreover, on two further occasions it is by no means certain that we should discard what Anna tells us in favour of what we learn from the crusader accounts.[50]

In other words, the conclusion which must be drawn from a considered reading of the *Alexiad*'s account of the First Crusade is that this is a source which contains an excellent supply of high-grade information, evidently drawn from a number of sources and eye-witnesses. The section of the text which deals with the First Crusade does not suffer from any of the chronological difficulties which appear elsewhere in the *Alexiad*. Instead, what we find is a well-ordered account, which has been subject to a considerable amount of editorial attention. There are problems with Anna's coverage: the author says nothing about the origins of the First Crusade; and what information there is about the events which followed the departure of Taticius from Antioch at the start of 1098 is convoluted and sketchy to say the least. In both cases, however, the logical explanation is that, for one reason or another, Anna's sources fail her. But, these failures notwithstanding, it should be stressed that the *Alexiad*'s coverage of the Byzantine perspective of the crusade – and of those crucial events of 1096–8 – is not the unreliable and untrustworthy work which modern scholars would have us believe.[51]

The *Alexiad* is, of course, a source of profound importance, not least since it fills in many of the gaps left by the crusader chroniclers whose focus essentially rests on the journey to the Holy Land and on Jerusalem. Anna Comnena's text provides us with invaluable information about relations between the Byzantines and the crusaders – and above all between the emperor and the crusade leaders – as well as about many other matters which are invariable only glossed over by the various Latin accounts, if indeed they are mentioned at all. Indeed, the *Alexiad* plays a key role in allowing us to build up a coherent picture of what was going on between the arrival of the crusaders in Constantinople and the fall of Antioch.

That Anna's account is of tremendous use in helping us to establish the historical narrative is by no means the only reason why the *Alexiad* is such a valuable source. For, above all, the text allows us a series of invaluable perspectives into the author's attitudes to the crusade and to the crusaders. It is not always easy, however, to know what we should make of Anna's opinions and of her interpretation of events. There is an obvious temptation, for example, to assume that because the author of the *Alexiad* was a woman we can use the text to draw conclusions not only about what the Byzantines in general thought about the crusade, but more specifically about how women perceived what was happening, about women's assessments of politics in twelfth-century Constantinople, or even about women's historiography in Byzantium as a whole. But the lack of comparative or analogous sources here makes such conclusions tenuous, and difficult to support: the fact that Anna's text is the only substantial surviving work from this period, and the only one by a woman from the Byzantine period as a whole, means that we have nothing with which we can compare Anna's views or even her style.[52]

The question of what we can learn from the *Alexiad* about women and gender in Byzantium, and about female perceptions of the crusade, is also complicated by the fact that Anna is so reticent about such matters. In fact, the author tells us very little about what it meant to be a woman or an imperial woman living and writing in the eleventh and twelfth centuries.[53] Indeed, the question of gender is largely hidden in the text, and it is only from Anna's occasional emotional outpouring about her husband that we are aware that the source was written by a woman.[54] It is true that close analysis of the literary style of the text does allow us to pinpoint occasions where Anna has obviously opened the seam of the material at her disposal to add a few comments *en passant*.[55] But few, if any, of these betray either the author's gender or her social and intellectual background.

Indeed, were it not for the odd comment about her father or her husband, or about her one-time fiancé, Constantine Ducas, it would be hard to guess that the text was written by a woman, if only because Anna does not mention things which we might expect her to mention. For example, even though the *Alexiad* is concerned with the life and reign of the emperor Alexius, the author says almost nothing about her own relationship with her father.[56] Nor does she mention things which we might expect an imperial princess to be interested in: we learn nothing about life at the court, description of Constantinople is limited to two or three passages,[57] and there is an almost total lack of reference to the imperial family, as Anna barely refers to her siblings, and fails entirely to mention her own children.[58]

Of course, the fact that Anna does not talk about things which we might expect her to talk about, and that we might be surprised that she does not go into any detail about her own family, says more about us than it necessarily does about Anna herself: for there is no reason why this author should conform to a model set out by the reader. Furthermore, the fact that much of the text deals with military matters, and is not about the court or about the family, is not enough by itself to assert, as one modern historian has done, that the *Alexiad* cannot have been written by a woman.[59]

The scope and quality of the text certainly make it difficult for us to get close to Anna Comnena. This is made no easier by the fact that the author of the *Alexiad* was not only related to the eponymous hero but was also herself at the very top of Byzantine imperial society: this too makes it hard to assess to what extent Anna's account is representative – stylistically or in terms of interpretation – of a woman in Byzantium in this, or indeed in any, period. Again, though, the dangers of generalizing here are obvious. The *Alexiad* is a work so markedly different in scale, tone and approach from so many of the primary sources for this period, that it is tempting to try to treat the text in isolation, and to see it as a one-off, distinct in terms of style if nothing else from what other writers were doing at the time. Certainly, Anna's account differs markedly from those of writers such as John Scylitzes, John Zonaras and Michael Glycas. Unlike these writers, who add only the occasional barbed comment to their dense, dry prose, Anna frequently intervenes in the text, offering an opinion here, a rude comment there, regularly reminding the reader that the crusaders (and all Westerners) are greedy and fickle, that they are incompetent, proud and treacherous.[60] These interventions and interruptions, opinions and comments have come to be interpreted as specifically female characteristics – both negatively and positively.[61]

There is, however, another source with which we can usefully compare the *Alexiad* here. The *Chronographia* of Michael Psellus, written at the end of the eleventh century, has obvious similarities with the *Alexiad*, for the author's style is broadly reminiscent of Anna's both in terms of the extent and frequency of authorial intervention and in terms of the nature of such intervention. Comparison of the texts yields two conclusions: first, contrary to the views of so many commentators, the visibility of the author and of the author's opinions in the text is not a characteristic unique to the *Alexiad*, and, consequently, cannot be reasonably labelled a feminine attribute.[62] And, secondly, there are obvious dangers of over-interpreting and reading too much into Anna's work, simply because the author was a woman.[63]

If we can find an analogy for Anna's intervention, then we should also add that it is possible to find parallels for at least some of her opinions, and particularly those about Westerners. Again, this allows us to present a context for the author's views, which is of some importance to our understanding of the *Alexiad*'s coverage of the First Crusade. For, rather than dismissing Anna's views of the crusaders as being tarnished by the fall-out after Antioch as well as by the fiasco of the Second Crusade (and therefore an example of bias towards her father), it should be stressed that one finds similar expressions of animosity towards Westerners, and identical charges that all Latins were obsessed by money, that they were fickle and untrustworthy and cruel, in a large number of Byzantine sources from the second half of the eleventh century onwards.[64]

In this respect, then, the *Alexiad* is an excellent example of a high-quality source which reveals a good deal about Byzantine attitudes in the eleventh and twelfth centuries generally. And even if it is not possible to separate the issue of whether Anna wrote as she did and had the opinions that she did because she was a woman, or because she was an imperial woman, or simply because she was a Byzantine, this conclusion alone goes some way to redressing the undeserved reputation for bias and inaccuracy which both the text and the author have acquired over the course of more than two hundred years. In a neat turn of irony, therefore, it is not so much the *Alexiad* but rather commentaries on this text which prove to be biased and prejudiced: Anna Comnena and her text have long been pulled apart by those who only see what it is that they want to see, without considering the context for this remarkable account and without stopping to question just how good and valuable a text it is for our understanding of the reign of Alexius I Comnenus in general and of the First Crusade in particular.

NOTES

[1] Anna Comnena, *Alexiade*, ed. B. Leib (3 vols., Paris, 1937–45); English trans. by E. R. A. Sewter (Harmondsworth, 1969). References will be cited from the Leib edn. (Sewter trans. in parentheses). For a commentary on the text, see Ia. Liubarskii, *Aleksiada* (Moscow, 1965).

[2] See, for example, A. Kazhdan and G. Constable, *People and Power in Byzantium* (Washington, DC, 1982), 156–7; F. Shlosser, 'The *Alexiad* of Anna Comnena as a source for the crusades', *Byzantinische Forschungen* 15 (1990), 397–406; R. Thomas, 'Anna Comnena's account of the First Crusade: history and politics in the reigns of the emperors Alexius I and Manuel I Comnenus', *Byzantine and Modern Greek Studies* 15 (1991), 269–312; J. France, *Victory in the East* (Cambridge, 1994), 110–12.

[3] Cf. J. France, 'Anna Comnena, the *Alexiad* and the First Crusade', *Reading Medieval Studies* 10 (1984), 20–38, at 22.

[4] Ibid., 26.

[5] While Anna Comnena's lack of comment on the origins of the First Crusade is certainly striking, so too is the failure of the principal Western primary sources to mention the Council of Clermont, or even to discuss the pope's preaching of the crusade in general in 1095 and 1096. Indeed Raymond of Aguilers and Albert of Aachen and even the *Gesta Francorum* say little or nothing about Urban II's contribution to the crusade, Raymond of Aguilers, *Historia Francorum qui ceperunt Jerusalem*, in *Recueil des Historiens des Croisades, Historiens Occidentaux*, 3; Albert of Aachen, *Liber christianae expeditionis pro ereptione, emundatione et restitutione sanctae Hierosolymitanae ecclesiae*, in *Recueil des Historiens des Croisades, Historiens Occidentaux*, 4; *Gesta Francorum et aliorum Hierosolimitanorum*, ed. R. Hill (London, 1962).

[6] For example, A. Buckler, *Anna Comnena* (Oxford, 1929), 469–78.

[7] See P. Magdalino, 'The pen of the aunt: echoes of the mid-twelfth century in the Alexiad', pp. 15–43 in T. Gouma-Peterson (ed.), *Anna Komnene and her Times* (New York, 2000), and also E. Albu, 'Bohemond and the rooster: Byzantines, Normans and the artful ruse', ibid., 157–68.

[8] John Zonaras, *Epitome Historiarum*, ed. M. Pinder and T. Büttner-Wobst (3 vols., Bonn, 1841–97), XVIII. xxii. 3, pp. 742–3. The crusade is also mentioned by Michael Glykas, who follows Zonaras here word for word, *Michaelis Glycae Annales*, ed. I. Bekker (Bonn, 1836), 621. A chronicle written in the thirteenth century by Theodore Skutariotes contains a short account of the crusade in which the author makes a number of unusual and interesting comments about Alexius' motivations for appealing to the West for support in the 1090s, *Bibliotheca Graeca Medii Aevi*, ed. K. Sathas (7 vols., Paris, 1872–94), 7: 184–5. Also see P. Charanis, 'Byzantium, the West, and the origin of the First Crusade', *Byzantion* 19 (1949), 17–36.

[9] For example, Anna Comnena, *Alexiad*, Proimion, 1. 3–4 (18–20); I: i. 1. 60–1 (72); III: viii. 1. 129–30 (124); IV: viii. 1. 166–7 (151–2); XII: iii. 3. 64 (378); XIV: vii. 3. 172–7 (458–62); XV: iii. 3. 194–5 (478).

[10] For Anna Comnena, see Buckler, *Anna Comnena*, 245 ff., and A. Kambylis, 'Zum "Programm" der byzantinischen Historikerin Anna Komnene', in K. Vourvenis and A. Skiadas (eds.), *Dorema – Hans Diller zum 70. Geburtsag* (Athens, 1975), 127–46.

[11] Stendhal, *Le Rouge et le Noir* (1830, repr. Paris, 2000), II: xxxiv, p. 583.

[12] E. Gibbon, *The History of the Decline and Fall of the Roman Empire* (London, 1776–88, repr. 3 vols., London, 1994), 3: 69. According to Gibbon, the author demonstrates 'an elaborate affectation of rhetoric and science', the result of which is that 'the genuine character of Alexius is lost in a vague constellation of virtues; and the perpetual strain of panegyric and apology, awakens our jealousy, to question the veracity of the author', 69. For Gibbon's views on Byzantium in general, as well as his comments on the *Alexiad*, see J. Howard-Johnston, 'Gibbon and the middle period of the Byzantine Empire', in R. McKitterick and R. Quinault (eds.), *Edward Gibbon and Empire* (Cambridge, 1997), 53–77.

[13] See, for example, R. Brown's remarks on the 'high-born feminine malice and sensual attraction' which lay behind the *Alexiad*'s portrayal of Robert Guiscard: *The Normans* (London, 1984), 90. Cf. Shlosser, 'The *Alexiad* of Anna Comnena', 397–8.

[14] Anna Comnena, *Alexiad*, VII: iii. 2. 98–101 (225–6).

[15] Ibid., II: x. 1. 94–5, (97–8); also III: v. 1. 117 (115).

[16] For the various plots against the emperor, see J.-C. Cheynet, *Pouvoir et contestations à Byzance (963–1210)* (Paris, 1990), 90–103.

[17] Anna Comnena, *Alexiad*, X: v. 2. 206 (308).

[18] Above, n. 2.

[19] According to Anna herself, the majority of the material that appears in the *Alexiad* was gathered in the 1140s, after the accession of Manuel I Comnenus, *Alexiad*, XIV: vii. 3. 175 (460).

[20] For example, *Alexiad*, I: xiii. 1. 47–51 (61–5). Also see Buckler, *Anna Comnena*, 307ff.

[21] It is worth noting here that, although it is not possible to establish when specific sections of the text were written, the writing of the *Alexiad* broadly corresponded with the Second Crusade – another papally endorsed initiative which was to cause great trouble for Byzantium.

[22] Anna Comnena, *Alexiad*, XI: iv-xii. 3. 20–52 (343–68). J. France, 'The departure of Tatikios from the Crusader army', *BIHR* 44 (1971), 137–47.

[23] Liubarskii, 'Zamechaniya k khronologii XI knigi "Aleksiada" Annyi Komninoi', *Vizantiiskii Vremmenik* 24 (1963), 47–56; R.-J. Lilie, *Byzantium and the Crusader States*, trans. J. Morris and J. Ridings (Oxford, 1993), 259–76.

24 The *Alexiad*'s report of the capture of Jerusalem, perhaps the defining event in the medieval period, is astonishingly curt. According to Anna, '[The crusaders] hurried to Jerusalem. Having encircled the town and made many raids, they captured [Jerusalem] after a month, massacring many Saracens and Jews in the city', *Alexiad*, XI: vi. 3. 32 (352).

25 Anna Comnena, *Alexiad*, XI: vii. 3. 33–4 (353). J. France, *Victory in the East* (Cambridge, 1994), 133; S. Runciman, *History of the Crusades* (3 vols., Cambridge, 1952–5), 1: 314–16.

26 Buckler, *Anna Comnena*, 469–78.

27 F. Chalandon, *Essai sur le règne d'Alexis I Comnène* (Paris, 1900), p. xvii; Runciman, *Crusades*, 1: 224–5, n. 1; Liubarskii, 'Zamechaniya', 47.

28 Anna Comnena, *Alexiad*, XIV: vii. 3. 175–6 (461).

29 Little is known about literacy in Byzantium in this period. It is not clear, then, how many accounts Anna had at her disposal, or what form these took. Nor is it possible to explain how Anna was able to get hold of these in the convent where she was effectively exiled between 1118 and her death in 1153. It has been argued that the convent in question was that of the Theotokos Kechairotomene, which had been established by the Empress Irene, Anna's mother, J. Howard-Johnston. 'Anna Komnene and the *Alexiad*', in M. Mullett and D. Smythe (eds.), *Alexios I Komnenos* (Belfast, 1996), 279. Also see P. Gautier, 'Le Typikon de la Théotokos Kécharitôménè', *Revue des Études Byzantines* 43, 5–165.

30 Anna Comnena, *Alexiad*, XIV: vii. 3. 174 (460). Anna was born in December 1083, *Alexiad*, VI: viii. 2. 60 (196). Also A. Kazhdan, 'Die Liste der Kinder des Alexios I in einer Moskauer Handschrift (GIM 53/147)', in R. Stiehl and H. Stier (eds.), *Beiträge zur alten Gesichte und deren Nachleben* (2 vols., Berlin, 1969–70), 233–7; K. Barzos, *He Genealogia tôn Komnenôn* (2 vols., Thessalonica, 1984), 1: 176–97.

31 For example, Buckler, *Anna Comnena*, 213–14. Curiously, though, Anna claims that her mother, Irene Doucaina, did accompany the emperor on campaign on at least one occasion, Anna Comnena, *Alexiad*, XIV: v. 3. 164 (452–3). We also learn that the empress went to Thessalonica with Alexius in 1105, *Alexiad*, XII: iii. 3. 60–4 (374–8). However, these two occasions appear to have been the exception rather than the rule, and there is no analogous evidence from the *Alexiad* or from any other Byzantine source which indicates that imperial women ever went on military expeditions: see B. Hill, 'Imperial women and the ideology of womanhood in the eleventh and twelfth centuries', in L. James (ed.), *Women, Men and Eunuchs: Gender in Byzantium* (London, 1997), 91–2.

32 Anna Comnena, *Alexiad*, XIV: vii. 3. 175 (460).

33 For some comments about George Palaeologus, including a detailed summary of his appearances in the *Alexiad*, see B. Skoulatos, *Les Personnages byzantins de l'Alexiade: Analyse prosopographique et synthèse*

(Louvain, 1980), 99–105. Also see D. Polemis, *The Doukai* (London, 1968), 153–5.

[34] Anna Comnena, *Alexiad*, XI: iii. 3. 17 (340–1).

[35] Ibid., X: vii-viii. 2. 213–20 (313–18).

[36] For Anna's account of the reconquest of Asia Minor, which focuses closely on John Doucas, see Anna Comnena, *Alexiad*, XI: v. 3. 23–7 (345–8).

[37] Anna Comnena, *Alexiad*, X: ix. 2. 223–5 (321–2); Howard-Johnston, 'Anna Komnene', 260 ff.

[38] See here Skoulatos, *Personnages*, 62–5, 186–7, 256–7, 71–3, 131–5.

[39] The *Alexiad*'s sequence of events is clearly flawed on many occasions outside the chapters on the crusade. See, for example, Buckler, *Anna Comnena*, 406–14; P. Diaconu, *Les Pétchénègues au Bas-Danube* (Bucharest, 1970), 112–34; Chalandon, *Essai*, 51–94. Also see Frankopan, 'Alexios I Komnenos' (unpublished D.Phil. thesis, Oxford, 1998), 18–20.

[40] Anna Comnena, *Alexiad*, X: viii. 2. 219 (317). In fact, Reifferscheid and Leib both state that there are six lacunae in the chapters which deal with the crusade. This view is dismissed by Liubarskii, *Aleksiada*, 566, n. 1032; 568, n. 1056.

[41] Anna Comnena, *Alexiad*, XI: vi. 3. 29 (350).

[42] Anna leaves a gap for indiction date at the very start of the coverage of the crusade, Anna Comnena, *Alexiad*, X: v. 2. 206 (308). The author also allows a space to fill how far a hill fort named Azala was from Nicaea, XI: ii. 3. 14 (339).

[43] Ibid., X: vii. 2. 214 (314).

[44] Bohemund landed at Kabalion, ibid., X: viii. 2. 215 (315). Richard, 'komes Prebentzas', made for Chimara. Liubarskii, *Aleksiada*, 563, n. 1008. For the identity of this individual, see H. Grégoire, 'Notes sur Anne Comnène', *Byzantion* 3 (1926), 312–14.

[45] Anna Comnena, *Alexiad*, X: ix-x. 2. 220–30 (318–26). Also see Runciman, *Crusades*, 1: 142 ff.; France, *Victory*, 104 ff.

[46] Anna Comnena, *Alexiad*, X: ix-x. 2. 220–30 (318–26). J. Hill and L. Hill, 'The convention of Alexius Comnenus and Raymond of St. Gilles', *American Historical Review* 58/2 (1953), 322–7; France, *Victory*, 111–21.

[47] Anna Comnena, *Alexiad*, X: xi. 2. 230–4 (326–9); J. Shepard, 'When Greek meets Greek: Alexius Comnenus and Bohemund in 1097–8', *Byzantine and Modern Greek Studies* 12 (1988), 185–277.

[48] Anna Comnena, *Alexiad*, XI: i. 3. 9 (335); XI: ii. 3. 12–13 (337); XI: iii. 3. 16–17 (340).

[49] Anna says that Peter the Hermit reached Constantinople by crossing over from Italy, which we know is wrong, ibid., X: v. 2. 210 (311). Peter's route is described in great detail by Albert of Aachen, *Liber*, I: vi-xv. pp. 274–82. Anna appears to think that Godfrey of Bouillon may have reached Byzantium via southern Italy: however, the author only implies this to have

been the case, *Alexiad*, X: ix. 2. 220 (318). Finally, Anna states that the crusade leaders included 'kings, dukes, counts and even bishops', *Alexiad*, X: x.
2. 228 (324). While the royal assignation is not strictly true, it is not far off
the mark, since Hugh of Vermandois was, after all, the brother of the king
of France. Cf. Liubarskii, *Aleksiada*, 567, n. 1044.

[50] Albert of Aachen and the *Gesta Francorum* both state that Peter the
Hermit was in Constantinople when his rabble was massacred by the Turks
in 1096, Albert, *Liber*, I: xix, p. 287; *Gesta*, 1: 4. The *Alexiad*, on the other
hand, is clear that Peter was present at the time of the rout, X: vi. 2. 211–2
(313). It is not clear why the *Alexiad* should be dismissed out of hand here,
cf. Runciman, *Crusades*, 1: 132–3, n. 1; Liubarskii, *Aleksiada*, 562, n. 994;
France, *Victory*, 93. The *Alexiad's* chronology also conflicts with that of
Albert of Aachen over the date of the outbreak of hostilities between
Godfrey of Bouillon and his men and the Byzantines at the start of 1097.
Anna's account is usually rejected here by modern historians: H. Mayer, *The
Crusades* (Oxford, 1972), 45 and n. 23; France, *Victory*, 114.

[51] Cf. France, who says that 'The *Alexiad* is at first sight a godsend to the
historians.' He goes on to state that 'for much of the work, she probably
relied on the recollections of elderly people', *Victory*, 110–11. The implication is clearly that this text is inconsistent, flawed and defective.

[52] A. Laiou, 'Observations on the life and ideology of Byzantine women',
Byzantinische Forschungen 9 (1985), 59. Also Laiou, 'The role of women in
Byzantine society', *Jahrbuch der Österreichischen Byzantinistik* 31 (1981),
233–60.

[53] B. Hill, *Imperial Women in Byzantium 1025–1204: Power, Patronage and
Ideology* (Harlow, 1999), 25.

[54] Bucker, *Anna Comnena*, 35 ff.

[55] For example, Anna's digression about the Gonatas tower at Nicaea,
Alexiad, XI: i. 2. 9–10 (335); Anna goes into detail to explain how the Latin
crossbow was fired, *Alexiad*, X: viii. 2. 217–8 (316–17). The author provides
a rambling passage in which she criticizes the Latin clergy for their blood-
thirstiness, *Alexiad*, X: viii. 2. 218–19 (317).

[56] With the notable exception of a long and painful scene at the very end
of the text, *Alexiad*, XV: xi. 3. 231–42 (505–15).

[57] Comment on Constantinople is limited to the passage about the burn-
ing of Basil the Bogomil at the start of the twelfth century, Anna Comnena,
Alexiad, XV: x. 3. 226–9 (502–4); to the trial of Michael Anemas, which
Anna appears to have witnessed in person, *Alexiad*, XII: vi. L. 3. 72–6, S,
384–6; and to a section dealing with the foundation of the
Orphanotropheion, *Alexiad*, XV: vii. 3. 214–8 (492–6).

[58] Barzos, *Genealogia*, 1: 198–265.

[59] Howard-Johnston, 'Anna Komnene', 260–302.

[60] See, for example, the opening section about the arrival of the First Crusade in Byzantium, Anna Comnena, *Alexiad*, X: v-xi. 2. 206–36 (310–31).

[61] For example, Gibbon, *Decline and Fall*, 3: 69; Shlosser, 'The *Alexiad* of Anna Comnena', 397–8. Cf. Hill, *Imperial Women in Byzantium*, 1–2.

[62] Cf. Hill's views on the Howard-Johnston hypothesis, *Imperial Women in Byzantium*, 2.

[63] R. Macrides, 'The historian in the history', in C. Constantinides, N. Panagiotakes, E. Jeffreys and A. Angelou (eds.), *Filellen: Studies in Honour of Robert Browning* (Venice, 1996), 205 ff. Cf. R. Scott, 'The classical tradition in Byzantine historiography', in M. Mullett and R. Scott (eds.), *Byzantium and the Classical Tradition* (Birmingham, 1991), 61–74.

[64] Above all, see J. Shepard, 'Aspects of Byzantine attitudes and policy towards the West in the 10th and 11th centuries', *Byzantinische Forschungen* 13 (1988), 67–118.

6

Philip Count of Flanders and Hildegard of Bingen: Crusading against the Saracens or Crusading against Deadly Sin?

MIRIAM RITA TESSERA

On the eve of his departure for the Holy Land in 1177, Philip of Alsace, count of Flanders, took care to write to Hildegard of Bingen, a German abbess inspired by God, rumoured to be a prophetess, to ask her illumination and advice about his crusader undertaking.[1] In 1177 the abbess's authority and her claim to be a weak woman sent by God to confound the powerful, including clergy, was firmly established: she was seventy-nine years old and she had already written her major works, the *Scivias*, the *Liber Vitae Meritorum* and the *Liber Divinorum Operum*, where she developed what has been called a 'theology of the feminine'.[2] Though a woman, she was so highly considered by lay-people and by clergy that in 1166 John of Salisbury, writing to his friend Master Gerard Pucelle, asked him to search in Hildegard's *visiones et oracula* for a forecast about the end of the papal schism.[3] Moreover, since Pope Eugenius III himself had approved her visions and writings during the synod of Trier 1147–8, the abbess could overcome the opposition due to her gender and be considered the speaking voice of God, justified by the biblical idea of prophecy which included women (like Deborah) as well as men.[4] The correspondence between Philip and Hildegard, not yet fully studied,[5] allows us to examine how different the perception of crusade was in the twelfth-century society where, notwithstanding her gender, Hildegard held a prominent position thanks to her prophetic role.[6]

Unlike most of Hildegard's letters, the correspondence with Philip of Alsace survives only in one manuscript, now in Wiesbaden, called the 'Riesencodex' because of its very large size.[7] According to Van Acker's convincing argument, the letter collection contained in the Riesencodex can be ascribed to the monk Guibert of Gembloux, Hildegard's secretary from June 1177, who edited the abbess's letters between 1177 and *c.*1180 while Hildegard was still living. The *Vita Hildegardis* (written *c.*1181–7) states the existence of a codex collecting the abbess's correspondence 'in one book, which contained both her letters and those addressed to her'.[8] Later on, this letter collection was inserted in the Riesencodex which was completed in Rupertsberg, Hildegard's cloister, *c.*1190.[9] So Hildegard was able to superintend the making of her letter collection by selecting and modifing the texts of the letters (which are likely to be authentic ones) to prepare a planned literary corpus and strengthen in this way her claim to a prophetic role in 1178–9. These were troubled years for Hildegard: in fact, she preferred to suffer the interdict because of an excommunicated knight's disputed burial rather than go against what she had learnt from divine vision.[10]

From the very beginning, the Riesencodex was conceived as a collection of Hildegard's complete theological and pastoral works: at fos. 328[r]–443[r] we find her correspondence, a careful choice of paired letters arranged in hierarchical order starting with Pope Eugenius III and going on to religious institutions and individuals. So the letter collection is a perfect *Prälatenspiegel*, a *speculum* of clergy, with only three letters addressed to laymen: those to Conrad III, Frederick I and, of course, Philip of Flanders.[11] This kind of *große Hildegardkomposition* portrays the abbess as a saint and a prophetess, the voice of conscience of her own age, able to expound causes and consequences of present events through the Spirit's shining shadow.[12] That is why every group of men classed in the letter collection turns to Hildegard to ask her for conclusive warning and advice with regard to a peculiar problem respecting its own status, such as pastoral duties for bishops, justice for secular princes or salvation for monks and priests.[13] The correspondence with lay rulers is inserted in the Riesencodex between the letters addressed to archbishops and bishops and those to abbots and abbesses, because, in the twelfth century, secular princes enjoyed some prerogatives of clergy as officers of justice, whose ultimate source is God alone, as Hildegard reminds in a letter probably written to Frederick I:

Every dominion and every reign indeed is from Him alone (*cf.* Romans 13:1), who disposes everything in good order, and it receives from Himself its name, because they have to guide, order and judge people according to His own rule and to show them the path of truth and justice.[14]

This 'trilogy' of justice begins with an impressive vision: Hildegard warns the king of Germany, Conrad, that 'the time in which you are living is an effeminate one, weak like a woman, and it also inclines to oppose injustice, which is attempting to destroy justice in Lord's vineyard'; moreover, she prophesies the coming of several ages when the world would be torn by the struggle between the *iustitia Dei*, embodied in the church, and secular injustice.[15] Then, writing to Emperor Frederick, the abbess describes the *rex iustus* as a man who 'was standing on the top of a high mountain and was watching over the valleys', to rule with the biblical *virga* the countries threatened by 'the fallacious multitude of those who destroy justice by the blackness of their sins'.[16] Having depicted this ideal prince, in the following letter to Philip of Flanders Hildegard then refers to the actual case: the lord has to comply with divine justice without putting his own interest before judgement, and he has to repent of the crimes he has committed.

Philip of Alsace, count of Flanders, took the cross on Good Friday, 11 April 1175, urged by Baldwin IV of Jerusalem's envoys – as the presence in Flanders of Arnulf, subprior of the Holy Sepulchre, between 1175 and 1177 suggests – and he promised to leave that very summer.[17] Despite Jerusalem's diplomatic pressure, the count did not sail for Acre until two years later, about Whitsunday 1177:[18] his delay may plausibly be ascribed both to the internal troubles of Flanders and of empire, and to Henry II of England's interference, as the Plantagenet was unwilling to lose his patronage over the Holy Land.[19] In his letter, which Philip sent to Hildegard through 'a very faithful servant of mine', regretting that he could not meet the abbess personally, the count pointed out that he was on the eve of his journey to Jerusalem and he was very busy with preparations. So this correspondence can be dated between the spring 1176, when the count could properly wonder 'if it would be useful for me to stay in that land or to return', because his heir-apparent – his brother Peter, count of Nevers – was still living, and the spring of 1177, when he was negotiating with the English king and he could well say that he could not meet the abbess of Rupertsberg personally because of 'so many ... affairs arising from day to day'.[20] It is easy to suppose that Hildegard's renown, spreading quickly through the North thanks to her relationship with the abbeys of Gembloux and Park and with the canons of Utrecht, reached Philip in a short time.[21]

Like many of his contemporaries, the count of Flanders wished Hildegard to advise him about the crusader expedition, on the basis of what the abbess could know from her visions about the state and fate of his own soul.[22] Relying on the biblical authority of St James's epistle (James 5: 16), Philip asked for the abbess's intervention because he was aware that his condition as layman prevented him from achieving a more perfect way of living; nevertheless, he also wanted to show his *pietas*, one of the virtues required in the ideal prince that the count tried consciously to embody during his lifetime, stating that: 'I love Christ's servants and friends with all my heart and I willingly honour them in all ways with highest reverence.'[23] As he himself acknowledged, Philip had inherited a deep religious feeling and a special care for ecclesiastical institutions from his mother Sybil of Anjou, who died in the Holy Land in about 1164 while attending the poor at the monastery of St Lazarus in Bethany.[24] On the eve of the 1177 crusade he granted a very long series of privileges to the churches belonging to his own demesne to purchase bread and wine for the sacrifice of the mass.[25]

In his letter, Philip insisted on the importance of Hildegard's role of *ancilla Christi*, mediating between the divine will and the *peccator et indignus* prince, who is stained with his own fault and who asks for the Lord's mercy thanks to the abbess's prayers. It is significant that the count mentioned the very bad *fama actuum meorum* just after having announced his departure for Jerusalem: since 1175, in fact, it was rumoured that Philip of Flanders had taken the cross to expiate the atrocities he committed during the war against England;[26] he was also charged with his brother Matthew's death which occurred during the siege of Driencourt 'because he himself, count of Flanders and Vermandois, who was very powerful in rousing those wars, could have much influence on restoring peace'.[27] Furthermore, on 12 August 1175 Philip had the knight Walter of Fontaines beaten to death because he was said to be Countess Isabel's lover: the count was pitiless towards the corpse and he ordered it to be exposed to public scorn.[28] As Hildegard referred to this well-known event in her answer, Philip's letter of enquiry, preserved in the Riesencodex, can be regarded as authentic, even if partly adapted.

Primarily, the count's journey to the Holy Land in 1177 was meant as a penitential pilgrimage carried out as a military *servitium divinum* in the East lasting one year or two, in accordance with Pope Alexander III's innovative view, which later on survived only in Flemish criminal law.[29] Notwithstanding this, Philip shaded the penitential significance of his crusade and he replaced it with a chivalrous notion of crusading which belonged to the tradition of the counts of Flanders because of their relationship with Byzantium long before the first crusade.[30] In fact, his own main concern in asking for the abbess's advice was 'what I ought to do to exalt the name of Christianity in these days and to bring low the terrible savagery of the Saracens, and if it would be useful for me to stay in that land or to return', according to what Hildegard could learn from God about Philip's soul. 'Ut nomen Christianitatis temporibus meis exaltetur':[31] the count's view mirrored the idea of the Christian reconquest originating from the reform papacy and guided by God to deliver the countries once belonging to the Christian faith from tyrannical Saracen oppression.[32] However, Philip conceived this idea of crusade in a secular way, shared with contemporary French epic poems, where Christendom was a 'geographical, social and cultural being' rather than a purely religious one.[33] In short: the count did not speak about the 'libertas Ecclesiae' at all and, furthermore, he turned to his own advantage the theological reading of the crusade as an enterprise ruled by God's will, which recurred in the Gregorian papacy's letters. As a result, the *iter Ierosolimitanum* changed into an occasion for personal prowess and knightly pride, deeply rooted values in the crusading tradition of Philip's family and of the county too.[34] Between 1138 and 1164, indeed, his father Thierry went four times on crusade to the Holy Land, because of his blood ties with the king of Jerusalem but also perhaps to gain a major fief in Syria.[35] Thierry's example was coupled with the great enthusiasm for crusading shown by the Flemish knights from the very beginning, as pointed out by Pope Urban II's letter in 1095 and, later on, by Bernard of Clairvaux's preaching.[36] So Philip's own prestige could be greatly increased by defending the kingdom of Jerusalem which, moreover, could fall under Flemish political influence, as occurred during Baldwin II's captivity in 1123–4 when the throne was offered to Count Charles the Good.[37]

Whatever may be the meaning of the mysterious sentence 'if it would be useful for me to stay in that land or to return', implying as it

does a possible long stay in the East,[38] it is clear that the count of
Flanders was looking to Hildegard for an unfailing confirmation,
that is a supernatural one, not only because of his religious disposi-
tion (which was indeed clear through his letter) but also thanks to the
political and chivalrous mission entrusted to him in the kingdom of
Jerusalem. In 1177 Philip seemed to think of his crusade as a penitential pilgrimage to redeem his honour and to appear the champion of
Christendom, albeit not without political profit: as he closed his letter, once again the count asked for the abbess's advice and prayers.

The reader is somewhat surprised at Hildegard's answer, for the
abbess changed direction completely, dealing with the struggle
against the Saracens only at the end of her warning to Count
Philip.[39] As usual in her writings, Hildegard ascribed what was
revealed to her not to her own wisdom, but to the divine light, that
is the *verum lumen* she can see as she remains fully conscious
throughout her vision.[40] In her letter to Philip, the abbess explained
the history of salvation as the history of God's justice, a subject the
Riesencodex had already dealt with in her letters to Conrad III and
Frederick I.[41] As the count had addressed her strongly in the biblical
promise that 'the effectual fervent prayer of a righteous man availeth
much', Hildegard dwelt upon the intrinsic nature of justice and she
went on to examine the dangerous temptation to consider as an act
of justice something which, in fact, is merely arbitrary, a topic she
had developed before when writing to a king of England.[42] God's
just judgement – the biblical *iustum iudicium* which was a recurrent
theme in medieval literary production thanks to Augustine's writings[43] – marks the whole history of Adam and of humankind, and it
reveals itself both in the expulsion of Adam from the Garden of
Eden after his fall (*praevaricatio eiusdem precepti*) and in the biblical
Flood, which in Hildegard's writings was the watershed between the
wicked ancient generation and the rising of a new world awaiting
Christ's coming.[44] However, the sacrifice of the cross fulfilled by the
mitissimus Agnus[45] replaced God's inflexible justice by redeeming
mercy, on condition that – and here Hildegard echoed the decrees
issued by the eleventh-century councils – the sinner acknowledged
his own guilt *per veram penitentiam*.[46]

The count of Flanders's own story followed the symbolic pattern
of Adam's fall too: that is why Hildegard addressed Philip as *filius
Dei*, because 'he himself moulded you in the image of the first
man'.[47] Then she referred to the classical image of the eagle gazing

at the sun, which in Hildegard's works is the symbol of man finding out the truth about himself if he turns his eyes to God ('so that you can see God with the clear eye of justice like an eagle gazing at the sun'),[48] and she urged the count to check the righteousness of his own judgement by looking at God's justice through a disturbing question: 'Why have you killed your neighbour without considering My own justice?' In this passage Hildegard seemed to hint at the arbitrary murder of Walter of Fontaines, especially since, having recalled Count Philip to the right way to administer justice by law and punishment – a duty Philip carefully attended – she warned him not to fall into God's curse on account of an unjust sentence passed in a fit of anger.[49]

At this point, in accordance with the history of humankind narrated before by Hildegard, the abbess brought into her letter the redeeming cross, the *signaculum crucis* able to secure God's mercy for the sinful count: 'You too, take refuge in the living God with the sign of the cross because of all your negligences and sins and all your unjust judgements.'[50] The sign of the cross, which is precisely the symbol of God's justice in Rupert of Deutz's contemporary works,[51] was related both to the spiritual power of Christ's cross and to the material sign of the cross tokening Philip's crusader vow. According to Hildegard, crusading deserves to be praised for its penitential significance because the crusade was an extraordinary opportunity that God's infinite mercy was offering to men to save themselves (Ezekiel 33: 11), as it was announced all over Western Christendom by Bernard of Clairvaux's well-known epistle 363 when he preached the Second Crusade.[52] But the abbess was not bound to Bernard only because they belonged to the same monastic world nor because of the influence the abbot's writings had on her literary production:[53] Bernard's preaching tour in Germany echoed as far as the cloister of Disibodenberg, as proved by one of Hildegard's letters written in 1147 or 1148, where the abbot of Clairvaux is described 'in his intense zeal and burning love for the Son of God, gathering men under the banner of the holy cross against pagan savagery'.[54] So the abbess shared with Bernard the monastic notion of *militia Christi*[55] conceived both as a spiritual fight against sin, the highest degree of perfection which belonged to the monk on the way of heavenly Jerusalem,[56] and as an armed fight led by the Christian knights against the pagans, those regarding 'their own will as God' and who are plunged into *incredulitate* and *infidelitate*.[57]

Having reminded the count of the remission of sins, Hildegard now prompted Philip to hold out against the infidels ready to destroy the *fontem fidei*, which was the earthly Jerusalem, but also the source and symbol of the Christian faith: 'And if the time shall come when the infidels seek to destroy the fountain of faith, then withstand them by God's grace, as hard as you are able.'[58] Once again, however, the abbess was referring to the military and knightly idea of crusading, so deep-rooted in Philip's mind, as a means to point out the penitential significance of the crusade. In fact, she urged the count of Flanders to reflect on *infidelitas*: this condition, embodied in the pagans' fighting against Christ and his church as instruments of the devil,[59] was a visible symbol of the sinful condition marking humankind as a whole after Adam's fall, and marking every human being who was determined to depart from God by his own will.[60] Therefore, crusading against the Saracens could be possible and useful to Philip only if preceded by an inner struggle, whose beginning, according to Hildegard, was the *sollicitudo* troubling the count's soul; expiation and true repentance (*vera penitentia*) would enable the soul to flee from the utter darkness of infidelity and to turn back to God. The meaning of Philip's conversion has to be found in the image of dawn 'which rises in the morning', which – as one of Hildegard's favourite symbols – stands both for the time of redemption heralded by Christ's coming, 'time of the shining dawn, that is full of justice', and for the time in which the soul, enlightened by the Holy Spirit, comes back to God and to spiritual life.[61]

So Hildegard's conclusion is completely devoted to the inner significance of Philip's crusade, far from the political and knightly care of the war against the Saracens: Hildegard admonished the count to purge his own heart, which was everyman's first and chief duty, thus serving the Lord 'so that you might live for ever in supreme blessedness'. As the abbess's authority was received in contemporary society without considering her gender, but with regard to her status of prophetess, her idea of crusade, very different from that of the count of Flanders, was not influenced by her female perspective: Hildegard's insistence on crusading against deadly sin rather than against the Saracens was related to the *ordo* to which she belonged, in this case ecclesiastical world as opposed to secular nobility.[62]

WIESBADEN, HESSISCHE LANDESBIBLIOTHEK, 2 (RIESENCODEX), FO. 341^{R-V}

PHILIPPUS COMES FLANDRIAE HILDEGARDI

Philippus, Flandriae et Viromensis comes, domicellae Hildegardi ancillae Christi salutem et plurimam dilectionem. Vestra noverit sanctitas me paratum esse ad faciendum quicquid scirem vobis placere, quia sancta conversatio vestra et vita honestissima sepissime meis insonuit auribus[63] omni fama suavior. Quamvis enim peccator sim et indignus, tamen Christi servos et amicos toto corde diligo et omnimoda veneratione libenter honoro, illius Scripturae memor: *Multum valet assidua iusti deprecatio* (Iac 5:16). Unde est quod ad pietatis vestrae gratiam mitto presentium latorem fidelissimum servientem meum, qui pro me misero peccatore vobiscum loquatur, cum ego tamen multo libentius ad vos venissem et vobis locutus fuissem quod desideravi; sed tot et tanta sunt negocia mea quae singulis diebus emergunt, quod ad haec vacare non/*(f. 341v)* poteram. Instat etiam iam tempus quo aggredi debeam iter Ierosolimitanum,[64] ad quod[65] opus mihi est magno apparatu,[66] super quo consilium vestrum mihi intimare dignemini per litteras vestras. Credo enim quod ad vos sepius pervenit fama nominis mei et actuum meorum, et multa Dei miseratione indigeo; unde et vos maxima precum instantia suppliciter exoro, ut pro me miserrimo et indignissimo peccatore apud Deum intercedere velitis. Rogo etiam humiliter ut, in quantum vobis concesserit divina misericordia, inquiratis a Deo quid mihi expediat et litteris vestris per latorem presentium mihi renuntietis consilium vestrum, quid et quomodo faciam, ut nomen Christianitatis temporibus meis exaltetur, et dira Sarracenorum feritas deprimatur,[67] et si utile mihi erit in terra illa morari vel reverti, iuxta id videlicet quod de statu meo forsitan audistis et divina revelatione cognovistis aut cognitura estis. Valete in Christo, soror dilecta, et scitote quod multum desidero audire consilium vestrum et quod maximam in vestris orationibus habeo fiduciam.

PHILIPPO COMITI FLANDRIAE HILDEGARDA

O fili Dei, quia ipse in primo homine te plasmavit, audi verba quae vigili mente et corpore in anima mea vidi et audivi, cum propter sollicitam inquisitionem tuam ad verum lumen aspexi. Deus preceptum

Adae in paradyso dedit et post prevaricationem eiusdem precepti eum, qui consilio serpentis consenserat, iusto iudicio de paradyso expulit. Cum iusto quoque iudicio homines qui eum omnino oblivioni tradiderant, ita quod eum nec desiderabant nec querebant, per diluvium dimersit, ubi illos qui eum amabant et querebant a diluvio per archam salvavit. Sed mitissimus Agnus, scilicet filius Dei, in sanguine suo, quem in cruce pendens effudit, omnia crimina et peccata, quae homo per veram penitentiam cognoscit, et[68] salvat. Nunc autem adtende, o fili Dei, ut puro oculo iusticiae in Deum/*(f. 341v)* velut aquila in solem aspicias, ita ut absque proprietate voluntatis tuae iudicia tua iusta sint,[69] ne a summo iudice, qui preceptum homini dedit, quem etiam in misericordia per penitentiam ad se vocat, tibi dicatur: Quare proximum tuum sine iusticia mea interemisti? Homines quoque qui iudicio rei sunt, illos secundum scripturas sanctorum, qui columpnae aecclesiae erant,[70] cum lege et cum timore mortis constringe, in omnibus tamen adtendens maledictionem hominis illius qui homicidium in ira sua perpetravit.[71] Tu etiam pro omnibus neglegentiis et peccatis ac pro omnibus iniustis iudiciis tuis cum signaculo crucis ad Deum vivum confuge, qui via et veritas est,[72] et qui etiam dicit: *Nolo mortem peccatoris sed ut magis convertatur et vivat* (Ezek. 33,11). Et si tempus advenerit quod infideles[73] fontem fidei destruere laborant, tunc eis, quantum per adiutorium gratiae Dei potueris, eis resiste. Ego enim in anima mea video quod sollicitudo, quam de angustiis animae tuae habes, aurorae quae in mane oritur similis est. Unde Spiritus Sanctus te in pura et vera penitentia ardentem solem efficiat, ut eum queras et ipsi soli servias, ita ut in summa beatitudine in eternum vivas.

NOTES

I am grateful to Susan Edgington who invited me to read this paper at the IMC 2000, and to the Hessische Landesbibliothek Wiesbaden and the Istituto Storico Olandese in Rome.

[1] H. van Werveke, 'Filips van de Elzas en Willem von Tyrus: een episode uit de geschiedenis van de kruistochen', *Mededelingen van de koninklijke Vlaamse Academie voor Wetenschappen, Letteren en Schone Kunsten van België, Klasse der Letteren* 33 (1971), 3–36; idem, *Een Vlaamse graaf van Europees formaat: Filips van de Elzas* (Haarlem, 1976), 50–61; J. Phillips,

Defenders of the Holy Land: Relations between the Latin East and West, 1119–87 (Oxford, 1996), 225–45; B. Hamilton, *The Leper King and his Heirs: Baldwin IV and the Crusader Kingdom of Jerusalem* (Cambridge, 2000), 119–31.

  ² S. Flanagan, *Hildegard of Bingen: A Visionary Life* (London, 1989), esp. 13–15; B. Newman, *Sister of Wisdom: St Hildegard's Theology of the Feminine* (Berkeley, CA, 1987), esp. 254–7.

  ³ John of Salisbury, *The Letters*, ed. W. J. Millor and C. N. L. Brooke (Oxford, 1979), vol. 2, no. 185, p. 224: 'Si non aliud occurrit quod nostratibus desiit, saltem visiones et oracula beatae illius et celeberrimae Hildegardis apud vos sunt; quae michi ex eo commendata est et venerabilis, quod eam dominus Eugenius speciali caritatis affectu familiarius amplectebatur. Explorate etiam diligentius et rescribite an ei sit de fine huius scismatis aliquid revelatum. Praedixit enim in diebus beati Eugenii quod non esset nisi in extremis diebus pacem et gratiam in urbe habiturus.'

  ⁴ C. Maier, 'Ildegarde di Bingen: Profezia ed esistenza letteraria', *Cristianesimo nella storia* 17 (1996), 271–303; as for Hildegard's comparison with Deborah see *Vita Sanctae Hildegardis*, ed. M. Klaes, CCCM 126, II, 6, 30–1.

  ⁵ S. Hildegardis *Opera*, PL 197, cols. 145–382, ep. XXVIII, 187C–188D; J. Johnen, 'Philipp von Elsass, Graf von Flandern, 1157 (1163)–1191', *Bulletin de la commission royale d'histoire* 79 (1910), 341–469 at 422–3; H. Lindeman, 'S. Hildegard en hare Nederlandische vrienden', *Ons Geestlijk Erf* 2 (1928), 128–60 at 156–7; R. Pernoud, *Storia e visioni di sant'Ildegarda* (Casale Monferrato, 1996), 78–83.

  ⁶ O. Engels, 'Die Zeit der hl. Hildegard' in A. Ph. Brück (ed.), *Hildegard von Bingen 1179–1979: Festschrift zum 800. Todestag der Heiligen* (Mainz, 1979), 1–29. For Hildegard, at least: A. Führkötter, *Hildegard von Bingen* (Salzburg, 1972); P. Dronke, *Women Writers in the Middle Ages* (Cambridge, 1984), 144–201.

  ⁷ Wiesbaden, Hessische Landesbibliothek 2, fo. 341^{r-v} (not yet edited by Acker); L. van Acker, 'Der Briefwechsel der heiligen Hildegard von Bingen: Vorbemerkung zu einer kritischen Edition', *Revue Bénédictine* 98 (1988), 141–68; 99 (1989), 118–54. See also M. Schrader and A. Führkötter, *Die Echtheit des Schrifttums der heiligen Hildegard von Bingen: Quellenkritische Unterschungen* (Cologne and Graz, 1956), 154–79; M. Klaes, 'Von einer Briefsammlung zum literarischen Briefbuch: Anmerkungen zur Überlieferung der Briefe Hildegards von Bingen', in E. Forster (ed.), *Hildegard von Bingen: Prophetin durch die Zeiten: Zum 900. Geburtstag* (Freiburg, 1998), 153–70.

  ⁸ *Vita S. Hildegardis*, 2, 1. 20: 'In unum volumen compilate et sue et ille, que ad se fuerant destinate'; Schrader and Führkötter, *Die Echtheit*, 184.

  ⁹ Acker, 'Vorbemerkung', 99 (1989), 129–34; A. Derolez, 'The manuscript transmission of Hildegard of Bingen's writings: the state of the problem', in

C. Burnett and P. Dronke (eds.), *Hildegard of Bingen: The Context of her Thought and Art* (London, 1998), 17–28 at 23.

[10] Hildegardis *Epistolarium*, CCCM 91, ep. XXIII; XXIV–XXIVR; H. Büttner, 'Die Beziehungen der heiligen Hildegard von Bingen zu Kurie, Erzbischof und Kaiser', in *Universitas: Festschrift A. Stohr* (Mainz, 1960), 2: 60–8. Cf. J. Oroz Reta, 'La Sibila del Rhin: misión profética de sancta Hildegarda de Bingen', *Latomus* 53 (1994), 608–34 at 618–20; Dronke, *Women Writers*, 196–201.

[11] Schrader and Führkötter, *Die Echtheit*, 158–60.

[12] Ibid., 175; R. W. Southern, 'Aspects of the European tradition of historical writing, 3: history as prophecy', *TRHS* 22 (1972), 159–80 at 170.

[13] B. Schmeidler, 'Bemerkungen zum Korpus der Briefe der hl. Hildegard von Bingen', in E. E. Stengel (ed.), *Corona Quernea: Festgabe K. Strecker* (Leipzig, 1941), 335–66 at 362–4.

[14] Berlin, Staatsbibliothek Preussischer Kulturbesitz, cod. lat. 4° 674, fos. 44ᵛ–45ᵛ, ed. Schrader and Führkötter, *Die Echtheit*, 130–1: 'Omnis enim potestas et principatus ab ipso solo exsistit (cf. Rom 13,1), qui omnia recta ordinatione disponit, et ab ipso nomen accepit, quoniam secundum ipsum regere, corrigere et iudicare populos debent et vias veritatis et iustitie ostendere'; cf. W. Berges, *Die Fürstenspiegel des hohen und späten Mittelalters* (MGH Schriften, 2; Leipzig, 1938), 24–6.

[15] S. Hildegardis *Opera PL* 197, cols. 145–382, ep. XXVI, 185B–186B: 'Tempora, in quibus es, veluti in muliebri persona, levia sunt, et etiam in contrariam injustitiam, quae justitiam in vinea Domini destruere tentat, se inclinant'; Maier, 'Ildegarde di Bingen', 283–5; for *tempus muliebre*: B. Widmer, *Heilsordnung und Zeitgeschehen in der Mystik Hildegards von Bingen* (Basle and Stuttgart, 1955), 260–6; Newman, *Sister of Wisdom*, 238–49.

[16] For Hildegard and Frederick I: Schrader and Führkötter, *Die Echtheit*, 124–31. Compare these texts with: *Analecta S. Hildegardis*, in *Analecta Sacra* 8, ed. J.-B. Pitra (Monte Cassino, 1882), ep. 73, 538, and ibid., ep. 112, 556.

[17] 'Régeste de Philippe d'Alsace', ed. H. Coppieters-Stochove, *Annales de la Societé d'Histoire et d'Archéologie de Gand* 7 (1906), 1–177 at 48–9, no. 125 (1175); 53, no. 137 (1176); 54–5, no. 141 (1176); 71, no. 198 (12 March 1177). The 'Arnold, sous-prieur de St. Sépulcre' mentioned here can be identified perhaps with the *Arnulfus subprior* who appears in three charters of Outremer, dated 1166, 1170–1 and 1178 respectively: *Cart St Sép*, 272, no. 139; ibid., 309, no. 158, and RRH 149, no. 561.

[18] *Sigeberti Continuatio aquicinctina*, MGH SS 6, 405–38 at 415; *Gesta regis Henrici*, RS 49, 1: 159; *La Chronique de Gislebert de Mons*, ed. L. Vanderkindere (Brussels, 1904), 121–2; *Chartes inédites concernant les comtes de Hainaut*, ed. C. Duvivier (Brussels, 1904), 89–94, no. 46 (24

April–12 June 1177, Philip's testamentary dispositions before leaving). Philip landed at Acre on 1 August 1177: WT 21, 13.

[19] Johnen, 'Philipp von Elsass', 422–6; H. E. Mayer, 'Henry II of England and the Holy Land', *EHR* 97 (1982), 721–39; J. Dunbabin, 'William of Tyre and Philip of Alsace', *Academiae Analecta* 48 (1986), 109–17.

[20] Coppieters-Stochove, 'Régeste de Philippe d'Alsace', 77, no. 215 (vers 1177); Johnen, 'Philipp von Elsass', 422–3 and Hamilton, *Leper King*, 119 (both of them date this letter perhaps before the death of Peter of Nevers).

[21] See Lindeman, 'S. Hildegard en hare Nederlandische vrienden', and P. Sejourné, 'Les Correspondants de Sainte Hildegarde à Utrecht', *Nederlandsch archief voor kerkgeschiedenis*, NS 16 (1921), 144–62.

[22] *Vita Sanctae Hildegardis*, 2. 4. 25–6: 'Confluebant ad eam undique utriusque sexus populorum examina, quibus per gratiam Dei utriusque vite affatim accomoda impendebat exhortamina. Ad salutem enim animarum suarum proponebat eis et solvebat questiones sanctarum scripturarum.' Cf. Hildegardis *Epistolarium*, ep. XLVIII, 118, rr. 29–30; see also Flanagan, *Hildegard of Bingen*, 158–64.

[23] Philip of Harveng wrote after 1167 a *speculum principis* addressed to Philip of Flanders in the form of a long letter: Philippi de Harveng, *Epistolae*, *PL* 203, cols. 1–180, 147B–151C, ep. 16 (see Werveke, *Een Vlaamse Graf*, 76–8).

[24] Th. de Hemptinne and M. Parisse, 'Thierry d'Alsace, comte de Flandre: biographie et actes', *Annales de l'Est* 43 (1991), 83–108 at 90; N. Huyghebaert, 'Une comtesse de Flandre à Bethanie', *Les Cahiers de Saint-André* 21 (1964), 1–13; Th. de Hemptinne, 'Les Épouses des croisés et pèlerins flamands au XIe et XIIe siècles: l'exemple des comtesses de Flandre Clémence et Sybille', in *Autour*, 83–95 at 92–5.

[25] Coppieters-Stochove, 'Régeste de Philippe d'Alsace', 62–70, nos. 162–96; Johnen, 'Philipp von Elsass', 426.

[26] Radulfi de Diceto, *Ymagines historiarum*, RS 68, 1: 398–9.

[27] *La Chronique de Gislebert*, 113: 'Ex eo quod in commotione guerrarum illarum ipse comes Flandrie et Viromandie potentissimus ad pacem componendam plurimum potuisset valere.'

[28] Radulfi *Ymagines*, 1: 402; *Gesta regis Henrici*, RS 49 (2 vols.), 1: 99–101; cf. Johnen, 'Philipp von Elsass', 418–20.

[29] C. Vogel, 'Le Pèlerinage pénitentiel', in A. Faivre (ed.), *En rémission des péchés: Recherches sur les systèmes pénitentiels dans l'Église latine* (Aldershot, 1994), paper VII, 113–53 at 145–8; J. Richard, 'Urbain II, la prédication de la croisade et la définition d'indulgence', in E.-D. Hehl *et al.* (eds.), *Deus qui mutat tempora: Menschen und Institutionen im Wandel des Mittelalters. Festschrift für Alfons Becker* (Sigmaringen, 1987), 129–35 at 134; *Papsturkunden für Templer und Johanniter*, ed. R. Hiestand (Göttingen, 1972), 251–3, no. 53, esp. 253 (Alexander III's letter, 29 June 1166).

[30] K. N. Ciggaar, 'Flemish counts and emperors: friends and foreigners in Byzantium', in V. D. van Aalst and K. N. Ciggaar (eds.), *The Latin Empire: Some Contributions* (Hernen, 1994), 33–62.

[31] C. Erdmann, *The Origin of the Idea of Crusade* (Princeton, 1977), 349–50, n. 138; P. Rousset, 'La Notion de Chrétienté aux XIe et XIIe siècles', *Le Moyen Age* 58 (1963), 191–203; J. van Laarhoven, 'Chrétienté et croisade: une tentative terminologique', *Cristianesimo nella storia* 6 (1985), 27–43; M. Pellegrini, 'L'idea di Christianitas nei cronisti latini della prima crociata', *Rivista di Bizantinistica* 1 (1991), 69–99; cf. R. Curtius, 'Der Kreuzzugsgedanke und das Altfranzösische Epos', in idem (ed.), *Gesammelte Aufsätze zur romanischen Philologie* (Berne and Munich, 1960), 98–105 at 102–5, esp. 102.

[32] J. Flori, 'Réforme, reconquista, croisade (l'idée de reconquête dans la correspondance pontificale d'Alexandre II à Urbain II)', in idem (ed.), *Croisade et chevalerie, XIe–XIIe siècles* (Brussels, 1998), 51–80.

[33] Curtius, 'Kreuzzugsgedanke', 103–5; J. Flori, 'Pur eshalcier sainte crestiënté: croisade, guerre sainte et guerre juste dans les anciennes chansons de geste françaises', *Le Moyen Age* 97 (1997), 171–87.

[34] J. Phillips, 'The murder of Charles the Good and the Second Crusade: household, nobility, and traditions of crusading in medieval Flanders', *Medieval Prosopography* 19 (1998), 55–76.

[35] Werveke, 'Filips van de Elzas', 27–31; Phillips, *Defenders*, 271–81.

[36] Hagenmeyer, *Kreuzzugsbriefe*, ep. II, 136–7; J. Phillips, 'Saint Bernard of Clairvaux, the Low Countries and the Lisbon Letter of the Second Crusade', *JEH* 48 (1997), 485–97.

[37] Cf. A. V. Murray, 'The origins of the Frankish nobility of the Latin kingdom of Jerusalem, 1100–18', *Mediterranean Historical Review* 4 (1989), 281–300; idem, 'Baldwin II and his nobles: factionalism and dissent in the kingdom of Jerusalem, 1118–34', *Nottingham Medieval Studies* 38 (1994), 60–85.

[38] Cf. Duvivier, *Chartes inédites*, 90, no. 46 (Philip's testamentary dispositions about a possible heir of his own) and WT 21, 13.

[39] Cf. Johnen, 'Philipp von Elsass', 423; Flanagan, *Hildegard of Bingen*, 165.

[40] Maier, 'Ildegarde di Bingen', 288–97; Dronke, *Women Writers*, 146–7; Flanagan, *Hildegard of Bingen*, 193–7.

[41] Cf. Hildegardis *Scivias*, CCCM 43, III, *visio* 10, c. 32, rr. 923–33; V. Ranff, 'Durch Mitwirken antworten: "Iustitia" und "Misericordia" als Ausdruck der interpersonalen Konstitution des Menschen', in Forster, *Hildegard*, 249–61.

[42] *Analecta S. Hildegardis*, 556, no. 112: 'Sed nigerrima avis de Aquilone ad te venit, et dicit: Tu possibilitatem habes facere quodcumque volueris; fac ergo hoc et illud, et causam hanc et illam, quia tibi non est utile ut

justitiam inspicias, quoniam si eam semper inspexeris, non es dominus, sed servus.'

[43] Deuteronomy 16: 18: 'ut iudicent populo iusto iudicio'; Aug. *Enarrationes in Psalmos*, CI, 12, ed. E. Dekkers and J. Fraipont, SL 40, ll. 16–17: '*Ego sicut fenum arui*: ego homo, post illam praevaricationem; hoc ego iusto iudicio tuo: tu autem quid?' Cf. Hildegardis *Liber divinorum operum* (*LDO*), CCCM 92, III, *visio* I, 2, ll. 5–9.

[44] For the biblical (Ezekiel 18: 24; Romans 5: 14) *praevaricatio*: cf. Hildegardis *Liber vitae meritorum* (*LVM*), CCCM 90, I, 44, ll. 720–4; *LDO*, I, *visio* 4, 73, ll. 13–20. For the Flood: cf. *LDO*, III, *visio* 5, 5, espec. ll. 16–21; *Scivias*, III, *visio* 2, 14.

[45] Cf. *Scivias*, II, *visio* 6, 23, ll. 942–57.

[46] The definition of *vera penitentia* was debated under Gregory VII and Urban II's pontificates: R. Somerville (ed.), *The Councils of Pope Urban II* (Amsterdam, 1972), 115; cf. *LVM*, II, 85, ll. 1596–1600: 'et de peccatis suis quantum potuerit *per veram penitentiam* se emundet, quatinus cum anima sua corpus suum exuerit, in illa vita mitius purgari, et debitis penis citius eripi mereatur' (cf. Ps. Aug. *De vera et falsa poenitentia*, 17, *PL* 40, 1127–8); *LDO*, I, *visio* 4, 27, ll. 10–14; cf. Hildegardis *Epistolarium*, ep. XXIII, 65, ll. 146–50.

[47] Cf. Hildegardis *Epistolarium*, ep. CIIIR, 259, ll. 3–4: 'O fili Dei per formationem hominis in quem Deus miracula sua constituit et signavit, quia, sicut speculum in quo queque videntur vasi suo imponitur, ita rationalis anima corpori veluti fictili vasi immittitur, quatenus per ipsam vivendo regatur et anima per fidem celestia contempletur'.

[48] The image of the eagle able to gaze at the sun without being blinded comes from Lucan, *Bellum civile*, 9, 902–5: Hildegardis *Epistolarium*, ep. LXIV, 147, l. 7: 'Homo sic videns in Deum, ut aquila in solem oculum ponit'; ibid., ep. XXXVIIR, 96, ll. 13–14; ibid., ep. CCLR, 531, ll. 26–8; *Scivias*, III, 13, 1, l. 54; *LDO*, III, *visio* 4, 10, ll. 53–4.

[49] R. C. van Caenegem, *Criminal Law in England and Flanders under King Henry II and Count Philip of Alsace* (Gent, 1982).

[50] Cf. Hildegard's vision of *sanctitas*: *Scivias*, III, *visio* 9, 3, ll. 215–18: 'Et in pectore suo *signum crucis* habebat circa quod etiam splendor magnus eodem in pectore velut aurora fulgens rutilabat', with her interpretation: ibid., 29, ll. 984–92.

[51] Ruperti Tuitiensis *De sancta Trinitate*, CCCM 23, XXX, *In Hiez.*, I, par. 32, p. 1690, ll. 1837–41 ('signaculo crucis, signaculo iustitiae Dei'); *signaculum crucis* can be found both in Ambrose's and Rufinus' writings.

[52] J. Leclercq, 'L'Encyclique de saint Bernard en faveur de la croisade', in idem, *Recueils d'études sur Saint Bernard et ses écrits*, 4 (Rome, 1987), 227–46; M. Meschini, *San Bernardo e la seconda crociata* (Milan, 1998), 75–84; the C version of Bernard's letter was found widely in the lands of the

empire. For Bernard and the crusade see also: P. Rousset, *Les Origines et les caractères de la première croisade* (Geneva, 1945), 152–68; É. Delaruelle, 'L'Idée de croisade chez Saint Bernard', in *Mélanges Saint Bernard* (Dijon, 1953), 53–67; B. Flood, 'St Bernard's view of crusade', *The Australasian Catholic Record* 47 (1970), 130–43; J. Leclercq, 'L'Attitude spirituelle de S. Bernard devant la guerre', *Collectanea Cisterciensia* 36 (1974), 195–225.

   [53] G. Iversen, 'Tradition och förnyelse i Hildegardis vision om dygderna', in M. Asztalos and C. Gejrot (eds.), *Symbolae Septentrionales in honorem J. Öberg* (Stockholm, 1995), 73–102; A. Lozar, 'Hildegard von Bingen und Bernard von Clairvaux', *Unsere Liebe Frau von Himmerod* 68 (1998), 8–18.

   [54] Hildegardis *Epistolarium*, ep. I, 3, ll. 3–5: 'Vexillo sancte crucis cum excelso studio in ardenti amore Filii Dei capiens homines ad bella pugnanda in christiana militia contra paganorum sevitiam'; for *vexillum crucis* see also: *LDO*, III, *visio* 4, 5, ll. 35–9: 'Tunc filius dei, ut prefatum est, diabolo nesciente occulte venit atque humanitate sua hamum illius, quo homines capiebat, confregit; quem etiam devictis hostibus suis pro signo triumphi *in vexillum crucis* suspendit et patri suo cum omni milicia celestis exercitus ostendit.' For the relationship between Bernard and Hildegard: E. Russel, 'Bernard et les dames de son temps', in *Bernard de Clairvaux* (Paris, 1953), 411–25 at 422–5; J. Leclercq, *La donna e le donne nel pensiero di San Bernardo* (Milan, 1997), 56–60.

   [55] '*Militia Christi' e crociata nei secoli XI–XII* (Milan, 1992); cf. *Analecta S. Hildegardis*, 547, no. 92, to a *miles Christi* about fighting as an allegory of the spiritual struggle against the devil.

   [56] Cf. Hildegard's frequent exhortation to become a *vivens/vivus lapis in coelesti Jerusalem*: see for instance Hildegardis *Epistolarium*, ep. CXCIX, 452, ll. 8–9; Flanagan, *Hildegard of Bingen*, 124–30.

   [57] *LVM*, III, 78, rr. 1493–1501; *LDO*, II, *visio* I, 16, ll. 37–44. Cf. for Hildegard's idea of *pagani*: ibid., III, *visio* 5, 24, ll. 13–19; *Scivias*, II, *visio* 3, 12, ll. 294–7: 'Ita etiam ecclesia repugnat nequissimis corruptoribus qui sunt errores haereticorum, scilicet tam Christianorum quam Iudaeorum et paganorum qui eam infestant, virginitatem eius, quae fides catholica est, corrumpere volentes'; ibid., III, *visio* 11, 24, ll. 470–5.

   [58] *Scivias*, III, *visio* 11, 42, ll. 874–6: 'Et sic in cruce fatigato, cum sitiret, *fons fidei* de gentili populo emanavit, de quo ipse bibens non erubuit, dicens etiam quod sic consummatum esset.'

   [59] See *LVM*, I, 53; *Scivias*, III, *visio* 7, 6; *LDO*, II, *visio* 1, 8, ll. 32–5; *LDO*, III, *visio* II, 17, ll. 1–12; cf. *Scivias*, II, *visio* 7, 22, rr. 520–3 'Sed quia diabolus novit se modicum tempus erroris sui habere, idcirco nunc festinat infidelitatem in membris suis perficere, quae vos pessimi deceptores estis qui fidem catholicam subvertere laboratis.'

   [60] Hildegard describes the vision of *infidelitas* in *LVM*, III, 11, ll. 250–74 and she explains it in ibid., 39–40, ll. 800–73; moreover, *infidelitas* is consid-

ered the mother of all sins: *LVM*, I, 66, ll. 976–84. See also *LVM*, III, 60–3 about *infidelitas* and *incredulitas*. Cf. *Scivias*, I, *visio* 4, 11, ll. 466–78; II, *visio* 6, 27, ll. 1054–68; ibid., 102; III, *visio* 12, 10–11.

[61] *LDO*, II, *visio* 1, 16, ll. 30–1: 'tempus rutilantis aurorae, id est plene ius-ticie'; see also *Scivias*, II, *visio* 5, 12, ll. 488–9; II, *visio* 5, 20, l. 726; Hildegardis *Epistolarium*, ep. CCIR, 457, ll. 23–6; *ibid.*, ep. CCXIV, 472, rr. 40–1; M.-A. Hönmann, 'Die Morgenröte (aurora) bei Hildegard von Bingen: Symbol für die "andere", die göttliche Dimension', *Erbe und Auftrag: Benediktinische Zeitschrift* 71 (1995), 486–95. Cf. *Scivias* II, *visio* 2, 5, ll. 130–2 (*rutilans ignis*); C. Maier, 'Die Bedeutung der Farben im Werk Hildegardis von Bingen', *Frühmittelalterliche Studien* 6 (1972), 245–355.

[62] In the edn. which follows, the diphthong *ae* has been used where the caudate *e* is found in the manuscript.

[63] Cf. Song of Songs 2: 14: 'Sonet vox tua in auribus meis.'

[64] Cf. 2 Timothy 4: 6: 'Et tempus meae resolutionis instat.'

[65] quod] quod quod R.

[66] apparatu] operatu *PL*.

[67] Cf. Beati Paulini *De vita Sancti Martini libri sex*, *PL* 61, V: 'Hic saevos vincens *dira feritate* tyrannos, tristia moestorum sitiens tormenta reorum, parcebat paulum.'

[68] et *add. interl.* R.

[69] Cf. Apocalypse 16: 7.

[70] Galatians 2: 9: 'Iacobus, et Cephas, et Iohannes, qui videbantur colum-nae esse'; cf. for *columnae ecclesiae* Hier. *In Hieremiam prophetam*, CC SL 74, I, 12, 3; id. *Comm. in prophetas minores*, *In Amos*, CC SL 76, III, 9, 11, 12; idem, *Comm. in IV epistolas Paulinas*, *Ad Galatas*, PL 26, I, 2 362B.

[71] Cf. Exodus 22: 3.

[72] Cf. John 14: 6: 'Ego sum via et veritas et vita.'

[73] in *add. interl.* R.

7

Women Warriors during the Crusades, 1095–1254

KEREN CASPI-REISFELD

This chapter examines the role played by women in crusader campaigns in the geographical region of Palestine as documented in
eye-witness accounts and crusader chronicles. Consideration of
these accounts, all authored by men, reveals a considerable level of
participation by women in the crusades. Women played a variety of
roles, some more in keeping with what may be conceived as conventional female roles, and some, as we shall see, that may be considered
unconventional according to contemporary mores.[1] Although participation by women in the crusades certainly diverged from the
original intent of their organizers and preachers, active participation
by women in the early crusades was certainly not explicitly forbid-
den. The religious motivation driving the crusade – personal
salvation – was equally applicable to every believing Christian,
whether male or female.[2]

Contemporary writers' lack of interest in female participation is
attributable to the organizers' assumption that women had no viable
contribution to make to this venture. Yet despite this negative attitude we find women from all walks of medieval life taking part in the
crusades. Women accompanied their husbands, mothers their sons,
daughters their fathers and sisters their brothers. Others joined the
crusades independently, without any link to a specific male. Thus
women became an integral part of this massive social-military movement.[3] However, the female image projected in eye-witness accounts
and other crusader chronicles revolves around feminine characteristics of vulnerability, weakness, frailty, motherhood and sensitivity.
The positive contribution by women to this social-military venture is
often obscured by these unflattering descriptions.

Women from different social strata made their contributions in a variety of spheres. Some women, mainly aristocratic, engaged in diplomacy that affected the course of the fighting; others provided moral or physical support to the soldiers on the battlefield. The most daring women, the female crusaders, assumed the dress of crusader warriors. Mounted on horses, dressed in armour and bearing lances, these women made straight for the heart of the fray, some losing their lives in the process.

Before examining the specific contribution of women in each of the above-mentioned spheres, it is worth noting how the nature of war as practised in the medieval period provided women with a chance to participate in the fighting, particularly in the case of sieges and invasions.[4] The success of a siege of a fortified city, where it related to the prevention of ingress and egress of persons and provisions, was largely a function of the number of besiegers, their patience and their familiarity with the countryside. Naturally, the more 'bodies' the besiegers could draft to their side, the greater their chances of success. As in the case of clergy, the elderly or other male noncombatants, the presence of women among the besiegers served as a way of physically increasing their numbers. Essentially, during sieges women played roles as pilgrims (as distinct from crusaders), whereas the fear-inspiring role of the military personnel, such as the knight or the archer, was obviously of greater significance. In describing siege activity by women, the chroniclers display no awareness that they were contravening church policy, which opposed active participation by women in the crusades.

The other types of warfare noted above, the more aggressive invasions and attacks, were less accessible to women. They were generally organized by a military leader who put his soldiers into action, and it was difficult for women to join such campaigns; nonetheless, accounts of instances where they managed to enjoy the fruits of the looting have been preserved. Most probably the female contribution to the attack in these cases lay primarily in the provision of emotional and physical support. In times of heightened distress, prior to the fall of the First Latin Kingdom for example, or when the male crusaders were involved in preparing for a different battle, women participants joined the invading and looting forces, their femaleness hidden by the uniform dress adopted by the Christian soldiers, men and women alike. The presence of women among the soldiers was camouflaged by the helmet that covered their hair and by their assumption of battle attire: chainmail and a coat. We even know of cases where leaders remained unaware that women had infiltrated their forces and were fighting alongside male crusaders.

It was mainly royal women, in particular the queens of Jerusalem, with vested interest in the Holy Land, who engaged in diplomacy during the crusades. During the period 1131–52, Queen Melisende was effective ruler of the Latin kingdom; as such, she actively negotiated with the ruler of Damascus. Her powers were limited, however, by her inability to lead the kingdom's military forces in battle against the Muslim troops surrounding the kingdom.[5]

While the king of Jerusalem was in captivity and she was therefore the highest ranking figure in the kingdom, Melisende's granddaughter Sybil participated in the negotiations between the Christian representation and Saladin.[6] We also find a woman initiating direct contact with Saladin. This was the lady Eschiva, who surrendered Tiberias to Saladin prior to the fall of the First Latin Kingdom.[7] Upon hearing that the king had been taken captive, she assumed that a similar fate or death had befallen her husband and sons; consequently, she turned the keys of the city over to the enemy. Concurrently, she sent a message to Saladin in which she agreed to surrender if she and her subjects were guaranteed safe passage to Tripoli.

When Louis IX was in Egyptian captivity, his wife Marguerite negotiated the Christian surrender at Damietta, Egypt, in 1250. Louis empowered her to negotiate, with the intent that she ensure his release and the removal of the Christian forces from Egypt. She took responsibility for making the arrangements for their departure until the boats arrived to evacuate the Christians.[8]

Outside the Holy Land, we find Eleanor of Aquitaine, queen consort of Louis VII of France and later of Henry II of England, and mother of Richard the Lion Heart, who, by virtue of her holdings, played an important role in the various lands where she lived. She also was a moving force behind French activity in the Levant during the Second Crusade.[9]

The most prominent role played by the majority of women who participated in the crusades was in the provision of various types of physical and emotional succour to the crusader army. Foremost among those who provided assistance of a physical nature were the washerwomen. This was the only group of women to receive official authorization to join the crusades, starting with the First Crusade.[10]

However, these washerwomen had to be old and physically unattractive in order not to arouse the men, who ostensibly had disengaged themselves from the women in their close environment. Another important task these women assumed was the removal of lice from the soldiers' heads. No skills except unattractive looks were necessary for this function.[11]

Of other supportive women, the most sought after by male crusaders were the prostitutes. Among female participants in the crusades, it was this group that most concerned the leadership. Undoubtedly, these providers of sexual services made an essential contribution to raising male morale, regardless of victory or defeat in battle. And, in cases of victory, no complaints were heard regarding this form of support. In cases of defeat, the leaders of the crusades criticized the sexual services the prostitutes provided and outlawed their activity. Even a Muslim chronicle notes the presence of these prostitutes and their self-image as contributing to the war effort.[12]

Chronicles from the First Crusade cite the role played by women in providing emotional and physical assistance to the Christian fighting forces, who were numerically inferior to the attacking Muslim force, at the battle of Dorylaeum in 1097.[13] Not only did the women in the camp provide the stunned Christian fighters with moral support, they also provided them with drinking water, an essential and fundamental matter whose importance should not be underestimated in the climatic conditions of the Middle East. The women came again and again onto the battlefield for various reasons. It is at least arguable that this unstinting support and encouragement made an important contribution in enabling the Christians to turn the tide and to win this engagement. For the crusaders, this victory opened the way south toward the Taurus Mountains. We find similar examples of feminine support during the prolonged siege of Antioch and Jerusalem, as described by William of Tyre, and during the Fatimid siege of Jaffa, in 1123, when women assisted the fighters both by bringing water and by providing ammunition – stones.[14]

Even when the crusader army left its home territory to fight strategic battles in Egypt (the Fifth Crusade to Damietta, Louis IX's crusade), Oliver of Paderborn[15] and Jean de Joinville mentioned assistance from a woman who sold provisions to the soldiers:

The next battalion to engage the enemy was the one led by the king's brother, the Comte de Poitiers. These troops were on foot, and the count was the man who was mounted. The Turks utterly routed them and led the Comte de Poitiers away captive. When the butchers and the other camp followers, including the women who sold provisions, saw this happen they raised a cry of alarm throughout the camp . . .[16]

This type of assistance – provision of water and entering the war zone – was consistently attested in the accounts of crusader–Muslim battles. The chronicles indicated that, in return for this form of assistance, the women received a portion of the booty divided among all sectors of the fighters. Thus we see that the role of these women, portrayed by the chroniclers as physically weak and taking a minor role in the crusader camp's battle, nonetheless received material recognition in the share of the loot.[17] Almost all the Christian chroniclers, all male, allow the women's assistance with water and mental support. This kind of military service was not antagonistic to the religious approach of these writers. Their unsympathetic approach towards the participation of women was not seen as incompatible with descriptions of feminine help. On the contrary, the women's zeal to help the male warriors emphasized the rightness of the male crusaders' behaviour. Muslim writers did not mention the provision of water, probably because this was not such an extraordinary situation to them.

A further aspect of emotional and physical assistance involved the most common type of medieval military encounter – the siege. We have already noted how the prevalence of sieges in medieval warfare facilitated the active participation of women. One siege task in which women assisted was filling in the moats that surrounded the fortified cities the crusaders wished to capture. There is the case of the woman killed while taking part in this task at Acre, whose dying wish was for her body to be left in the ditch.[18] We can assume that, like this woman, there were others who had played similar roles in earlier sieges, joining the Christians engaged in filling moats in order to allow the crusaders easier access to the city walls. Most of them did not die during their work so they did not receive the honour of being the hero of an episode in a Christian chronicle. It seems as if the chroniclers wrote about female assistance only when it served their tendencies to glorify the crusaders, that is the male warriors. Despite this chauvinist attitude, those unknown women affected warfare directly and helped to change its course from defeat to victory.

In the aftermath of battle, women were allowed to take revenge on the Muslims. After a naval battle and a solemn triumph in March 1190 the Christians brought the enemy to shore: 'Our women pulled the Turks along by the hair, treated them dishonourably, humiliatingly cutting their throats; and finally beheaded them. The women's physical weakness prolonged the pain of death, because they cut their heads off with knives instead of swords.'[19] The importance of this incident is the recognition of the women's ability to use knives and swords. The cruel action needed some strength and skill. We can assume that the execution was carried out by semi-skilled women, in order to get rid of the Muslim captives with maximum humiliation and suffering. In mentioning this killing by the Christians the writer intended to emphasize the superiority of the Christian male warriors over the Muslims, but it also attests unwittingly the women's ability to use medieval weapons.[20]

In his description of the aftermath of the capture of Damietta, Oliver of Paderborn implied that almost all the Christians took part in the siege and battles. Plunder and spoils that were left in the Egyptian cities were divided among the soldiers, clergy, servants, women and children.[21] In spite of their non-participation in the battles, women received some share of the plunder. How did those women arrive in Egypt? The Christian troops were transported by ship from the crusader kingdom to the Egyptian shore. Unlike the infantry march which was not limited in its number of participants, the number of soldiers who could be transported by sea was limited by the capacity of the ships. Since a fleet of ships took a finite number of soldiers and their equipment, the appearance of women in the crusades to Egypt leads us to a surprising conclusion: women's participation in the naval crusades was authorized by the leaders of the campaigns, despite the fact that bringing them by ship reduced the space for male troops. The leaders took women in preference to men. The only possible conclusion is that their contribution to the crusade army was essential, and not only as washerwomen or prostitutes. Reward for their contribution to the campaign took the form of permission to share in the plunder and spoils.

Examination of the written sources also reveals the presence of a unique, daring and little-recognized group of female participants in the crusades – women who took part in the actual fighting between the Christian and Muslim forces. Crusader chronicles noted the presence of women in the ranks of the fully outfitted crusader army stationed outside the city walls prior to the conquest of Jerusalem in 1099: 'Even women, regardless of sex and natural weakness, dared to assume arms and fought manfully far beyond their strength . . .'[22]

William of Tyre, a male writer, singled out the activities of women in the crusader battle in front of Jerusalem's walls.[23] Admittedly, this chronicler was not an eye-witness to the events and may have used poetic or legendary sources. Although his evidence is anecdotal it suggests that women's involvement in this military action was not marginal. What is significant is that he does not criticize female involvement in military actions. It seems that women's assistance was willingly accepted and the help of those women was more than anticipated. This unexpected behaviour[24] is a function of an emergency period and situation confronting the crusade leaders and battle planners. Any help was accepted to gain the target of the crusades: the defence of Christendom.

During the Third Crusade, if 'Imad ad-Din is to be believed, there were women killed in the fighting who 'were not recognized as women until they had been stripped of their arms'.[25] These females who mounted horses were in no way identifiable as members of the so-called weaker sex: attired and outfitted like male soldiers, they played an actual role in battle. The chainmail coat disguised their sex and obscured their feminine characteristics. Although they probably intended a political message regarding the behaviour of the male Christian warriors, Muslim chroniclers showed their amazement at the women's bravery – soldiers' bravery by any standard – and the fact that they had only been identified as women after their deaths. In those days, 'It was believed that in a civilized, godly society women should not have been fighting. Conversely, women were regarded as being particularly susceptible to evil', as Helen Nicholson has written.[26] The mismatch between the Muslims' and the Christians' chronicle versions makes us look at the evidence more carefully. The political and physical disparity between the two armies made it possible to describe women warriors only on the Muslims' side, and not on the Christians' side. A Christian writer could not write about a woman warrior without humiliating the Christian warriors for their need of women's support, as well as emphasizing strangeness, barbarity, fearfulness and godlessness. And what a Christian chronicler could not write about, a Muslim writer could. Their surprise at the

presence of women on the battlefield was engendered by their identification of fighting ability as a masculine quality. The women
crusaders were depicted with male attributes ('manfully', 'men's
clothes'); nevertheless, the absolute feminine sign was revealed at the
end of this episode – the feminine body. It is assumed that the reve-
lation of the bodies was made by Muslims and not by Christians.

Other female crusaders found their way into the crusader chronicles – the rare examples of aristocratic women who led a fighting
force composed mainly of men. Noble and wealthy women could
add their services to the crusade troops as sponsors or leaders, as in
this example from 1190:

> Another person who arrived by sea was a noblewomen who was very
> wealthy. She was a queen in her land, and arrived accompanied by five
> hundred knights with their horses and money, pages and valets . . . They
> rode out when she rode out, charged when she charged, flung themselves
> into the fray at her side, their ranks unwavering as long as she stood
> firm.[27]

Other women were active participants in warfare. As the duchess of
Aquitaine and Poitiers, Eleanor of Aquitaine engaged her vassals to
join the Second Crusade and swell the numbers of the soldiers.[28]

Still other women joined the ranks of the archers; armed with
bows and arrows they, like the other Christian crusaders, shot at
their Muslim adversaries:

> [an] old (Muslim) soldier who penetrated the trenches that day told me
> that on the other side of the parapet was a woman dressed in a green
> mantle, who shot at us with a wooden bow and wounded many Muslims
> before she was overcome and killed.[29]

Her qualification with the bow was highly esteemed by the Arabic
historian. She wounded or even killed more than one Muslim.
Evidently no Christian writer could bring himself to express admi-
ration for the woman's skill with the bow, or even to mention her
presence.

Examination of various chronicles indicates that women died in
the following engagements: Dorylaeum (1097);[30] the siege of
Antioch (1098);[31] campaigns against the Turks (1101);[32] defence of
the crusader fortress (1126);[33] the battles preceding the fall of the
First Latin Kingdom (1186–87);[34] the battles preceding the founding
of the Second Kingdom (1189) and the siege of Acre (1190).[35] These

women cannot be identified by name, nor can the extent of their participation in the battles during which they lost their lives be established. But the very fact that chroniclers who are well known for their lack of sympathy for the so-called weaker sex mentioned these women killed in battle provides ample evidence that this occurrence was not anomalous. Women, indeed, fought and died in crusader campaigns, and we can conjecture that the dimensions of this phenomenon were broader than their reflection in the literary sources.

Let us not forget that most of the evidence for Christian women fighting is from Muslim sources. None of the Christian writers mentions these episodes from the women warriors' point of view. Is it possible that such evidence is intended as a slur by the godly Muslim upon the godless Christian? It is certainly possible that the Muslims exaggerated the role of women warriors, as Helen Nicholson has said.[36] But it is also necessary to look for women fighting in Europe at the same time. The crusaders came from all over Europe, and their actions in the Latin East are a reflection of what was happening there. Orderic Vitalis describes Juliana, daughter of King Henry I of England, shooting her father with a crossbow.[37] He wrote about Helwise, countess of Evreux, who rode armed with the horsemen and showed as much ardour as the knights.[38] Ramon Muntaner mentions some Catalan women who behaved like real warriors: some women defended Gallipoli when the men were away on campaign.[39] Another woman went out with a lance and shield to defend herself against King Philip III's troops, who were besieging her town.[40]

Apparently these women were quite familiar with the atmosphere of the battlefield from their experience in Europe.[41] Megan McLaughlin gives more evidence for women warriors from different social strata. Noblewomen from southern France and Catalonia not only joined their husbands' campaigns, but also possessed their own castles and made use of their own retainers for both offensive and defensive warfare, like the Lombard princess Sichelgaita and Countess Adelaide of Milan.[42] Beside these noblewomen there were widows who were forced into warlike careers on behalf of their territories. Countess Blanche of Champagne is known for her triumph over her enemies. Matilda de Braose, Sybilla of Flanders and Therasia of Portugal are wives without any husbands around, who protected their homes.[43] The author of the *Histoire des ducs* described Matilda de Braose as 'a beautiful woman, very wise and doughty and very vigorous. People said nothing about her husband compared to what they said about her, she was responsible for keeping up the war against the Welsh and conquered much from them.'[44] Matilda of Tuscany is well known as 'the most prudent war leader and most faithful soldier of St Peter'.[45] Another type of woman warrior is represented by Nicola de la Haye, sheriff of Lincoln. She engaged in warfare by virtue of office.[46]

McLaughlin observed a change in female participation in warfare between the eleventh century and later periods. In the early Middle Ages the basic military unit was a lord with his vassal warriors. Battles were actually engagements of small groups, one against the other. Armies made up of multiple domestic contingents fought the most common type of feudal warfare. The domestic group was trained together in the lord's household. The girls and women of a noble house would have been exposed to military practices from an early age. The responsibility to protect the lord's household was usually the lord's and his warriors', but in his absence the warriors defended their home with his substitute – sometimes it was his wife or daughter who led the fighting force against the enemies.[47] In emergency circumstances the women joined the military forces, together with other warriors. Necessity led women like Matilda de Braose or Matilda the empress to take active roles in war.[48]

The crusade was one of the most important events in the life of any Christian man or woman. So is there any reason why women should not have fought as crusaders in the Latin East? It seems that they had permission to join the crusades, they had the knowledge to ride a horse and use weapons and sometimes they were in such desperate situations that they had no choice but to fight. This changed in the East following the changes in the military unit in the West from a small group of warriors into a bigger and more professional group. Domestic wars became wars between states, in which there was no place for amateur warriors, still less for women warriors. From this point in time, the participation of women in war declined until it was anomalous.

In conclusion, several factors have contributed to the obscuring of women's military roles: first, their natural desire was not to call attention to themselves, mostly because their actions were not the expected behaviour of decent Christian women who were not part of the aristocratic elite. It seems that in the military world their main goal was to camouflage themselves in the surroundings. Secondly, the chroniclers largely overlooked their participation in conformity with Church doctrine which viewed women as inferior to men. As religious, the chroniclers observed this tendency and edited out women's participation on the battlefield. Nonetheless, the story of brave women is not entirely absent from the accounts of the male chroniclers. Thirdly, women adopted the clothing uniformly worn by all warriors according to their role in battle. The use of helmets to cover the head, hair and face helped the women to hide some of their sexual characteristics. The *brunea*, the tunic of leather covered with iron rings, was not stiff, and would fit both men and women. The *hauberk*, or coat of mail, had the same characteristic: the numerous small iron rings made the mail shirt available to different bodies of different shapes and sizes. It also hid the physical differences between male and female warriors. Lastly, it has been assumed that women lacked combat skills, but women warriors are shown riding horses, using spears and swords. These activities were not intuitive. They needed some learning and practice, which could have been acquired before the crusade, in Europe. There was a change in the way soldiers were trained during the period of the crusades. If in the early crusades children were trained on the estate, in their masters' home, in the later period special venues for military training outside the estates and devoted solely to this purpose can be found.[49] Women had no entrée to these schools, but earlier, when training took place on the estates, young women had the opportunity to be exposed to fighting methods along with the boys. Male–female role separation was enhanced by the implementation of special training for specific martial arts. However, emergency situations during the crusades inspired anomalous actions. Women took on new roles and became warriors. Extraordinary situations prepared the ground for extraordinary actions: women as warriors.

In feudal Europe, custom gave some women the formal right to influence battles. Women such as Matilda of Tuscany and Empress Matilda sent troops to help their allies in battles. During the Second Crusade Eleanor of Aquitaine summoned her own vassals to join the French forces. We have heard about Countess Ida of Boulogne,[50] Sybilla of Flanders, Nicola de la Haye and other anonymous women who took part in different military actions. Those women knew what to do with military equipment.

There is also a shift in the dimensions of female participation in crusade battles over the decades. More frequently attested during the First Latin Kingdom, female participation declined during the crusades and in the time of the Second Latin Kingdom women were enlisted to the military forces only in time of crisis. Emphasis was once again placed on the acquisition of the classic women's skills such as weaving and sewing. Consequently, the development of a diminished role for women in battle both in Europe and in Palestine can be discerned, and certainly in the events which linked them: the crusades.

In summation, the extant sources, both Christian and Muslim, indicate that female participation in the crusades was not seen as a natural or inevitable phenomenon. Nonetheless, once they had joined the crusades, women gained recognition for contributions made in a variety of spheres, including ones for which their upbringing had not necessarily prepared them. The crusades provided them with an opportunity to realize their talents and their training, and also to contribute to their success. Some of these women even stepped out of conventional female roles, becoming female crusaders in what started out as an all-male venture.[51]

NOTES

[1] W. Porges, 'The clergy, the poor and the non-combatants on the First Crusade', *Speculum* 21 (1946), 1–23.

[2] C. Tyerman, 'Who went on crusades to the Holy Land?', in *Horns*, 13–26; L. A. Brady, 'Essential and despised: images of women in the First and Second Crusades: 1095–1148', MA thesis (Windsor, Ontario, 1992), 5; M. Purcell, 'Women crusaders: a temporary canonical aberration?', in L. O. Frappell (ed.), *Principalities, Powers and Estates* (Adelaide, 1979), 57–64; J. A. Brundage, 'Prostitution, miscegenation and sexual purity in the First Crusade', in *CS*, 57–65.

[3] M. McLaughlin, 'The woman warrior: gender, warfare and society in medieval Europe', *Women's Studies* 17 (1990), 193–209; H. Solterer, 'Figures of female militancy in medieval France', *Signs* 16 (1991), 522–49; H. J. Nicholson, 'Women on the Third Crusade', *JMH* 23 (1997), 335–49.

[4] P. Contamine, *War in the Middle Ages* (Cambridge, 1994); R. C. Smail, *Crusading Warfare 1097–1193* (Cambridge, 1956); C. Marshall, *Warfare in the Latin East 1192–1291* (Cambridge, 1994); J. F. Verbruggen, *The Art of Warfare in Western Europe during the Middle Ages from the Eighth Century to 1340* (2nd edn., Woodbridge, 1997); D. Nicolle, *Medieval Warfare Source Book* (2 vols., New York, 1996); J. France, *Victory in the East: A Military History of the First Crusade* (Cambridge, 1994).

[5] WT (trans. Babcock and Krey), 2: 182, 185; H. E. Mayer, 'Studies in the history of Queen Melisende of Jerusalem', *Dumbarton Oaks Papers* 26 (1972), 94–182, at 127–8.

[6] *Itinerarium Peregrinorum et Gesta Regis Ricardi*, trans. H. J. Nicholson (Aldershot, 1997), 37, 39; P. Edbury, *The Conquest of Jerusalem and the Third Crusade: Sources in Translation* (Aldershot, 1996),77.

[7] *Conquest of Jerusalem*, 48.

[8] *Joinville and Villehardouin: Chronicles of the Crusades*, trans. M. R. B. Shaw (Harmondsworth, 1963), 249–51, 256.

[9] A. Kelly, *Eleanor of Aquitaine and the Four Kings* (Cambridge, 1950), 33–4.

[10] E. Siberry, *Criticism of Crusading 1095–1274* (Oxford, 1985), 45; for later crusades see J. Prawer, *A History of the Latin Kingdom of Jerusalem* (London, 1972), 2: 18; Porges, 'The clergy, the poor', 1–23.

[11] *The Crusade of Richard Lion-Heart by Ambroise*, ed. and trans. M. J. Hubert and J. L. La Monte (New York, 1941), ll. 5695–8.

[12] Prawer, *Latin Kingdom*, 18. *The Chronicle of the Third Crusade* describes the washerwoman as one 'who would not be a burden on the army nor a cause of a sin' (p. 235). A young, beautiful and married woman is the opposite of this description. Therefore only an old, ugly and probably single woman could be a washerwoman.

[13] *Gesta Francorum et Aliorum Hierosolimitanorum*, trans. R. Hill (London, 1962), 19; Fulcher of Chartres, *A History of the Expedition to Jerusalem 1095–1127*, trans. F. R. Ryan (Knoxville, TN, 1969), 85; Peter Tudebode, *Historia de Hierosolymitano itinere*, ed. and trans. J. H. Hill and L. L. Hill (Philadelphia, 1974), 34.

[14] WT, 367; Fulcher, *History*, 241.

[15] Oliver of Paderborn, *The Capture of Damietta*, trans. J. J. Gavigan (London, 1948), 38, 73.

[16] Joinville, *Chronicles*, 233.

[17] *Third Crusade Chronicle*, 89; Oliver, *Capture*, 56.

[18] *Third Crusade Chronicle*, 106.

[19] Ibid., 89.

[20] The military skills learning appears in D. Nicolle, *Medieval Warfare Source Book* (New York, 1996), 1: 250–1; McLaughlin, 'Woman warrior', 202; Solterer, 'Figures', 534–5.

[21] Oliver, *Capture*, 56.

[22] WT, 362.

[23] Solterer, 'Figures', 540. WT described events up to his death in 1185, therefore his chronicle cannot refer to the Third Crusade, as Solterer claims.

[24] McLaughlin, 'Woman warrior', 194, 196, 199.

[25] F. Gabrieli (trans.), *Arab Historians of the Crusades* (Berkeley, CA, 1969), 207.

[26] Solterer, 'Figures', 540–1; Nicholson, 'Women', 340–2.

[27] Gabrieli, *Arab Historians*, 207; Nicholson, 'Women', 340.

[28] Kelly, *Eleanor*, 29–34.

[29] Gabrieli, *Arab Historians*, 218; Beha Ed-din, *The Life of Saladin 1137–1193*, trans. C. W. Wilson, *PPTS* 13 (London, 1897), 261.

[30] WT, 1: 173; for the First Crusade see Porges, 'The clergy, the poor', 10.

[31] Peter Tudebode, *Historia*, 37; *Gesta*, 29.

[32] Fulcher, *History*, 145, 165.

[33] Ibid., 295. Fulcher wrote that only the soldiers escaped from the fortress city, leaving behind their women and children. The abandonment of the noncombatants is considered rightful by the chronicler. This is his attitude towards women.

[34] Nicholson, 'Women', 338–9.

[35] *Itinerarium*, 106; Ambroise, ll. 3625–60.

[36] Nicholson, 'Women', 342.

[37] Orderic Vitalis, *The Ecclesiastical History of Orderic Vitalis*, ed. and trans. M. Chibnall (Oxford, 1975), 6: 212–15; Nicholson, 'Women', 343.

[38] Contamine, *War*, 241.

[39] Ramon Muntaner, *The Chronicle of Muntaner*, trans. Lady Goodenough (2 vols., London, 1920), 1: 311–12.

[40] Nicholson, 'Women', 343–4.

[41] McLaughlin, 'Woman warrior', 203; Solterer, 'Figures', 522–49; Marshall, *Warfare*, 175.

[42] McLaughlin, 'Woman warrior', 198.

[43] Nicholson, 'Women', 344–5; McLaughlin, 'Woman warrior', 199.

[44] Nicholson, 'Women', 345.

[45] McLaughlin, 'Woman warrior', 199.

[46] Ibid.

[47] Ibid., 201–3; see also R. Mazeika, '"Nowhere was the fragility of their sex apparent": women warriors in the Baltic crusade chronicles', in Alan V. Murray (ed.), *From Clermont to Jerusalem* (Turnhout, 1998), 234–43.

[48] Nicholson, 'Women', 345–6. Jean A. Traux, 'Anglo-Norman women at war: valiant soldiers, prudent strategists or charismatic leaders?', in D. J. Kagay and L. J. A. Villalon (eds.), *The Circle of War in the Middle Ages* (Woodbridge, 1999), 111–25, at 112–15; R. Mazeika, 'Nowhere', 234–43.

[49] Nicolle, *Source Book*, 1: 250–1.

[50] Traux, 'Anglo-Norman women', 111–25.

[51] A female skeleton wearing scale armour was excavated at Caesarea in 1982, constituting additional archaeological evidence for female warriors in the crusading period: K. Itolum and R. L. Hohlfelder (eds.), *King Herod's Dream: Caesarea on the Sea* (New York, 1988), 225–6.

8

The Head of St Euphemia:
Templar Devotion to Female Saints

HELEN J. NICHOLSON

In 1986, Caroline Walker Bynum wrote:

> In the period from the twelfth to the fifteenth century, in contrast to the
> early Middle Ages, positive female figures and feminine metaphors took
> a significant place in spirituality alongside both positive male figures and
> misogynist images of women. Devotion to the Virgin and to women saints
> increased; the proportion of women among the newly canonized rose
> sharply ... female erotic experience, childbirth and marriage became
> major metaphors for spiritual advance, for service of neighbor and for
> union with the divine. Such ideas and images were not, however, created
> by or especially attractive to women. As Simone Roisin has demonstrat-
> ed, the Virgin Mary appeared more often to men than to women in
> northern European visions.[1]

These assertions were based not only on her own research but also
on the research of Joan Ferrante, Donald Weinstein and Rudolf
Bell, Jane Tibbets Schulenburg and others.[2] Thus the devotion that
is the subject of this chapter is not at all surprising. Templar devotion to female saints fits into the wider pattern of Catholic devotion
to female saints in the twelfth to fifteenth centuries. It would be a
greater cause for remark if the Templars had *not* been devoted to
female saints. We certainly should not, as some populist historians
have tried to do, claim that Templar devotion to female saints
demonstrates their heresy. On the contrary, the Templars' devotion
to female saints clearly demonstrates their orthodoxy.

The Templars' devotion to the Blessed Virgin Mary has received
some attention from historians, although there is a tendency to
assume that it derived from their connections with the Cistercian

order. These connections have recently been questioned by Dominic Selwood, and so we have to reconsider the derivation of the Templars' Marian devotion.[3] I would contend that it fits into the pattern described by Caroline Walker Bynum. It is clear from the Rule, from charters of donation to the order, the admission ceremony and prayers recorded by the order during the trial of the order (1307–12) that the Blessed Virgin Mary was regarded as the patron saint of the order of the Temple. Candidates for admission to the order were told that the order was established in honour of the Blessed Virgin, and promises were made on admission 'to God and our lady St Mary'. There were also various legends linking the Templars to Mary.

The modern icon of St Euphemia in St George's Patriarchal Church, Istanbul. Photograph © Judi Upton-Ward

During the trial, some of the brothers of the order declared proudly
that the cords which they wore around their waists as a symbol of
chastity had touched the pillar, or other objects, in the church of the
Blessed Mary at Nazareth where Mary received the Annunciation.
In short, the evidence indicates that the brothers did regard the
Blessed Virgin as their lady in a personal way.[4] But this is only what
we would expect during this period; the Templars' Marian devotion
was typical of its age. Mary was regarded as Queen of Heaven as
well as Mother of God; all Catholics would wish to serve her and
seek her favour as a matter of course, as noble ladies on Earth
should be served.

The Templars were also involved in devotion to other female
saints. In this they followed the pattern of devotion which Caroline
Walker Bynum has described. This might seem surprising; after all,
as an order dedicated to military activity in defence of Christendom,
what help could female saints give them? We might expect Templars
to concentrate their veneration on male, military saints such as St
George, who would be able to sympathize with their military activity. George, like the Templars, had been an active warrior; he had
patiently died a horrible martyrdom at the hands of pagans because
of his Christian faith. His life was an obvious model for the
Templars.

It is clear that the Templars did have a devotion to St George. He
appears on some seals of the order and in a fresco in the order's
chapel at Cressac (Charente) in France; and a few anecdotes regarding the Templars' military activity mention St George. Again, he is
mentioned in a prayer recorded by the order during the trial of the
order.[5] However, during the trial proceedings he received less attention than St Euphemia.

The great martyr St Euphemia is still honoured by the Greek
Orthodox Church. Her relics are in the patriarchal church of St
George, Constantinople (Istanbul). Her feast day is kept on 16
September, the day of her martyrdom and death at the hands of the
pagan proconsul Priscus, under the Emperors Diocletian (284–305)
and Maximian (285–305). A feast day is also observed on 11 July, in
commemoration of her miraculous condemnation of heresy during
the Fourth Ecumenical Council of Chalcedon in 451. Euphemia is
regarded as having great power against pagans and heretics.[6]

A pilgrim guide to the Holy Land by one Philip, written in the
thirteenth century, recorded that the Templars had the relics of St

Euphemia at Castle Pilgrim ('Athlit), and stated that they had been miraculously brought there from Constantinople. This suggests that they were booty from the Fourth Crusade. The Templars' relics of St Euphemia were taken to Cyprus after Castle Pilgrim was abandoned in 1291, and during the trial of the order the relic was in the order's treasury at Nicosia. Subsequently the relic passed with the rest of the order's possessions to the Hospital of St John, and is recorded as being on Rhodes in 1395. The Hospitallers carried it with them when they surrendered the island to the Ottomans at the end of 1522, and brought it to their new home on Malta. Later in the century a new reliquary was made for the relic. It is recorded in the *Acta Sanctorum* as being on Malta in the sixteenth and the early seventeenth centuries, but I have not been able to ascertain whether it is still there. In the absence of firmer evidence, it is assumed that the reliquary was carried off as plunder by Napoleon Bonaparte's troops in June 1798 with the other reliquaries in the co-cathedral, in which case it went to the bottom of the Mediterranean with Napoleon's flagship *L'Orient* at the battle of the Nile on 1 August 1798.

As the body of St Euphemia of Chalcedon still remains intact and incorrupt in the patriarchal church of St George in Constantinople, and its history and movements can be traced in detail from St Euphemia's martyrdom at the end of the third century or beginning of the fourth to the present day, clearly the Templars' and Hospitallers' relic of St Euphemia was not authentic. A glance at the *Acta Sanctorum* indicates that many non-authentic relics of St Euphemia have existed. However, the important point for the purpose of this chapter is that the military orders believed that their relic of St Euphemia was genuine, and would bring them the saint's intercession on their behalf before God.[7]

It appears that the Templars, and later the Hospitallers, valued their relic of St Euphemia highly. They publicized their possession of it, carried it with them on their orders' travels, and took care to house it properly. Evidence given by Templars during the trial of the order certainly indicates that St Euphemia's relic was valued by the order. During the trial in France, a group of Templars submitted a defence to the papal commissioners, stating among other things that the body of St Euphemia had come to Castle Pilgrim by the grace of God, in which place God had done many miracles through it, and it would not have lodged itself with the Templars if they were criminals, nor would any of the other relics which were in the possession of the order. This argument that only worthy people may possess holy relics was also used by the Teutonic order to justify its plundering of the relics of St Barbara from the Pomeranians in a raid on Sartowitz in the 1240s.[8]

This indicates that the order of the Temple was proud of the possession of the relics of St Euphemia. It is not clear exactly what relics of her body the order claimed to possess. Some witnesses refer to the body or the relics, but others refer only to the head, kept in a silver reliquary. By 1560 the Hospitallers claimed to have the head and part of the body. The Templars also possessed the head of St Policarp, which had been given to the order by the abbot of the Lord's Temple in Jerusalem for safekeeping. One Brother Guy Delphini, when asked whether the cord he wore around his waist had touched the supposed idol of the Templars, retorted that it had not; it had touched the relics of St Policarp and St Euphemia.[9] This brother certainly knew about the order's relics, realized their spiritual significance and was proud of what this meant for him and for his order. Likewise, the brothers issuing their statement about the spiritual value of the order cited their possession of St Euphemia's relics as proof positive that the order was holy and in God's favour.

The order also held the head of another female saint at its house in Paris, which received rather less attention during the trial. Brother William of Arreblay, who had been almoner to King Philip IV of France, testified before the papal commissioners that he had often seen on the altar in the Temple of Paris a silver head, which he often saw being adored (this is a technical term for the respect paid to relics by Catholics) by the leading officials of the order, and which he had understood to be the head of one of the 11,000 virgins who had been martyred with St Ursula at Cologne at the beginning of the fourth century. However, since his arrest, he saw that he must have been mistaken; he had thought that it looked like the head of a woman, but now he realized that it had had two faces and a beard – a rather odd mistake to make, considering that he had seen the head many times. Presumably many investigators of heresy had been persuading him that his memory had been faulty. In any case, the papal commissioners asked him if he would recognize the head again, and he assured them that he would; so orders were sent to the relevant officials that a search should be made for the head.

When the head arrived, it fitted the original description perfectly; a large silver reliquary containing the skull of a young woman, wrapped and stitched into a white linen cloth with a piece of red muslin around it. To clinch the matter, a small piece of parchment was sewn on to the cloth, on which was written: 'Head no. 58' (*et erat ibi quedam cedula consuta in qua erat scriptum caput LVIIIm*). This female martyr's head was certified genuine.[10]

The supposed graveyard of St Ursula and her martyred maidens had been excavated at Cologne in 1155. Although many of the bodies were placed in a church in Cologne, where they can still be seen, many were distributed among the faithful. The *Acta Sanctorum* contains a long list of the locations of many of these heads, all over Western Europe; the Teutonic order had one at their commandery of the Holy Trinity in Venice; presumably the Templars' head passed to the Hospital after 1312.[11]

While only one of the Templars interrogated during the trial mentioned this head, it is reasonable to assume that when the order acquired it, it did so with a specific devotionary purpose; and it is reasonable to assume that the officials of the order who showed devotion to this young female martyr on the many occasions described by William of Arreblay did so because they believed that she could assist them in their spiritual journey. Likewise, Brother Guy Delphini and the other brothers of the Temple who spoke of their devotion to St Euphemia must also have seen her intercession on their behalf as beneficial to them. But why should these warriors assume that these young women would have had any sympathy with their calling; and why should they see these young women as having any relevance to their vocation? To answer this question it is necessary to consider their legends, which were recorded in the *Golden Legend* of Jacobus de Voragine, written in the second half of the thirteenth century. St Euphemia of Chalcedon was a senator's daughter. In the late third century or early fourth century she was arrested for her faith, as part of the Emperor Diocletian's persecutions of Christians. She openly avowed her faith in Christ before the pagan governor Priscus and refused to renounce Christ even under torture. Nothing was able to harm her. Instruments of torture were miraculously destroyed, and wild beasts were unable to kill her; she remained calm and firm in her faith throughout her sufferings. Eventually the executioner cut off her head, and she passed (apparently painlessly) to glory.

St Ursula's story was less securely dated, but apparently occurred around the same time. She was the daughter of a British king, who was betrothed to a pagan king's son who agreed to become a Christian for her sake. She requested that before her marriage she be allowed to go on pilgrimage to Rome with 11,000 virgin companions. On their way back to Britain they were captured by the Huns at Cologne, and as they refused to renounce their faith they were all martyred.[12]

What have these stories to do with the Templars' vocation? In a word, everything. The Templars were an order dedicated to dying as martyrs on the battlefield, with a promise of direct entry to heaven when they did so. The opening clauses of their Rule declared that this was the reward which they should seek; Bernard, abbot of Clairvaux, depicted them seeking martyrdom in his letter of encouragement to the order, *De laude novae militiae*.[13] Popes giving privileges to the order also emphasized their dedication to self-sacrifice in the interests of Christendom. Pope Innocent II described this in his great bull of exemption for the order, *Omne datum optimum*:

> As true Israelites and warriors equipped for divine battles, aflame with the true flame of charity, your deeds fulfil the saying of the Gospel, where it is said: 'Greater love has no man than this, than a man lay down his life for his friend'. Following the voice of the supreme shepherd, you are not afraid to lay down your lives for your brothers and to defend them from the incursions of the pagans . . .[14]

In the same way, Pope Celestine II described the order in his *Milites Templi* of 1144:

> The Knights of the Temple of Jerusalem, new Maccabees in the time of grace, denying secular desires and leaving their own possessions, have taken up their cross and followed Christ . . . They do not fear to lay down their lives for their brothers and to defend pilgrims against the incursions of the pagans as they go and return on their journey to the holy places.[15]

Likewise, there were many anecdotes recorded outside the order of the Templars' propensity for martyrdom. In the original *Itinerarium Peregrinorum*, for instance, are recorded the martyrdoms of Jakelin de Mailly, marshal of the order, at the Spring of Cresson, 1 May 1187; of Nicholas, a Templar, after Hattin, 4 July 1187; and of Gerard de Ridefort, master of the order, at Acre, 4 October 1189. Jakelin de Mailly is compared to St George, Nicholas was so eager to be martyred that he encouraged all the other Templars by his example, while Gerard de Ridefort is described as *felix* (literally 'fortunate', but meaning 'blessed' when applied to martyrs and saints), winning the laurel wreath he had earned through his prowess in many battles. The writer declares that he became a fellow of the college of martyrs: *martyrum collegio sociandus haberet*. Other accounts of Gerald's death, even more laudatory than that in the *Itinerarium*, are recorded by the contemporary *trouvère* Ambroise and in a contemporary Latin poem about the siege of Acre. James of Vitry, bishop of Acre, writing probably between 1216 and 1228, recorded an anecdote of a Templar who rode eagerly to death against the Christians, bidding his horse Morel ('Blackie') to carry him to paradise. The anonymous composer of *Du Bon William Longespee* describes the martyrdoms of the Templars at Mansurah in February 1250. In the final version of the First Crusade Cycle, written right at the end of the thirteenth century or the start of the fourteenth, one of the major characters, Harpin de Bourges, joins the order of the Temple; we then find him preaching martyrdom to one of the other major characters.[16] In short, the Templars' vocation was martyrdom, and therefore it is only to be expected that they should have taken martyr saints as their spiritual patrons.

There were, however, many male warrior martyr saints whom they could have selected. Why was St Euphemia apparently more favoured than St George? The facile answer would be that in an order that did not officially admit women (although it had female associate members) and in which all men were celibate, devotion to female saints gave the brothers an outlet for their natural sexual drive. This is certainly one explanation that applies to all male religious devotion to female saints, but it is only a small part of the story.

It must be remembered that in Latin and in French (the two languages most used in literature in the Middle Ages) the word for 'soul' is female. Hence the journey of the soul was, during the period under discussion, often expressed in terms of the female soul seeking the male God; as father or as bridegroom, or even as baby. Male religious were encouraged to describe themselves in female terms and to think of themselves as female in relation to God, for their 'female' soul was seeking God. This view of the journey to God was underlaid by early Christian writings, based on the Greek concept of the male as spiritual and the female as physical; to 'become male' meant to become spiritual (so even men must aim to become male!); while to 'be female' meant to recognize one's physicality and imperfection in the sight of God (all humans, therefore, must begin their spiritual journey by recognizing themselves as 'female'). Caroline Walker Bynum has pointed out that medieval men embracing this view of themselves did not necessarily regard themselves as equal to women; some might regard themselves as having a sort of superior female-ness. 'To become female' was a metaphor for renunciation and conversion.[17]

This, then, was the negative side of being female: all Templars must realize that humans start their spiritual journey far from God, and devotion to female saints helped them to do so. Yet there were also more positive aspects to this devotion. These female martyr saints offered an example of those who were weak yet became strong in Christ. Ennodius of Arles (473–521), bishop of Pavia, had written a poem of praise to St Euphemia on this theme: Euphemia was a *puella fortis*, a *virago*.[18] If Euphemia, a weak young girl, could over-come pagan men, how much more should the physically strong Templars be able to face the Muslim hosts without fear!

What was more, these female virgin saints could offer the Templars virtues that they sorely needed. The virtues of these female martyrs included chastity, patience, long-suffering, modesty and humility. These were also virtues of male saints, but to a lesser degree; male saints were more noted for 'active' virtues, female for 'inactive' or passive virtues. The brothers of a military religious order who joined the order to fight for Christ, however, were far more likely to embody the excessively active virtues expected in a warrior: self-confidence, aggression, the desire to seek one's own honour and glory and to avenge oneself if insulted, and with little emphasis on chastity. These warrior qualities were likely to damage the community of the brothers, undermining discipline in the house and on the battlefield, where the brothers must fight as a unit under the command of a leader, not as a group of independent glory-seekers. Hence the brothers of the Temple were very much in need of the 'passive' virtues of female virgin saints, in order to transform them into an effective military force and dedicated religious men.[19] Moreover, if they were captured on the battlefield by the Muslims, the examples of St Euphemia and St Ursula's maiden would teach them to accept death readily rather than abandoning their faith.

Few works were written to educate the Templars in their faith – they were not well educated in a literary sense and apparently edu-cation was discouraged in the order.[20] Of those few works that were produced, for the brothers of the British houses, two make interest-ing points on female examples of virtue. One, the 'Life of St Thaïs', was one of the three works produced for Brother Henry d'Arcy, pre-ceptor of Temple Bruer, Lincolnshire, 1161–74. This was a retelling of the popular story of the converted prostitute. The poet justifies his subject by explaining at the end of the poem that, as Thaïs was forgiven of her sins after repentance and penance, so may we be. As the Rule expected that many Templars would have lived unchaste lives before joining the order, the example of Thaïs was intended to show them that if she, supposedly a weak woman, could abandon the lusts of the flesh through the grace of God, then so could they. Again, in the translation of the Old Testament Book of Judges pro-duced for the leading brothers of the Temple in England, Richard of Hastings and Osto of St Omer, during the third quarter of the twelfth century, the translator added a note to the story of Jephthah's daughter. She lamented that she was going to die while still a virgin, but the translator stated that he did not lament this. In other words, all Templars should note that it is an excellent thing to die while still a virgin.[21]

In short, the order of the Temple in England put some emphasis on female religious of the past as good examples for Templars to follow. The whole of the order promoted the cult of St Euphemia of Chalcedon, while the Temple at Paris venerated one of St Ursula's maidens. These devotions would have encouraged the brothers to seek humility, patience and long-suffering in their everyday lives and encouraged them to stand firm in their faith and face martyrdom boldly on the battlefield.

It is, however, difficult to tell how far individual brothers took up these devotions. The most detailed information we have for the lives of individual brothers comes from the trial depositions, but the French depositions and some others were distorted through the methods of interrogation used. At least one outsider, however, expected the brothers to look to female saints for support – and not only to the Blessed Virgin Mary. During the trial of the order, a well-wisher writing to encourage the Aragonese Templars compared them to St Susanna, the chaste wife who was falsely accused of fornica-tion: 'May Jesus Christ, who aided St Susanna in her trials and tribulations, also give you comfort.'[22] The whole order, therefore, could be represented by a holy woman, looking helplessly yet patiently to God to justify its cause. If God did not act, then, like St

Euphemia and St Ursula's maiden, the whole order should go submissively to its death.

This chapter has outlined the evidence for Templar devotion to two female saints, apart from the Blessed Virgin Mary, and has attempted to demonstrate the role this could have played within the inner spiritual life of brothers of the order. As stated at the beginning, this pattern of devotion fits into the wider pattern of Catholic devotion to female saints in the twelfth to fifteenth centuries. The fact that these relics of female saints were treasured and venerated demonstrates that the Templars were in the mainstream of Catholic devotion of their day.

NOTES

[1] Caroline Walker Bynum, '... And woman his humanity', in her *Fragmentation and Redemption: Essays on Gender and the Human Body in Medieval Religion* (New York, 1992), 151–79: here 152–3.

[2] See her footnote ibid., 357, n. 5.

[3] Dominic Selwood, *Knights of the Cloister: Templars and Hospitallers in Central–Southern Occitania 1100–1300* (Woodbridge, 1999), 89, n. 124; 143 and n. 4.

[4] For this see ibid., 202, 210; for the Templars and the Cistercians see also nn. 124, 143 and n. 4; Helen Nicholson, *Templars, Hospitallers and Teutonic Knights: Images of the Military Orders, 1128–1291* (Leicester, 1993), 117–18. See also *Le Procès des Templiers*, ed. Jules Michelet, Documents inédits sur l'histoire de France (Paris, 1841–51), 1: 419; *Der Untergang des Templerordens mit urkundlichen und kritischen Beiträgen*, ed. Konrad Schottmüller (Berlin, 1887), 2: 65; 'Deminutio laboris examinantium processus contra ordinem Templi in Anglia, quasi per modum rubricarum', ibid., 2: 78–102, at 93; *Annales Londonienses*, ed. William Stubbs, in *Chronicles of the Reigns of Edward I and Edward II*, RS 76 (London, 1882), 1: 180–98, at 195. I am currently working on a longer study of this material.

[5] Paul de Saint-Hilaire, *Les Sceaux des Templiers et leurs symboles* (Puiseaux, 1991), 95, 115; Paul Deschamps and Marc Thibaut, *La Peinture murale en France: Le Haut Moyen Age et l'époque romane* (Paris, 1951), 132–6; *Das Itinerarium Peregrinorum: Eine zeitgenössische englische Chronik zum dritten Kreuzzug in ursprünglicher Gestalt*, ed. Hans E. Meyer (Stuttgart, 1962), 249; *Itinerarium peregrinorum et gesta regis Ricardi*, ed. William Stubbs, in *Chronicles and Memorials of the Reign of Richard I*, RS 38: 1

(London, 1864), bk 1, ch. 2, p. 7; *Quinti belli sacri scriptores minores*, ed. Reinhold Röhricht, Société de l'orient Latin (Geneva, 1879), 99–100, 130–1, 157; *Procès*, 1: 120–4.

[6] For my information on the cult of St Euphemia in the Greek Orthodox Church today I am indebted to the research of Dr Judith Upton-Ward, formerly of Fatih University, Istanbul. See also St Euphemia's entry in the *Acta Sanctorum*, Sept. V (16 September); and her liturgy in *He Agia Endoxos Megalomartus kai Paneuphemos Euphemia* (Kateríni, 1997), 30–1.

[7] 'Philippi descriptio Terrae Sanctae', ed. W. A. Neumann, 'Drei mittelalterliche Pilgerschriften III', *Oesterreichische Vierteljahresschrift für katholische Theologie* 9 (1872), 76; *Procès*, 1: 143–4, 419; *Untergang des Templerordens*, 2: 136; Francesco Tommasi, 'I Templari e il culto delle reliquie', in G. Minnucci and F. Sardi (eds.), *I Templari: Mito e storia. Atti del convegno internazionale di studi alla magione Templare di Poggibonsi-Siena* (Singalunga and Siena, 1989), 191–20, here 209; *Acta Sanctorum* (Paris and Rome, 1868), Sept. V (16 September), 252–86, here 262, C–D.

[8] *Procès*, 1: 143–4; Peter von Dusburg, *Chronik des Preussenlandes*, ed. Klaus Scholz and Dieter Wojtecki (Darmstadt, 1984), 138–40, section 36.

[9] *Untergang des Templerordens*, 2: 136, 209, 210, 215; Tommasi, 'I Templari e il culto', 207; *Procès*, 1: 419.

[10] *Procès*, 1: 502, 2: 218.

[11] *Acta Sanctorum* (Paris, 1885), October IX (21 October), 73–303; Tommasi, 'I Templari e il culto', 207.

[12] Jacobus de Voragine, *The Golden Legend: Readings on the Saints*, trans. William Granger Ryan (2 vols., Princeton, 1992), no. 139, 2: 181–2; no. 158, 2: 256–60. I have not yet been able to see the new edn. of this text, Iacopo da Varazze, *Legenda aurea*, ed. Giovanni Paolo Maggioni (Florence, 1998).

[13] *La Règle du Temple*, ed. Henri de Curzon, Société de l'histoire de France (Paris, 1886), section 9; 'Liber ad milites Templi de laude novae militiae', in *S. Bernardi opera*, ed. Jean Leclercq, C. H. Talbot and H. M. Rochais (8 vols., Rome, 1957–77), 3: 213–39, here 217.

[14] *Papsturkunden für Templer und Johanniter, Archivberichte und Texte*, ed. Rudolf Hiestand (Abhandlungen der Akademie der Wissenschaften in Göttingen, phil.-hist. Klasse, dritte Folge, 77; Göttingen, 1972), no. 3; reissued in nos. 17 (Eugenius III), 27 (Hadrian IV), 93, 121, 133 (Alexander III), 208, 217, 222, 224 (Clement III), 233 (Celestine III).

[15] *Papsturkunden* (1972), no. 8.

[16] *Itinerarium Peregrinorum*, ed. Mayer, pp. 180–1, p. 248, l. 6 – p. 249, l. 20, p. 260, ll. 3–7, p. 313, l. 31–p. 314, l. 3; *Itinerarium peregrinorum*, ed. Stubbs, bk 1, chs. 2, 5, 29, pp. 7–9, 16–17, 70; Ambroise, *Estoire de la guerre sainte: Histoire en vers de la troisième croisade*, ed. Gaston Paris (Paris, 1897), ll. 3021–34; 'Ein zeitgenössisches Gedicht auf die Belagerung Accons', ed. Hans Prutz, *Forschungen zur deutschen Geschichte* 21 (1889),

449–94, here 478–9, ll. 767–86; James of Vitry, sermon 37, pp. 412–13, in *Analecta novissima spicilegii solesmensis: altera continuatio*, 2: *Tusculana*, ed. J. P. Pitra (Paris, 1888); 'Du Bon William Longespee', ed. Simon Lloyd, in 'William Longespee II: the making of an English crusading hero', *Nottingham Medieval Studies* 35 (1992), 110–21; *The Old French Crusade Cycle, VIII: The Jérusalem Continuations: The London–Turin Version*, ed. Peter R. Grillo (Tuscaloosa, AL, 1994), ll. 15267–74, 16704–8.

[17] Bynum, *Fragmentation*, 155–6.

[18] Ennodius of Arles, *Carmina*, bk 1, v. 17, in *PL* 63, col. 351; also in *Acta Sanctorum*, Sept V, 252 E.

[19] On 'feminine' virtues and their application to men and especially male religious, see Caroline Walker Bynum, *Jesus as Mother: Studies in the Spirituality of the High Middle Ages* (Berkeley, CA, 1982), 128, 138, 259–62; Bynum, *Fragmentation*, 35–7, 108–9, 156, 165–6, 171, 175–9, 218; Joan Ferrante, *Woman as Image in Medieval Literature: From the Twelfth Century to Dante* (New York, 1975), 45, 69, 107, 127.

[20] The evidence is set out and discussed by Alan Forey, 'Literacy and learning in the military orders during the twelfth and thirteenth centuries', in Helen Nicholson (ed.), *The Military Orders*, 2: *Welfare and Warfare* (Aldershot, 1998), 185–206, here 205–6.

[21] 'The Life of St Thaïs', ed. R. C. D. Perman, 'Henri d'Arci: the shorter works', in *Studies in Medieval French Presented to Alfred Ewert in Honour of his Seventieth Birthday*, ed. E. A. Francis (Oxford, 1961), 279–321, here 284–5, ll. 137–146; cf. *Règle*, 52, clause 49. *Le Livre des Juges: Les Cinq Textes de la version française faite au XII siècle pour les chevaliers du Temple*, ed. le Marquis d'Albon (Lyons, 1913), p. 46, ch. 11, v. 45.

[22] Heinrich Finke, *Papsttum und Untergang des Templerordens* (2 vols., Münster, 1907), 2: 28.

9

Captivity and Ransom: The Experience of Women

YVONNE FRIEDMAN

A part from what James Brundage so aptly called the *militia cubi-culi* – the feudal service in the nuptial chamber that women rendered by marrying – and the help women extended during siege warfare, female crusaders have been seen as virtually non-existent.[1] Indeed, Maurice Purcell declared that there was no such creature as a woman crusader until the thirteenth century, and then only briefly.[2] Yet there is one part of crusader history in which women seem numerically dominant: the sphere of captivity. Women were often the first and sometimes the only ones taken captive on both the Muslim and the Christian sides.[3] For this reason their experiences of captivity and the need for their ransom would seem to be central to the history of warfare in the Latin East, even if their military contribution was negligible.

However, this centrality is not reflected in the written record. As the chroniclers were all male, the place of women in their narratives of captivity is at best very marginal. The women's story was considered unimportant, unless it suited a wider, predominantly male discourse. In the literary chanson *Les Chétifs* all the captives – the heroes of the story – are men, and in *Chanson d'Antioche*, although depicted as warriors, women often appear only as comic relief.[4] However, when describing warfare both Christian and Muslim chronicles use the formula: 'All the men were killed and the women and children were taken captive.' Did this reflect reality, or was it a literary topos influenced by the biblical precedents?[5] Were women really the majority of captives? Having no reliable statistics for numbers and gender of captives, we have to investigate the different arenas that may lead to captivity, namely the battlefield, sieges and conquests of cities and raids into enemy territory, and search for the place of women in them.

Women were not supposed to be on the battlefield. Assuming that they did not usually fight, women were not on the spot at the end of the battle and would not be a considerable part of the booty taken afterward. But most medieval wars were not decided on the battle-field. After the First Crusade, with its famous battles and the three battles of Ramle, sieges and skirmishes were the rule. Pitched battles were few and risky. However, during the expeditions called the cru-sades there were famous battles in which the line between soldiers and civilians was not easy to draw. The camp where the noncombat-ants were left might be only metres from the battlefield and in case of defeat women were exposed to the enemy's fury even if they did not take part in the actual fighting.

This was also the case when a city was taken by storm, as in Caesarea in 1101 when 'very few of the male sex were left alive. But a great many of the women were spared.'[6] Thus while we do not know of women taken captive after the Muslim victory at the battle of Hattin, the conquest of Frankish cities and strongholds in the wake of the battle swelled the number of female captives.[7] The same situation applied to raids made explicitly for booty and captives. Raids into hostile territory to take hostages and slaves were normal procedure both in Muslim and Christian warfare: here the women were valuable trophies and loomed large in the number of captives. In a frontier society where people of different religions lived in prox-imity and the borders between their spheres of domination changed as continuously as in thirteenth-century Palestine, the danger of cap-tivity for women became pressing. As captives were not taken only as a result of great, heroic battles, the danger was just as real for civil-ians travelling in a caravan, or inhabitants besieged in their city by the enemy.[8] The sum made up from battles, conquests and skirmish-es seems to point to the predominance of women as captives.

Sometimes the women were left to their fate by their men and taken prisoner. Thus in 1126 Bursuq ibn Bursuq captured some women and their children, while the men of the besieged town fled: 'The men of the besieged town had with much difficulty and danger escaped the hand of the enemy. They had chosen to seek safety alone rather than be caught in the wretched bonds of captivity with their wives and children.'[9] This may seem a far cry from chivalrous ideals, but it is also evidence that captivity was a common event for women.

Perhaps the men thought they would be able to ransom their wives later. Anyway, in this case, as in the instances where men were killed and women spared and taken captive, the outcome was captivity only for the women. Nor were the Franks the only warriors to leave their wives undefended and run away. After the battle at Antioch the Turks behaved no differently: 'Those Turks who had swift and good horses escaped, but the stragglers were abandoned to the Franks.' As Fulcher of Chartres goes on to say, in the tents outside Antioch the crusaders found women left behind while the men ran away, so apparently many of the 'stragglers' were women.[10] In 1101, when the crusaders lost the battle at Paphlagonia, they likewise left the unde-fended women together with the rest of the spoils of war to be taken by the Turks:

> So great a fear took possession of them all that not one of the princes remained who was not despairing of life and planning escape, great and small, noble and lesser men . . . Moreover, the Christians left their tents and all their equipment with all their wagons, with their delicate and beloved wives, with all the goods which are needed by so many nobles and so great an army . . . The Turks . . . cruelly attacked these noble women and eminent matrons, as many Gauls as Lombards, seized them wickedly and held them in fetters, sending over a thousand into barbarous lands where the language was unknown; they plundered them like dumb ani-mals and sent them into perpetual exile into the land of Khorasan as if they were in a cage or prison.[11]

Even if these numbers were exaggerated, there must have been a large number of women taken captive, of whose fate we have no inkling. They were not heard of later in the narrative, and apparently were never ransomed.

The predominance of female captives in the Latin kingdom may be corroborated by a comparison between the laws of the Latin kingdom and parallel sources. Prawer showed that the late twelfth-century *Assise* on confiscation and the thirteenth-century *Assise* on disinheri-tance bear many close resemblances to the Roman law and the twelfth-century Provençal code *Lo Codi*.[12] In his minute comparison between the texts, Prawer did not note one main difference, namely the place of women. Both *assises* repeat the Roman law stating that a son who declined to ransom his father from captivity would lose his inher-itance, and in the same way a father who did not free his son who had been hostage for him was to forfeit his fief. The version of the *Assises* adds a female equivalent to both cases: a son had to ransom his father or *mother*, and they had the same duty toward their son or *daughter*.[13] The Provençal lawgiver probably meant to include all cases of family relations without giving any special thought to gender. The fact that the promulgator of the *Assises* found it necessary to add the mother and daughter to the law dealing with fathers and sons may point to the predominance of female captives in the Latin kingdom and the need to deal with their case explicitly.

The fate of a captive was usually determined by his rank. In both Christian and Muslim society the main factor deciding the chances for survival, the conditions of captivity and the possibility of returning home was the price the captor expected to fetch for his captive, and this was set by the prisoner's rank. Did gender play an important role too? Christians and Muslims alike killed prisoners of war, both male and female, without compunction.[14] The main reason to keep captives alive seems to have been mercenary: if it was deemed worthwhile to sell a woman as a slave on the market, or in the case of an important person to await her ransom, then her life might be spared. This was not only applicable to females. Generally speaking, captives were treated according to their rank. Knights and nobles, although they were military opponents, often inspired awe and honour for their prowess in battle, and were considered worth their price. Commoners were usually treated more harshly, sometimes tortured for the fun of it, or killed because it was considered expedient or as part of a strategy of terror.[15] Torture was sometimes used to make the captive raise his price. In this respect women fared no better than men. In Tripoli the Franks tortured a woman severely to extract money, and were lucky enough to obtain important intelligence from her instead.[16] The only reason we are told about this apparently not unusual case is because of the unexpected outcome. Torturing a female captive out of greed would not be a fact worthy of mention in itself, and gender was no shield against the atrocities of war.

As civilians, women were at a disadvantage from the outset. As a rule, they were noncombatants, and they were usually lower down on the social ladder than the men. We have a clear case of this economic evaluation in the terms of capitulation offered by Saladin to the inhabitants of Jerusalem in 1187: a woman's freedom could be bought for half the price of a man's, and a child's for a tenth.[17] While it was often cheaper to ransom a wife or daughter than a male relative, the incentive for the captor to keep them alive was weaker as they were worth less. If the women survived in spite of their lower market value, the reasons must have been different from the importance of their rank, and connected to their gender. Thus, when Fulcher of Chartres explains why the Muslim women of Caesarea were spared he ventures as a reason: 'They could always be used to turn the hand mills.'[18] But then he goes on to describe how the captured women were bought and sold among the captors according to another criterion: 'the comely and the ugly'. It is not at all clear why the women needed to be handsome in order to turn the hand mills and what difference their looks would make if that was really the reason they were spared.

According to the Latin chroniclers, the Muslims made no secret of the importance of gender when choosing whom they would take captive. While rank and price were important, the good looks of the women were decisive. Thus, already at Civetot: 'They put them all to the sword, regardless of age. They took away only young girls and nuns, whose faces and figures seemed to be pleasing to their eyes.'[19] According to Albert of Aachen, the women were quick to learn the lesson that beauty might save their lives, and at the next encounter, at the battle of Dorylaeum, they acted accordingly:

> Stunned and terrified by the cruelty of this most hideous killing, girls who were delicate and very nobly born were hastening to get themselves dressed up, they were offering themselves to the Turks so that at least, roused and appeased by love of their beautiful appearance, the Turks might learn to pity their prisoners.[20]

Nor was this criterion for survival used only on the battlefield. After the conquest of Antioch a knight called Folbert of Bullon was caught in a raid on his way to Edessa together with his wife and his retinue:

> He was overcome there and beheaded with the rest after putting up no great resistance. His wife, because she was greatly pleasing to their eyes on account of her beautiful face, was taken prisoner and led away into the the fortress of Azaz. The prince and lord of the fortress ordered her to be treated honourably while he found out if she might be worth some great sum of money in ransom.[21]

While the captive's looks probably saved her life, her rank was undoubtedly decisive in determining how she was treated in captivity, as it did not make sense to maltreat a valuable lady and thus diminish her value. In this case the beautiful captive was given to one of the leading Muslim warriors instead of wages and she became his wife. Thus an attractive woman had far better chances of survival than an old or ugly one and apparently also a better chance of survival than a male of the same rank.

What was the fate of women in captivity? Was there more concern for female captives than for male prisoners? Was any priority given to setting women free because of the more severe hardships awaiting them in captivity, or was the possibility of losing her freedom just one of the facts a woman in a fighting society had to live with? The sexual abuse of female captives was more or less taken for granted. Women were raped during the conquest of a city as a matter of course, and this was considered a normal part of warfare.[22] Usually, even after the rumble of war quieted, the capture of a woman had clear, sexual undertones. 'Imad ad-Din al-Isfahani, Saladin's secretary and chronicler, described the fair women taken captive in Nazareth and Sepphoris. He described the female captives of Jerusalem in almost the same words, making no secret of the importance of gender:

> Women and children together came to 8,000 and were quickly divided up among us, bringing a smile to Muslim faces at their lamentations. How many well-guarded women were profaned, how many queens were ruled, and nubile girls married, and noble women given away, and miserly women forced to yield themselves, and women who had been kept hidden stripped of their modesty, and serious women made ridiculous, and women kept in private now set in public, and free women occupied, and precious ones used for hard work, and pretty things put to the test, and virgins dishonoured and proud women deflowered, and lovely women prostrated, and untamed ones tamed, and happy ones made to weep! How many noblemen took them as concubines, how many ardent men blazed for one of them, and celibates were satisfied by them, and thirsty men sated by them, and turbulent men able to give vent to their passion.[23]

Notwithstanding 'Imad ad-Din's boisterous verbosity, his description shows very clearly what was expected of a female captive. His flowery language allows for the differences of rank between female captives, but shows clearly that sexual abuse was considered the norm and the conqueror's right, regardless of the captive's former standing.

The Muslim law of war took this as a matter of course. In his *Kitab al Jihad* Tabari rules accordingly how a Muslim woman taken captive was to behave: 'If the prisoner is a woman who is subjected to physical hardship, she must at first endure persecution, but if she fears death, she is permitted to submit to the enemy demands unwillingly.'[24] In other words, sexual conquest was a normal part of warfare and a woman could not be expected to save her honour under such circumstances. As a result of this realistic view, women were not blamed and no recriminations called for. But, nonetheless, heroic women were described as preferring death to defilement.

The assumption that it was virtually impossible to keep one's chastity and honour in captivity made Usamah ibn-Munqidh see captivity as a fate worse than death for a noble woman. Usamah, the noble warrior from Shaizar whose autobiographical anecdotes give much insight into everyday life in a frontier society, describes his valiant mother leading his sister to the balcony of their house during an attack on it. When asked about her actions she explained:

> I have given her a seat on the balcony and sat behind her so that in case I had found that the Batinites had reached us, I could push her and throw her into the valley, preferring to see her dead rather than to see her captive in the hands of the peasants and ravishers.

Both daughter and son praised the mother's solicitude for honour.[25]

Usamah also tells the story of the Kurd Abu-al-Jaiysh, whose daughter Raful was taken captive by the Franks. Greatly troubled because of that, when her father found that his daughter had thrown herself from the back of the horse that carried her away and had drowned, his anguish was abated.[26] We may well doubt, with Robert Irwin, the accuracy of Usamah's anecdotes, but they seem to display the ideology, if not the reality, of Muslim society in the twelfth century, that is, that for a woman honourable death is preferable to captivity.[27]

The Christian chroniclers of the First Crusade had an altogether different agenda. Their depiction of victory includes the most horrendous descriptions of massacres of women and children, but not rape. No Christian chronicler of the First Crusade would boast about the rape of women as 'Imad ad-Din al-Isfahani did. The conquests of Antioch and Jerusalem were seen as a holy war of extermination, a biblical war of cleansing the holy places of the polluting unbelievers.[28] Sexual abuse would contaminate the purity of the crusaders. Fulcher of Chartres proudly describes the fate of the female captives after the battle of Antioch: 'In regard to the women found in the tents of the foe, the Franks did them no evil but drove lances into their bellies.'[29] It has been claimed that this was meant as a euphemism for sexual abuse,[30] but I tend to take the good chaplain's words literally. It is true that Raymond d'Aguilers blamed the crusaders for enjoying 'dancing girls' in Antioch, and the crusaders probably did indulge themselves after the conquest of a Muslim city, but their ideology was one of sexual purity and savage killing of female captives during conquest.[31] To support this we have the testimony of a contemporary from the victims' side, telling us about the fate of Jewish women in Jerusalem in July 1099. In a letter found in the Geniza, the Karaite elders from Ascalon, lamenting the crusaders' conquest of Jerusalem, wrote: 'We have not heard – thank God, the Exalted – that the cursed ones known as *Ashkenaz* violated or raped women, as others [do].'[32] In both these cases the emphasis of the writer shows that a different treatment was the norm, and the Frankish behaviour of homicide, but not rape, was exceptional and worthy of special mention.

The assumption that violation was the norm led later Christian chroniclers to reach the same conclusion as the Muslim ones: for a real lady captivity was worse than death. Thus Joinville, half a century later than Usamah, describes Louis IX's queen Margaret as preferring death to captivity. With her husband already taken captive in Mansurah and herself close to giving birth to their child, the queen implored the old knight who slept by her bed to guard her:

> I ask of you, said she, by the troth that ye have plighted me, that if the Saracens take this town, ye will cut off my head before they take me prisoner. And the knight made answer: Be ye certain that I will do it willingly; for I had it in my mind that I would kill you before they took us.[33]

The valiant queen survived and negotiated the ransom of her saintly spouse. But clearly, notwithstanding her advanced pregnancy, she was expected to prefer death to certain defilement. Nobody seems to have thought that her husband ought to have had the same set of priorities, although Louis IX suffered greatly in captivity. The reason for the difference of moral expectations is clearly connected to the dread of sexual abuse connected with women's captivity.

At the end of the twelfth century there seems to have emerged an idea of chivalrous concern for motherhood as a mitigating factor when deciding the fate of captives. Baha ad-Din, Saladin's chronicler and propaganda agent, proudly tells the story of a Frankish mother who asked to cross the lines and be brought before Saladin. When the weeping and wailing woman was asked what was the matter she answered:

> 'Some Muslim thieves got into my tent last night and carried off my child, a little girl. All night long I never ceased begging for help, and our princes advised me to appeal to the King of the Muslims. "He is very merciful," they said. "We will allow you to go and seek him and ask for your daughter." Therefore they permitted me to pass through the lines, and in you lies my only hope of finding my child.' The Sultan was moved by her distress, tears came into his eyes, and acting from the generosity of his heart, he sent a messenger to the market-place of the camp, to seek her little one and bring her away, after repaying her purchaser the price he had given.[34]

The child was promptly found and returned to the mother without asking any price for it. The story is intended to enhance Saladin's prestige by demonstrating his mercy and chivalrous behaviour. A society that sees mercy for a mother, even if she comes from the enemy, as a commendable asset promotes different ideals from those we have seen before. It should, however, be noted that Muslim law stipulated that captive children should not normally be taken from their mothers when dividing the spoils of war.[35] But Baha ad-Din does not emphasize the religious context, rather his master's chivalrous behaviour. At the time of the Third Crusade chivalry is no longer characterized only by courage and valour on the battlefield.[36]

William of Tyre tells a corresponding story about Baldwin I. On an expedition to Arabia, Baldwin encountered a captive woman, the wife of a Bedouin chieftain, who was in labour. Baldwin had mercy on the woman and left her a bed, food and a maid to take care of her. He even gave her his mantle as a cover and two camels for milk. This spectacular show of generosity is described as a part of the king's chivalrous magnanimity.[37] Curiously, none of Baldwin I's contemporaries mentions this chivalrous story. Fulcher of Chartres, who went with the king on this expedition, knows nothing about it. If this event of merciful regard for motherhood ever took place it was not considered worth recording at the beginning of the twelfth century. William of Tyre, writing in the early 1180s, elaborated on the details of the story. He also claimed that Baldwin was given his due: later, at the siege of Ramle (1102) when Baldwin was forced to flee, the lady's grateful husband saved the fugitive king's life and showed him the way to safety.[38] According to contemporary chroniclers, the same Baldwin had no moral scruples about smoking out the women and children from the caves between Ascalon and Egypt. He killed some of the women together with their children and showed no merciful regard for motherhood.[39] The rank of the chieftain's wife may have played a definitive role in Baldwin's decisions and explain his different reactions to the plight of mothers in captivity, or the difference in reaction may have stemmed from the ideals current in each narrator's period.

Life in captivity is very seldom described in Latin sources. If described at all, it is usually the grim fate of a male captive that is dwelt upon as a background and contrast to his later, often miraculous, redemption. Women have no part in those stories. As sexual abuse was taken for granted, it was probably very unpleasant for a male writer to think about the life of a conquered wife or daughter, and the less one knew about it the better. The Arabic sources give more information, but they also prefer to describe the fate of enemy women they conquered and not vice versa. Usamah ibn-Munqidh mentions some cases of captive women who were married to their captors and started a new life in captivity. From his point of view this was a case of happy ending. Did captivity become a new home?

The answer of Usamah is ambiguous, as the anecdotes he provides point out both possibilities. He claims that 'the Franks are an accursed race, the members of which do not assimilate except with their own kind'. The proof for this maxim is the story of a beautiful captive Christian maid whom his uncle sent as a present to the ruler of Ja'bar, Shihab-al-Din Mulik ibn Salim. He took her as wife and their son became ruler of Ja'bar. In spite of her exalted position as the mother of the reigning ruler, the former captive escaped back to the Franks after her husband's death. She preferred life with a Frankish shoemaker, while her son was the lord of the castle of Ja'bar.[40] Perhaps her life in captivity had not been as successful as Usamah assumed. The same situation – that is, forced marriage with the captor and subsequent conversion and life in the new home – was probably quite widespread on the Latin side too. Fulcher of Chartres mentions converted Muslim women starting new families in the Latin East as a proof of successful assimilation: 'We who were Occidentals have now become Orientals,' he wrote in the 1120s. The new, local wives – 'Saracens who have obtained the grace of baptism' – and in-laws described by Fulcher were probably also the result of captivity.[41]

Another episode which allows us to study the subject of inter-religious contacts in and after captivity is an account from Ibn Hijja's *Adab* compendium *Thamarat al-awraq*.[42] The original story was told by a prefect of Cairo in *c*.1230, and written down in the fifteenth century. The same episode is included in the *Arabian Nights* as the romantic tale of nights 894–6.[43] The historical setting is Acre in 1184. An Egyptian cotton dealer hires a store in Acre and is attracted by one of his customers, a beautiful Frankish woman. The merchant tries to arrange an amorous meeting between them, and after he has paid 50 Tyrian dinars a meeting is fixed for the night. During their meeting on the roof of the merchant's dwelling, he is struck by religious qualms, being aware that he is disobeying Allah with a Christian, and decides to abstain from her. The irritated woman leaves at dawn, and when the cotton dealer sees her again in the shop, he feels remorse for his chaste decision, and asks for a second chance. This is granted, for 100 dinars. Though he yields to her costly conditions, the same thing happens the next night. On the third morning, the compensation demanded for the nocturnal indignity is even higher: 'By God's name, you shall not rejoice with me save for 500 dinars or else you shall die in agony.' He is, however, prevented from carrying out his decision to pay, because a herald announces the end of the truce between the Latins and the Muslims and the merchant has to leave the city in a hurry. He moves to Damascus, and there starts on a new line of commodities: slave-girls.

Three years later, in 1187, after the battle of Hattin, the Egyptian dealer is asked to sell a concubine to the triumphant sultan Saladin. The payment is 100 dinars, 90 in cash, and instead of the remaining ten, the merchant is entitled to take one of the Frankish woman prisoners. When the now wealthy dealer enters the captives' tent, he immediately identifies his admired one from long ago in Acre. She, on the other hand, does not recognize him until he reminds her of past events: 'You surely remember your words, "Thou shall not see me but for 500 dinars," now I take you for 10 dinars.' The Frankish captive immediately expresses her wish to become Muslim. In the more literary version of *Arabian Nights* this is because she realizes Allah's providence. It should, however, be noted that according to canon law a Muslim captive or slave who converts has to be set free, and the same applies in Muslim law. Although we know from James of Vitry that this was not always carried out,[44] our young lady may have had ulterior motives.[45] Apparently, the conscientious slave-trader is also unsure, as he consults a jurist before marrying her. This time the story has a happy ending. The marriage is arranged, and the girl becomes pregnant immediately.

The next step is the ransom of captives. In an agreement signed between Saladin and the Franks all Christian captives are released. A Latin legate arrives at Damascus to conduct an inquest about missing captives, and the wealthy merchant has to bring his wife, the former captive girl, to the court of Saladin. When asked what she prefers, the new convert replies: 'O, my master the Sultan. I became Muslim and am expecting; the Franks will have no more use for me.' She is allowed to stay.

As in the case of the wife of the ruler of Ja'bar, marriage to the captor brings with it social advancement. The lady described in the literary version of the *Arabian Nights* was the wife of a knight, and to round off the romance her mother sends her the chest with the money once paid for her in Acre. The heroine described more realistically by Ibn Hijja seems to have originated from a lower social stratum. She was not exactly a chaste virgin before becoming a captive. The presence of women in Acre who were willing to come to a stranger's rented house for a night, at a price, is well attested in the angry outbursts of James of Vitry.[46] So it is not surprising that our captive woman had no reason to remember her former customer. She seems to have decided on her change of lifestyle because of her pregnancy. Her new life in Damascus may well have bettered her social position. The romantic story did of course also emphasize the fantasies of the Muslim conqueror whose victory, both on the battlefield and in bed, was now complete. But in this case life in captivity may have been better than at home, or at least preferable to what would await a released captive returning home.

Was there any priority in setting women free because of the more severe hardships awaiting them in captivity? We have already seen that in the crusader *assises* mothers and daughters were explicitly mentioned as needing ransom, but not as having any precedence. In the few known cases of women being ransomed, their rank and not their gender is emphasized, as in the case of the Turkish lady who was ransomed for 15,000 bezants in 1104, an enormous sum demonstrating her importance. Indeed, she was seen as worth the same as the ruler of Edessa.[47] I have not found any evidence for priority in ransoming women in crusader society in the East, although, as I have shown elsewhere, the situation was different at a rather later period in Spain. Jewish law also differed on this matter, giving women priority in ransom, as their suffering was supposedly worse. However, in the event of a general crisis, as after the conquest of Jerusalem in 1099, it seems that in fact the Jews ransomed whomever they could, without giving preference to gender.[48]

For women, redemption from captivity did not always mean the end to their plight. Their experiences in captivity would haunt them and make the return home difficult, if not impossible. Renier Brus's wife was taken captive together with the citizens and mercenary soldiers of Banyas in 1132. She was released two years later via diplomatic efforts as part of the truce between King Fulk of Anjou and the Damascenes. Thus the negotiations for the release of the lady of Banyas were conducted on the highest possible level and successfully concluded. Her story did not, however, have a happy end:

> She was returned to her distinguished husband after an absence of two years, and he graciously (*devotione*) restored her to her wifely position. But later, however, he discovered that her conduct while with the enemy had not been altogether discreet. She had not satisfactorily preserved the sanctity of the marriage couch as a noble matron should. Accordingly, he cast her off.[49]

The lady ended her life in a convent in Jerusalem, and after her death Renier promptly remarried. William of Tyre, who reports the story, clearly thought that Renier's behaviour was commendable, and the lady was to blame for her fate. This is one of the main differences between Jewish and Muslim mores of ransoming women and the crusaders' ethics. Both Jews and Muslims assumed automatically that a woman in captivity could not preserve 'the sanctity of the marriage couch',[50] but as their religious laws enabled them to divorce a violated wife and remarry, marital problems following captivity could be solved one way or another. Except in the case of a Cohen, the Jewish husband was obliged to receive his wife back, and, even if he did not want to continue the marriage, he had to pay for her ransom. The Geniza shows that the ransom of a captive woman could be a way to acquire a second wife, or force the first one to give permission for her husband to marry another.[51] Canon law permitted no such alternative, and the repudiation of the unwanted wife still left

the husband bound to her until her death. Baldwin I tried to get rid
of his Armenian wife in 1108, claiming that she had been violated in
captivity, but the Church did not dissolve his marriage.

> When she reached her husband, the king, suspicious, and not unreason-
> ably, of the barbars' sexual incontinence, banished her from his bed,
> changed her mode of dress, and sent her to live with other nuns in the
> monastery of Anne, blessed mother of the virgin mother of God. He him-
> self was glad to live the celibate life, because 'his struggle was not against
> the flesh and blood, but against the rulers of the world'.[52]

In this case it seems that the king's suspicions were unfounded and
used only as a pretext to rid himself of his wife, but suspicions were
enough to warrant her forced entry into a convent.

Not only married women had a difficult time returning from captivity. Albert of Aachen tells the story of the nun of Trier who was
redeemed and returned to the crusader army in 1098:

> She complained that she had been taken in a vile and detestable union by
> a certain Turk and others with scarcely a pause. Then, while she was utter-
> ing her wretched moans about these wrongs to the audience of Christians,
> . . . Henry of Castle Esch . . . was affected by her misfortune, and he
> employed diligence and every argument of pity he could with Duke
> Godfrey until advice for repentance was given her by Lord Adhémar, the
> venerable bishop. At last, when advice about an unchaste act of this sort
> had been received from the priest, she was granted forgiveness for her
> unlawful liaison with the Turk, and her repentance was made less bur-
> densome because she had endured this hideous defilement by wicked and
> villainous men under duress and unwillingly.[53]

To Albert's great shock, the nun decided to return to her former captor the next night rather than face the 'less burdensome repentance'
laid upon her. In his opinion the reason for her change of mind was
either that she was deceived by flattery and vain hopes or because
her 'own lust was too much to bear'. Considering the nun's description of her rape, that seems unlikely. It may well be that the poor nun
realized that after her violation she was not to receive any pity, but
rather would be seen as a sinner in need of harsh repentance. She
might have understood that there was no real future for her in her
former camp. We have already seen that some female captives preferred to stay in captivity, rather than face their former society and
be seen as contaminated.

Nor was the return problematic only for women who had been raped or married to their captors. Because the enemy was perceived as sexually incontinent, even suspicion was enough to blemish the reputation of a returning captive, as in the case of the Armenian queen in 1108. To warrant suspicion it was enough to be female, notwithstanding age. Thus, Baldwin II gave his four-year-old daughter as a hostage to release himself from captivity and ransomed her in 1125. Despite the little princess's tender age and the fact that hostages were usually treated better than captives, Yvette never married. While her three sisters made politically advantageous matches, she joined the convent of Bethania in Jerusalem and became an abbess. *L'Estoire d'Outremer* insinuated that the reason was connected to her time in captivity.[54] The suspicions connected to captivity made the return troublesome for Muslim and Jewish captives too. Thus a bride mentioned in a marriage contract in the Geniza was described as one who lost her virginity during the siege of Acre. Accordingly, her contract was less advantageous than a regular *Ketubah* and she had to agree to her husband's right to take another wife if he wanted to, but at least she had a chance at starting a new life.

Most female redeemed captives had no such chance, however, and they were often in need of economic help. Entering a convent may not have been an option for a Latin woman not of royal or noble stock, and her worth on the marriage market was considerably devalued. Women returning from captivity who could not opt for marriage were in an economic quandary. Geniza sources show that Jewish communities took responsibilty for the care of released captives, but we do not know of any lay organization in crusader society that assumed comparable responsibilities for returning women. We may, however, note that the military orders understood the responsibility for captives in the same way. The general chapter of the Hospitallers decided in their statutes of 1182 that the order's almoner should give every freed captive 12*d.* to start his new life.[55] Gender is not mentioned in the statutes, so apparently men and women received the same sum.

Thus, while female prisoners of war had better chances of survival than male ones, especially if they were young and attractive, their lot in captivity was harder than that of men and usually included sexual abuse. Therefore their ransom, except in cases of dignitaries, was often more problematical. The main difference was, however, in the event of what was supposed to be the happy return. While male captives often had to face economic difficulties, these were only one facet of returning women's plight. Christian women had fewer options than the Muslim and Jewish returning captives although they too had serious difficulties trying to be reabsorbed into society. For crusader ladies the convent was often the only institution that would receive them. In Frankish society organized for war, the women paid a heavy price both during and after the time when bugles of battle sounded.

NOTES

The research for this chapter was aided by a grant from the Irwin Moskowitz foundation and the Ingeborg Rennart Center for the Study of Jerusalem. I would like to thank Lucy Cavendish College, Cambridge, where I was Visiting Scholar during 2000, for their warm hospitality.

[1] J. A. Brundage, 'The marriage law in the Latin kingdom of Jerusalem', *Outremer*, 271; R. Rogers, *Latin Siege Warfare in the Twelfth Century* (Oxford, 1992), 8–9, 52, 61.

[2] M. Purcell, 'Women crusaders: a temporary canonical aberration?', in L. O. Frappell (ed.), *Principalities, Powers and Estates: Studies in Medieval and Early Modern Government and Society* (Adelaide, 1979), 57–67.

[3] For example, Albert of Aachen (AA) 1: 21; cf. 1: 12; 4: 45; 7: 40; 8: 19.

[4] See Susan B. Edgington, Chapter 11, below.

[5] Numbers 31: 9; Deuteronomy 21: 10–17; 1 Samuel 30: 3.

[6] Fulcher of Chartres, *A History of the Expedition to Jerusalem 1095–1127*, trans. R. Ryan (Knoxville, TN, 1969), 2. 9. 6.

[7] Cf. 'Imad ad-Din al-Isfahani's description of the female captives of Sepphoris and Nazareth', F. Gabrieli (trans.), *Arab Historians and the Crusades* (London, 1969), 163.

[8] J. Brodman, *Ransoming Captives in Crusader Spain: The Order of Merced on the Christian–Islamic Frontier* (Philadelphia, 1986), 1–6; J. Bradbury, *The Medieval Siege* (Woodbridge, 1992), 301–2, 312–13 *et passim*.

[9] WT 13, 20. William does not identify the town; he says it was undistinguished: 'municipium quoddam non magni nominis'.

[10] Fulcher, *History*, 1. 23. 5.

[11] AA 8: 18–19.

[12] J. Prawer, *Crusader Institutions* (Oxford, 1980), 431–68; Miryam Greilsammer (ed.), *Le Livre au roi* (Documents relatifs à l'histoire des croisades, 17; Paris, 1995), chap. 16, 177–84.

[13] *Assises de la Cour des Bourgeois*, in *RHC Lois* 2, no. 240, p. 170; Prawer, *Crusader Institutions*, 445, 449.

[14] For example, Beha ed-Din, *Saladin*, PPTS, 272–5, 279, 281. Cf. Ambroise, *L'Estoire de la Guerre Sainte*, ed. G. Paris (Paris, 1897); *GF* 15; Gaston Raynaud (ed.), *Les Gestes des Chiprois: Recueil des chroniques françaises écrites en orient* (Publications de la Societé de l'Orient Latin, 5; Geneva, 1887), no. 350, p. 182.

[15] T. S. Asbridge and Susan B. Edgington (ed. and trans.), *Walter the Chancellor's The Antiochene Wars: A Translation and Commentary* (Aldershot, 1999), 132–6; Bradbury, *Medieval Siege*, 100, 312–13.

[16] AA 11: 14.

[17] M. R. Morgan, *La Continuation de Guillaume de Tyr (1184–1197)* (Paris, 1982), 69. Cf. Beha Ed-din, *Saladin*, PPTS 13, 120.

[18] Fulcher, *History*, 2. 9. 6.

[19] AA 1: 21. There is no doubt about the aim as Albert adds: 'and beardless and attractive young men'.

[20] AA 2: 39.

[21] AA 5: 5.

[22] Bradbury, *Medieval Siege*, 94, 101, 322. For the trope of rape in chivalrous literature see Kathryn Gravdal, *Ravishing Maidens: Writing Rape in Medieval French Literature and Law* (Philadelphia, 1991).

[23] 'Imad ad-Din al-Isfahani, *Kitab al-Fath al qussi fi'l-fath al-qudsi*, trans. H. Masse as *Conquête de la Syrie et de la Palestine par Saladin* (Documents relatifs à l'histoire des croisades; Paris, 1972), 34 (Nazareth) and 50; Gabrieli, *Arab Historians*, 163.

[24] Tabari, *Kitab al-Jihad*, ed. J. Schacht (Leiden, 1933), 196–7; M. Khadduri, *War and Peace in the Law of Islam* (Baltimore, 1955), 174.

[25] Usamah ibn-Munqidh, *An Arab-Syrian Gentleman and Warrior in the Period of the Crusades*, trans. P. K. Hitti (New York, 1929), 156.

[26] Ibid., 179.

[27] Robert Irwin, 'Usamah ibn Munqidh: an Arab-Syrian gentleman at the time of the crusades reconsidered', *Crusade Sources*, 71–88.

[28] Penny Cole, '"O, God, the Heathen have come into Your Inheritance" (Ps. 78.1): the theme of religious pollution in crusade documents, 1095–1188', in Maya Schatzmiller (ed.), *Crusaders and Muslims in Twelfth-Century Syria* (Leiden, 1993), 84–111.

[29] Fulcher, *History*, 1. 23. 5.

[30] Sarah Lambert, oral communication, Leeds, July 2000.

[31] RA, vi, p. 48.

[32] S. D. Goitein, 'Geniza sources for the crusader period: a survey', *Outremer*, 312. In a note, Goitein gallantly apologized to Raymond of St Gilles as he formerly took the word *Ashkenaz* to mean that only German crusaders did not rape captives while the Provençals probably did. In fact the

writer uses the word to mean all crusaders in the same way Muslim sources call them all Franks. The text of the letter is in Cambridge University Library: MS TS 20.113 and TS 10J5, fo. 6.

[33] Jean, sire de Joinville, *Histoire de Saint Louis*, ed. and trans. Natalis de Wailly (Paris, 1874), ch. 78, 398, 218; trans. Joan Evans, *The History of St. Louis* (Oxford, 1938), 119.

[34] Beha ed-Din, *Saladin*, 41.

[35] Giulio Cipollone, *Christianità – Islam: Cattività e liberazione in nome di Dio. Il tempo di Innocenzo III dopo 'il 1187'* (Pontificia Universitas Gregoriana Miscellanea Historiae Pontificiae, 60; Rome, 1992), 193.

[36] Cf. the same trend in Western literature at the end of the twelfth century: Richard W. Kaeuper, *Chivalry and Violence in Medieval Europe* (Oxford, 1999); Linda Paterson, 'Knights and the concept of knighthood in the twelfth-century Occitan epic', in W. H. Jackson (ed.), *Knighthood in Medieval Literature* (Woodbridge, 1981), 23–38; Jean Flori, 'De la chevalerie féodale à la chevalerie chrétienne? La Notion de service chevaleresque dans les trés anciennes chansons de geste françaises', *'Militia Christi' e crociata nei secoli XI–XIII* (Miscellanea del Centro di studi medioevali, 13; Milan, 1992), 67–101.

[37] WT 10, 11, pp. 464–5: *'humanitas et clementia'*. William emphasizes the woman's importance: *'quedam illustris femina, cuiusdam magni et potentis principis uxor'*.

[38] WT 10, 21.

[39] AA 7: 40.

[40] Usamah, *Arab-Syrian Gentleman*, 160.

[41] Fulcher, *History*, 3. 37. 3–4.

[42] Ibn Hijja al-Hamawi (Abu Bakr ibn Ali), *Thamarat al-awraq* (Cairo, 1971), 236–9. I am grateful to Dr Joseph Drory for letting me use his paper, 'New data on Muslims in Palestine under the crusades', 17th International Conference of CISH, Madrid 1990, before publication, and for his translation of the *Adab*.

[43] R. F. Burton (ed.), *Thousands Nights and a Night*, vol. 9 (London, 1885), 19–24; B. Z. Kedar, 'The subjected Muslims of the Frankish Levant', in J. M. Powell (ed.), *Muslims under Latin Rule 1100–1300* (Princeton, NJ, 1960), 87–8.

[44] R. B. C. Huygens (ed.), *Lettres de Jacques de Vitry* (Leiden, 1960), 2, 87–8.

[45] B. Z. Kedar, *Crusade and Mission* (Princeton, NJ, 1984), 76–9, 215.

[46] Huygens, *Lettres,* 87.

[47] AA 9: 45. The lady is not named. The negotiators offered to exchange her for Baldwin le Bourq. For the date see AA 9: 46.

[48] Geniza fragments TS NS J 270; ENA 2808; TS 16.250; CUL Add. 3388; TS 20.138; TS NS 176, 2–3 (unpublished). In the letter from 1099 (TS

10J5, fo. 6) the writer explicitly said that they tried to ransom whomever they could get. For the fate of Jewish women see my forthcoming book *Encounter between Enemies: Captivity and Ransom in the Latin Kingdom of Jerusalem* (Leiden: Brill).

[49] WT 16, 19, cf. Ibn al-Qalanisi, *The Damascus Chronicle of the Crusades*, ed. H. A. R. Gibb (London, 1932), 217, who dates it December 1132 and also stresses the capture of women.

[50] '*Maritalis thori reverentiam non satis caute . . . observaverat*', WT 16, 19.

[51] M. A. Friedman, 'New sources from the Geniza for the crusader period and for Maimonides and his descendants' (Hebrew), *Cathedra* 40 (1986), 63–82, at 71.

[52] Guibert of Nogent, *The Deeds of God through the Franks*, trans. R. Levine (Woodbridge, 1997), 164; see also H. E. Mayer, 'Études sur l'histoire de Baudouin Ier roi de Jérusalem', in idem (ed.), *Mélanges sur l'histoire du royaume latin de Jérusalem* (Paris, 1983), 73–91, on Baldwin's homosexuality and marital problems.

[53] AA 2: 37.

[54] Margaret A. Jubb (ed.), *A Critical Edition of the Estoires d'Outremer et de la naissance Salehadin* (Westfield Publications in Medieval Studies, 4, London, 1990), 45: 'Dont il avint ke sa fille ki en ostages avoit esté, quant ele fu revenue, ses peres le vaut marier, et ele dist ke jamais n'avroit mari, ains vaurroit estre noune.'

[55] 'Idem etiam elemosinarius cuilibet capto cum primo a jugo captivitatis evellebatur, duodecim denarios de consuetudine erogavit', Cart. Hosp. 1: 428.

10

Women in Medieval Colonial Society: The Latin Kingdom of Jerusalem in the Twelfth Century

SYLVIA SCHEIN

In his *De recuperatione Terre Sancte* of *c.*1306–7 Pierre Dubois proposed a specific curriculum of studies for girls who would, once trained, immigrate to the Latin kingdom of Jerusalem when it was recovered. They would be trained within a school system that should comprise elementary schools in every province and a single high school at the papal curia; pupils would be recruited mainly from the ranks of the nobility. The girls would study grammar, the basics of the Catholic faith, and surgery; only the most talented among them should also study logic, some of the foundations of natural sciences, medicine and one foreign language. In the East the most attractive would be given in marriage to Oriental Christian magnates and even to Muslims in order to convert their husbands to the Catholic faith. These who benefited from training in medicine or surgery would be able to provide medical assistance to local women, either Oriental Christians or Muslims, and act among them as missionaries.[1]

If Dubois's plan has anything at all in common with the position of women in the historical kingdom of Jerusalem, it is that they enjoyed more legal rights, held a more important position and carried out more functions than their contemporaries in the West. The subject-matter of this study is the position of the noblewoman (*nobilis femina, nobilis mulier, femme noble*) in the twelfth-century kingdom of Jerusalem; it aims to demonstrate that in the kingdom women had a better legal status and more freedom of action within both state and society than in the West, for instance in England or France.[2]

The factors which contributed to create this phenomenon are all typical of colonial societies at a certain stage of their development[3] and in no way connected to, or an outcome of, the image of women, which in all medieval colonial states was the stereotypical image as developed in Western Europe during the early Middle Ages.[4] These factors are the following: because the survival rate among girl-children born to Frankish settlers was higher than that among boys, women inherited their fathers' fiefs more often than elsewhere; a relatively short male lifespan (thirty to thirty-five years) produced a large number of female heiresses, girls or widows who either inherited fiefs or had to act as guardians for their young children; a conjuncture of constant warfare and a general shortage of manpower, and especially military manpower, created a situation in which women had to take up functions which in Europe were traditionally fulfilled by men.[5]

The specific position of women in the Latin kingdom of Jerusalem is reflected in its laws and their enforcement. An examination of marriage and inheritance laws shows first of all that, in comparison with the West, the law of the kingdom was more favourable to women; secondly, that in practice laws were less rigidly enforced than in Europe.

Marriage law did not achieve its final form until the 1160s. Its history is related by the jurist Philip of Novare who wrote his *Livre de forme de plait* in about 1250 and revised it in the 1260s in an attempt to reconstruct the lost *assises* of the twelfth century. According to him, in the early years of the kingdom noble women could marry freely without the consent of their feudal lords. Then the lords, and especially the kings of Jerusalem, began to establish their right to control marriages, thus weakening the right of families over the marriages of their daughters. This led to the opposition of the nobility and a new rule was introduced (probably in the 1160s under King Amalric): the king or another feudal lord was to propose three barons to a female heiress (either one who had reached the marriageable age or a widow) from among whom she was obliged to choose her husband. Although required to choose her husband from the three candidates proposed by her lord, under pain of losing her fief by *commise*, the heiress could refuse all of them on the grounds of disparagement or misalliance. Thus the king and other feudal lords found themselves forced to propose to an heiress candidates of her own social rank and of similar wealth or else she, with the advice of her family, might refuse the marriage. All this refers to heiresses who held fiefs which owed *servize de corps*; lords did not have any authority over marriages of heiresses who held fiefs which did not owe *servize de corps*. This gave to the family of an heiress more choice and undoubtedly presupposed its advice and consent, and thus considerably limited the control of overlords. Referring to the law, Philip of Novare complains that, in the third phase of its development, it favoured the strengthening of the royal power and, consequently, the weakening of the *lignages*. Actually, as already pointed out by Peter Edbury, it was clearly a concession to the nobility.[6]

Law also regulated the age of marriage. An heiress under the age of twelve could not be coerced to marry.[7] As for widows, they could not be forced to remarry before one year and one day had elapsed;[8] moreover, they could not be forced to remarry once they were over sixty. John of Ibelin, lord of Jaffa and Ascalon, who wrote his monumental *Livre des Assises de la Haute Cour* in the 1260s and, like Philip of Novare, attempted to reconstruct the *assises*, reasoned that requiring women over sixty to marry was contrary to God's will and to the dictates of reason, because there is no possibility that the marriage would produce offspring. He drew an analogy between an heiress's duty to remarry and the military obligations of male fief holders. Men, he claimed, are excused from military service when they reach the age of sixty. While male fief holders render *servize de leur corps*, through military service, female fief holders render a comparable bodily service through marriage in the interest of their feudal lords.[9]

A comparison with France and England emphasizes the relatively weak authority of the feudal lords of the kingdom of Jerusalem over marriages of daughters and widows of their vassals. For example, in twelfth-century England, monarchs and other feudal lords collected a fee for permission to marry, a custom unknown in the kingdom of Jerusalem. Until 1215 English feudal lords could force a husband of their own choice upon a widow, as is demonstrated by paragraph 8 of Magna Carta which stated that 'a widow should not be compelled to remarry so long as she prefers to remain without a husband'.[10] However, the baronial revolt and the reform of 1258 clearly show that the English monarchs continued to enforce marriages as well as disparagement.[11] In France it was not until the middle of the thirteenth century that the *Établissements de Saint*

Louis stipulated that at least three candidates should be offered by both the family and the lord to an heiress (either a girl of marriageable age or a widow) and she should choose the best and the most suitable among them.[12]

Several examples demonstrate the greater freedom enjoyed by heiresses in the kingdom of Jerusalem in comparison with their counterparts in the West. One such example is that of Constance, widow of Raymond of Poitiers, prince of Antioch. Constance married Raymond in 1137 while under ten years of age; when she became a widow in 1148, she was about twenty years old and the mother of four children, the eldest of whom, Bohemond, the heir to the principality, was five years old. Two years later, in 1150, King Baldwin III of Jerusalem offered Constance three candidates: Yves of Nesle, count of Soissons, Walter of Falconberg, whose family (the Saint-Omer) had in the past held the principality of Galilee, and Ralph of Merle, a baron from the county of Tripoli. According to William of Tyre, 'any of these seemed with justice quite capable of protecting the region'. But Constance refused them all because, according to William, '[she] dreaded the yoke of marriage and preferred a free and independent life. She paid little heed to the needs of her people and was far more interested in enjoying the pleasures of life.'[13] William, however, was wrong. She did not dread the yoke of marriage but refused to consider a marriage as her obligation; she probably refused all the three candidates offered to her by the king, her overlord, because she did not want to marry any of them. This became evident when, in 1153, she married Renaud of Châtillon, having asked the consent of King Baldwin III only after she had chosen a husband for herself. William of Tyre remarked somewhat unkindly (and inaccurately) that 'many there were, however, who marvelled that a woman so eminent, so distinguished and powerful, who had been the wife of a very illustrious man, should stoop to marry an ordinary knight'.[14]

Another example reads like an episode from a *chanson de geste*. In 1158 the beautiful Theodora, the niece of the Byzantine Emperor Manuel Comnenus, married King Baldwin III; when the king died in 1163, his widow, then only seventeen years old and childless, retired to Acre which she had received from her husband as her dower to be held for life if she were widowed. King Amalric, brother of Baldwin III, did not want his widowed sister-in-law to remarry, as he did not wish Acre, the largest and richest city in the kingdom and traditionally a part of royal domain, to pass into other hands; if Theodora remained a widow, Acre would revert to the crown at her death. In the winter of 1166/7, Theodora, then a widow for about three years and living in retirement in Acre, eloped with her cousin Andronicus Comnenus, the Byzantine governor of Cilicia, a married man in his forties. The couple eloped to Nur-ad-Din's court in Damascus and lived there happily with their two children; Theodora died before 1182 when Andronicus became the emperor of Byzantium. As Theodora's children were born out of wedlock the dower lands of Acre returned to the crown.[15] Still, the story once again shows how little control the kings could have over their female vassals.

The law of the kingdom ruled that, in the absence of male heirs, the eldest daughter should have the same rights as an eldest son and should inherit the entire fief. This practice changed in 1171 when the High Court altered the law so that when cases of female inheritance arose, all daughters should divide a fief equally between them: the eldest should receive the homage of her sisters and should herself do homage for the whole fief to the king.[16] In the kingdom of Jerusalem this right to inherit included the crown, which was uncommon in Europe.

Women also had the right to a part of their deceased husbands' property through the dower (*dos*) right. Moreover, widows with children who were minors had the right to act as their guardians, enabling them, as the child's surviving parent, to act as regents. According to John of Ibelin, 'when a man who held a fief dies and he leaves a wife and children below age, the mother should have the *bailliage* over all that the children inherit from their father'.[17] The dower (*dos, douaire*) was particularly important as it granted women, upon the death of their husbands, control over considerable immoveable and moveable property, land as well as chattels, money, rents or services. According to John of Ibelin and other jurists, the common usage in the kingdom of Jerusalem was 'that all wives should have as *dos* half of all their husbands had owned at the time of their death'.[18] As this law dates from the early twelfth century it is an extremely early one in comparison to Europe. In France dower only became common after 1214;[19] in both France and England the dower was only a third or even less of the husbands' property.[20] In England Magna Carta's guarantee that a widow would have her marriage portion, dower and inheritance without any hindrance was often violated in the thirteenth century.[21]

Inheritance law thus enabled women in the kingdom to rule territories and to enjoy considerable revenues. Theodora Comnena received Acre as her dower upon the death of her husband King Baldwin III in 1163.[22] After the death of her husband, Hugh of Ibelin, Lord of Ramle, in *c*.1169, Agnes of Courtenay enjoyed for life the usufruct of half of the revenues of Ramle as her dower.[23] Maria Comnena, upon the death of her husband, King Amalric, received Nablus as her dower (1174) which she ruled together with Barisan the Younger of Ibelin, lord of Ramle, whom she married in 1177.[24]

The right to inherit their fathers' fiefs meant that very often women became the rulers of fiefs and lordships which they transmitted to their husbands. Helvis of Ramle, the daughter of Baldwin I of Ramle, inherited the lordship in *c*.1138 and transmitted it to her two husbands, first to Barisan-le-Vieux of Ibelin (d. *c*.1150) and then to Manasses of Hierges.[25] Stephanie of Milly, the daughter of Philip of Milly, who inherited the lordship of Oultrejourdain following the death of her sister Helena of Milly in 1174, transmitted it to her third husband, Renaud of Châtillon (1177).[26] Juliana of Caesarea inherited Caesarea upon the death of her brother, Walter II of Caesarea, during the siege of Acre (*c*.July 1189–12 July 1191). She transmitted it to her second husband, Aymar of Lairon, and upon her death (between 1213 and 1216) to her son by her first husband, Guy of Beirut, Walter III lord of Caesarea (*c*.1216–29).[27] In 1198, following the death of her brother Humphrey IV of Toron, Isabelle of Toron (Tibnin in Lebanon), the widow of Roupen III of Armenia, inherited the lordships of Oultrejourdain, Hebron, Toron, Chateau-Neuf and Belinas, which she transmitted to her daughter Alice of Armenia. She, in turn, passed them on to Raymond Rupin, her son from her second marriage to Raymond of Antioch (d. 1194).[28]

This situation applied not only in fiefs and lordships but often to the crown itself. Thus Queen Melisende, as the heiress of King Baldwin II, was crowned together with her husband Fulk of Anjou on 14 September 1131, thus transmitting the crown to her husband Fulk and, following the latter's death (in 1143), to their son Baldwin III.[29] Sybille, the daughter of King Amalric and Agnes of Courtenay, transmitted the crown to her husband Guy of Lusignan; she, as the eldest daughter of Amalric, was considered 'li plus apareissanz et li plus dreis heirs dou roiaume' following the death of the childless Baldwin IV in 1185 and that of her son by William of

Montferrat, Baldwin V, who died in summer of 1186 at the tender age of nine.[30] Sybille was crowned alone by the patriarch and then she conferred the crown upon her husband Guy of Lusignan. Following her death (on 25 July 1190) the crown passed to her half-sister, Isabella, another daughter of King Amalric. When she inherited the crown of Jerusalem, Isabella's marriage to Humphrey IV of Toron was annulled as invalid on the grounds that she had been only eight and therefore under the canonical age when the marriage was contracted. As the queen of Jerusalem Isabella married and transmitted the crown to three husbands. In 1190 she married Conrad of Montferrat; after his death by the hands of the Assassins in 1192, after only one week of widowhood (whereas the law of the kingdom stipulated at least a year of widowhood), she married Henry of Champagne, who died in 1197. A year later, in 1198, Isabella married King Amalric of Cyprus. She died in 1205 aged about thirty-three, leaving five daughters, including the thirteen-year-old Maria of Montferrat as the heiress to the throne.[31]

Men who married heiresses therefore often lost the fiefs and the titles they had gained upon the death of the wives, if the wife had an heir, an issue of an earlier marriage, or the couple did not have a male heir. Consequently Guy lost his position as king of Jerusalem following the death of Queen Sybille (on 25 July 1190); as the couple did not have a male heir, the crown passed to Sybille's sister, Isabella.[32] Among the knights who entered into possession of seigneuries through marriages and lost them were Walter III of Beirut and Aymar of Lairon. The former married Helena of Milly, the heiress to the lordship of Oultrejourdain, and in 1166 became lord of this lordship by virtue of this marriage. Following the death of his wife in 1168 and that of his daughter early in 1174, Walter's rule of the lordship came to an end and in 1174 Oultrejourdain passed into the hands of Helena's sister, Stephanie of Milly.[33] Aymar of Lairon, the second husband of Juliana of Caesarea, became the lord of Caesarea upon their marriage in c.1193; when Juliana died sometime between 1213 and 1216 Aymar lost the lordship, which then passed to Juliana's eldest son, Walter III of Caesarea.[34]

Women also held and ruled fiefs and lordships by their right of guardianship (*bailliage*) while widowed mothers of minors.[35] Thus, following the death of Fulk of Anjou in 1143, Queen Melisende acted as regent for her son Baldwin III who was then thirteen and therefore still under age; the kings of Jerusalem came of age at fifteen.[36] Ermengarde of Tiberias, the widow of Elinard of Bures, prince of Tiberias (d. 1153), ruled the principality of Galilee on behalf of her minor son Walter, until he came of age in 1159.[37] In turn, the wife of Walter of Bures, Eschiva of Tiberias, ruled the principality following his death in c.1170 until her marriage to Raymond of Tripoli in 1174.[38] Stephanie of Milly, of Oultrejourdain, acted as guardian for her son, Humphrey IV of Toron.[39]

The right to inherit and to hold land guaranteed to women financial control over the land, including the right to alienate it. In 1177, as the widow of William of Montferrat, Sybille, then the countess of Jaffa and Ascalon, granted land in Ascalon to the Order to St John 'for the salvation of William's soul'.[40] Similarly, in 1174, Eschiva of Tiberias granted land to the Hospital for the salvation of the soul of her husband, Walter of Bures,[41] while about twenty years earlier Ermengarde of Tiberias granted land to the Order to St Lazarus of Jerusalem.[42] In 1164, Mary Brisebarre, the lady of Beirut and the widow of Guy II Brisebarre of Beirut who had died in 1156, gave to the Order to St Lazarus 10 besants annually from the revenues of the casale of Musecaqui near Beirut.[43] In 1180, a certain Ahuhisa, lady of Palmarea, granted estates and privileges there to the monastery of Mount Tabor.[44]

As demonstrated above, women in the Latin kingdom of Jerusalem were granted more rights and enjoyed more freedom of action than their contemporaries in the West. This was dictated by the specific condition of a society in a state of constant war that exposed women in Outremer to great hazards. In 1101, the Armenian wife of King Baldwin I was allegedly raped by pirates on the voyage from Laodicea to Jaffa and therefore the king repudiated her and she was forced to take the veil at the convent of St Anne in Jerusalem.[45] Other women were subjected to Muslim captivity.[46]

Some women found themselves forced to command the defence of their homes against the Muslim enemy. Thus, in 1187, while the entire army of the kingdom was destroyed at the battle of Hattin, Maria Comnena, the widow of King Amalric and the wife of Balian of Ramle, defended Nablus, which she had received as her dower from Amalric, against the forces of Saladin.[47] When Saladin conquered Tiberias on 1 July 1187, Eschiva of Tiberias, whose husband Raymond of Tripoli was with the king's army, was commanding a small garrison which held out in the castle of Tiberias. She surrendered Tiberias only on 5 July, following the disaster of Hattin (4 July

1187). Saladin allowed her to go with all her household to Tripoli.[48] The constant and often intensive state of warfare also caused famines and epidemics. The famine in the Christian camp besieging Acre in 1190 caused an epidemic among whose victims were Queen Sibylle of Jerusalem and her two little daughters by Guy of Lusignan, Alice and Maria (25 July 1190).[49]

The examination of the position of women in the kingdom of Jerusalem shows that their legal status was superior to that of their contemporaries in the West. It also shows that what dictated their position in the kingdom was neither feudal nor canon law but rather conditions in a society in a state of constant war. In the kingdom of Jerusalem laws were often neglected or adapted to new conditions created by conquest; the law of survival took precedence over all others.

A NOTE ON LIFE EXPECTANCY

According to J. C. Russel the average length of life of females was about twenty-five to thirty years.[50] It is known, however, that Queen Isabella of Jerusalem died at the age of about thirty-three; Queen Melisende died at the age of forty-one.[51] Maria Comnena, who married King Amalric in 1167, must have been at the time of her death in 1217 over sixty years old.[52] Another queen of Jerusalem, Agnes of Courtenay, who died before late summer of 1186, must have been about fifty as she may have been born c.1136.[53] The length of life of other noble women is more difficult to establish as their date of death is seldom known. However, Mary of Beirut, who died in 1166, may have been about forty.[54] Helena of Oultrejourdain who died in 1168 may have been under twenty.[55] Juliana of Caesarea who died between 1213 and 1216 may then have been about sixty as she married her first husband Guy Brisebarre soon after 1166.[56] The dates of the deaths of Stephanie of Milly of Oultrejourdain and of Echive of Galilee are unknown; in 1187, however, Stephanie, who married for the first time in 1162/3, may have been about forty.[57] Echive who married for the first time before 1166 may have been about thirty-three.[58] Helvis of Ramle who married in c.1137/8, at about fifteen, disappeared from history in 1158/60, being then about forty years old.[59] It follows, therefore, that the average length of life was about forty-four and not, as argued by Russel, twenty-five to thirty, and thus it was higher than that of men, which was thirty to thirty-five according to Russel.[60]

NOTES

[1] *Pierre Dubois, De recuperatione Terre Sancte. Dalla Respublica Christiana ai primi nazionalismi e alla politica anti-mediterranea*, ed. A. Diotti (Florence, 1997), 53–69, 184–5; W. J. Brandt, 'Pierre Dubois: modern or medieval?', *AHR* 35 (1929/30), 507–21; Sylvia Schein, 'The future *regnum Hierusalem*: a chapter in medieval state planning', *JMH* 10 (1984), 101–3; Shulamith Shahar, *The Fourth Estate: A History of Women in the Middle Ages*, trans. Chaya Galai (London and New York, 1983), 155–7.

[2] There are number of studies dealing with specific aspects of the subject of women in the kingdom of Jerusalem, none, however, addresses the subject of colonial society and the comparison with contemporary Europe. See Jean Richard, 'Le Statut de la femme dans l'Orient Latin', *La Femme, 2: Recueils de la Société Jean Bodin pour l'Histoire Comparative des Institutions*, 12 (Brussels, 1962), 377–87; J. A. Brundage, 'The marriage law in the Latin kingdom of Jerusalem', in *Outremer*, 258–71; H. E. Mayer, 'Studies in the history of Queen Melisende of Jerusalem', *Dumbarton Oaks Papers* 26 (1972), 93–189; Bernard Hamilton, 'Women in the crusader states: the queens of Jerusalem (1100–1190)', in Derek Baker (ed.), *Medieval Women* (Oxford, 1978), 143–73; Sarah Lambert, 'Queen or consort: rulership and politics in the Latin East, 1118–1228', in Anne J. Duggan (ed.), *Queen and Queenship in Medieval Europe: Proceedings of a Conference Held at King's College, London, April 1995* (Woodbridge, 1997), 153–69.

[3] Not only to medieval but also to early modern colonial societies (for example, United States and Australia). See on this topic, for example, Roger Thompson, *Women in Stuart England and America: A Comparative Study* (London and Boston, 1974); Margaret Strobel, *European Women and the Second British Empire* (Bloomington and Indianapolis, IN, 1991). The claim that in medieval, and likewise in early modern colonial societies, women enjoyed a better legal status than in the West is demonstrated by the *Assises de Romanie* (Morea), a private legal treatise, the final version of which was compiled between 1333 and 1346. According to the Morean law lords had no control over marriages of vassals of liege ranks and, while a woman of simple homage required her lord's permission to marry, she could not in any case be forced to marry. See Peter W. Topping, *Feudal Institutions as Revealed in the Assises of Romania: The Law Code of Frankish Greece* (Philadelphia, 1949), art. 31, 80 and pp. 136, 150–4.

[4] For this image see Eileen Power, *Medieval Women,* ed. M. M. Postan (Cambridge, 1975); Georges Duby et al. (eds.), *A History of Women, 2:*

Silences of the Middle Ages (Cambridge, MA, 1992); Henry Kraus, 'Eve and Mary: conflicting images of medieval woman', in idem (ed.), *The Living Theatre of Medieval Art* (Bloomington, IN, 1967), 41–62. For the image of women in the Iberian kingdoms see H. Dillard, *Daughters of the Reconquest: Women in Castilian Town Society* (Cambridge, 1984). Such a study for the kingdom of Jerusalem is still a *desideratum*.

5 For the kingdom of Jerusalem as colonial society see J. Prawer, *The Latin Kingdom of Jerusalem: European Colonialism in the Middle Ages* (London, 1972), 469–533; 'The crusading kingdom of Jerusalem – the first European colonial society? A symposium', in *Horns*, 341–66. See also appendix to this chapter, 'A note on life expectancy'.

6 *Livre de Philippe de Navarre*, 86, in *RHC Lois* 1: 558–9; P. W. Edbury, 'Feudal obligations in the Latin East', *Byzantion* 47 (1977), 345–7. See also *Livre de Jean d'Ibelin*, 227, *RHC Lois* 1: 359–61; Richard, 'Le Statut', 379; J. Prawer, *Crusader Institutions* (Oxford, 1980), 30–1; Brundage, 'Marriage law', 259–60, 268. For Philip de Navarre see Jonathan Riley-Smith, *The Feudal Nobility and the Kingdom of Jerusalem, 1174–1277* (London, 1973), 126–7. Though these legal treatises were all composed by thirteenth-century jurists they can be used for the twelfth century. First of all, one of the main aims of those jurists was to reconstruct the lost (in 1187) twelfth-century *Letres du Sepulcre*. Secondly, though the jurists themselves express doubts as to whether they were describing actual laws or merely custom, and this finds expression in their law-books in the recurring phrase 'assise or usage', they preserve the memories of jurists who lived before 1187, and remembered the assises and customs, such as Ralph of Tiberias. Thirdly, those jurists often used twelfth-century chronicles and diplomatic material. Moreover some of the legislation regarding women as defined by thirteenth-century jurists appears in twelfth-century sources. See Riley-Smith, *Feudal Nobility*, 133–44.

7 *Livre de Philippe de Navarre*, 86, p. 559; *Livre de Jean d'Ibelin*, 171, p. 263. This was the conventional Romano-canonical rule proclaiming the minimum age for marriage of females as twelve: W. Onclin, 'L'Age requis pour le mariage dans la doctrine canonique médiévale', in Stephan Kuttner (ed.), *Proceedings of the Second International Congress of Medieval Canon Law: Monumenta iuris canonici,* ser. C, vol. 1 (Vatican City, 1965), 237–47; Brundage, 'Marriage law', 261–2.

8 Writing in the 1170s, William of Tyre argues that: 'it was our custom, approved by a long usage, not to consider the remarriage of a widow, especially of one who was pregnant, within one year after the death of her husband, for that would not be honorable mourning' (WT, trans. Emily Alwater Babcock and A. C. Krey (New York, 1976), 2: 419). See also *Livre de Philippe de Navarre*, 86, p. 559; *La Clef des Assises de la Haute Cour*, 225, *RHC Lois* 1: 595; *Livre au Roi*, 30, *RHC Lois* 1: 696. For the *Livre au Roi*

see now its new edn.: *Le Livre au Roi: Introduction, notes et édition critique*, ed. Myriam Greilsammer (Paris, 1995).

[9] *Livre de Jean d'Ibelin*, 228, pp. 362–4; Brundage, 'Marriage law', 270–1.

[10] James C. Holt, *Magna Carta* (Cambridge, 1965), 318 and see 45–8, 113–16; Eleanor Searle, 'Seigneurial control of women's marriage: the antecedents and function of merchet in England', *Past and Present* 82 (1979), 3–14.

[11] Scott L. Waugh, 'Marriage, class and royal lordship in England under Henry III', *Viator* 16 (1985), 181–207.

[12] *Établissements de St Louis,* 67, ed. Paul Violet (Paris, 1881), 2: 99–103.

[13] WT 16, 18 (Engl. trans. 2: 213).

[14] Ibid. 16, 26 (Eng. trans. 2: 224). Constance bore Renaud two children (Renaud and Agnes, later of Hungary). In 1160 Renaud was captured by the Moslems and held captive until 1175; Constance died in 1162/3, before his release. See J. Prawer, *Histoire du Royaume Latin de Jérusalem*, 1 (Paris, 1969), *passim.*

[15] WT 18, 22; 29, 2 (Eng. trans. 2: 275, 345, 346). William of Tyre's argument that the queen was 'treacherously abducted' by Andronicus is hardly convincing. See also Hamilton, 'Women in the crusader states', 157–62.

[16] *Livre de Jean d'Ibelin*, 148–50, pp. 224–5; *Livre au Roi*, 34–5, pp. 628–31; *Livre de Philippe de Novare*, 71–2, pp. 542–3; Richard, 'Le Statut', 378–9; *Documents relatifs à la successibilité*, 6, *RHC Lois* 2: 408.

[17] *Livre de Jean d'Ibelin*, 178, p. 280; Riley-Smith, *Feudal Nobility*, 185–228 *et passim.*

[18] *Livre de Jean d'Ibelin*, 177, pp. 279–80; *Livre de Geoffroey Le Tort*, 16, *RHC Lois* 1: 449. *Livre de Jacques d'Ibelin*, 68, p. 467. According to the *Livre au Roi,* when for some reason a fief of a vassal is confiscated, the *douaire* of his wife is to be reserved as she should have a half of that fief 'tant comme elle vivera, por son vivre. Car la raison juge que por la mauvaistie dou baron, ne deit mie perdre la feme son douaire . . .' *Livre au Roi*, 21, p. 620. See also ibid., pp. 622–4, 628.

[19] F. R. P. Akehurst (trans.), *The 'Coutumes de Beauvaisis' of Philippe de Beaumanoir*, 13, 430–45 (Philadelphia, 1992), 154–8.

[20] Janet Senderowitz Loengard, *'Of the Gift of her Husband*: English dower and its consequences in the year 1200', in Julius Kirshner and Suzanne F. Wemple (eds.), *Women of the Medieval World: Essays in Honor of John H. Mundy* (Oxford, 1985), 215–55.

[21] Above n. 10. Waugh, 'Marriage', 196 and n. 40.

[22] Hamilton, 'Women in the crusader states', 158–9.

[23] Bernard Hamilton, 'The titular nobility of the Latin East: the case of Agnes of Courtenay', in *CS* 197–201, esp. 199.

[24] *L'Estoire d'Eracles Empereur et la Conqueste de la Terre d'Outremer*, 23, 3, *RHC Oc* 2: 5 (infra: *Eracles*); H. E. Mayer, *Das Siegelwesen in den*

Kreuzfahrerstaaten (Abhandlungen der Bayrischen Akademie der Wissenschaften. Phil.-Hist. Klasse, Neue Folge, 83; Munich, 1978), 53.

[25] WT 17, 13 (Eng. trans. 2: 204); H. E. Mayer, 'Carving up crusaders: the early Ibelins and Ramlas', *Outremer*, 107–29.

[26] WT 21, 3 (Eng. trans. 2: 401); E. Rey, 'Les Seigneurs de Mont-Réal et de la Terre d'Outre le Jourdain', *ROL* 4 (1896), 21.

[27] J. L. LaMonte, 'The lords of Caesarea in the period of the crusades', *Speculum* 22 (1947), 152–4; Steven Tibble, *Monarchy and Lordship in the Latin Kingdom of Jerusalem 1099–1291* (Oxford, 1989), 120.

[28] Rey, 'Les Seigneurs de Mont-Réal', 22–3.

[29] Mayer, 'Studies in the history of Queen Melisande', 95–182.

[30] *Eracles*, 23, 17–21, pp. 26–33; Hamilton, 'Women in the crusader states', 168–72.

[31] *Eracles*, 151–4, 195–6, 258–63, 305; S. Runciman, *A History of the Crusades*, 3 (Cambridge, 1954), 30–104 *passim*; Riley-Smith, *Feudal Nobility*, 111–20 *et passim*. For the law stipulating a year of mourning see above n. 8. See also *Livre au Roi*, 30, pp. 626–7; Brundage, 'Marriage law', 270 and n. 71.

[32] Hamilton, 'Women in the crusader states', 172; Riley-Smith, *Feudal Nobility*, 114–15.

[33] *RRH* Add. no. 454; Rey, 'Les Seigneurs de Mont-Réal', 20; Runciman, *A History of the Crusades*, 2: 335, n. 1; B. Hamilton, 'Miles of Plancy and the fief of Beirut', *Horns*, 141–2.

[34] LaMonte, 'The lords of Caesarea', 152–4.

[35] *Livre de Jean d'Ibelin*, 178, pp. 280–1; *Livre de Philippe de Navarre*, 22, p. 495; *Livre au Roi*, 35, pp. 630–1; *Livre de Geoffroy Le Tort*, 18, p. 440; Riley-Smith, *Feudal Nobility*, 161–2, 185–6.

[36] *Livre de Jean d'Ibelin*, 169, p. 259; Mayer, 'Studies in the history of Queen Melisende', 113–15. Melisende refused to relinquish power to her son who he came of age in 1145 and ruled until 1152: ibid., 115–58; Hamilton, 'Women in the crusader states', 152–3.

[37] *RRH*, no. 297.

[38] *RRH*, no. 522; WT 21, 5 (Eng. trans. 2: 404).

[39] See n. 26 above.

[40] *RRH*, no. 553. Sibylle remarried in 1180. See H. E. Mayer, 'The double county of Jaffa and Ascalon: one fief or two?', in *CS* 182–3.

[41] *RRH*, no. 522.

[42] Ibid., no. 297; *Cartulaire de S. Lazare*, ed. A. de Marsy, *AOL* 2 (1884), n. 13, pp. 132–3.

[43] *RRH*, no. 401; *Cartulaire de S. Lazare*, no. 23, p. 141; M. E. Nickerson, 'The seigneury of Beirut in the twelfth century and the Brisebarre family of Beirut-Blanchegarde', *Byzantion* 19 (1949), 162–3.

[44] *RRH*, no. 594; B. Z. Kedar, 'Palmarée Abbaye Clunisienne du XIIe siècle en Galilée', *Revue Bénédictine* 93 (1983), 260–9.

[45] Guibert of Nogent, *Gesta Dei per Francos*, 7, 48, *RHC Oc* 4: 259; WT 11, 1 (Engl. trans. 1: 461–2); Hamilton, 'Women in the crusader states', 144–7.

[46] See the article by Y. Friedman, Chapter 9, above.

[47] *Eracles*, 23, 46, p. 68.

[48] *Eracles*, p. 69 n.; *Chronique d'Ernoul et de Bernard Le Tresorier*, ed. M. L. de Mas Latrie (Paris, 1971), 169–70.

[49] *Eracles*, 25, 10, p. 151 and see also p. 154 n; Hamilton, 'Women in the crusader states', 172. Sybille born in *c*.1157 was thus about twenty-six years old. See also 'A note on life expectancy', above.

[50] Josiah C. Russel, 'The population of the crusader states', in *A History of the Crusades*, ed. K. M. Setton, vol. 6 (Madison, WI, 1989), 298.

[51] Ibid., 297, n. 6.

[52] Hamilton, 'Women in the crusader states', 161–73.

[53] Ibid., 159, 170.

[54] M. E. Nickerson, 'The seigneury of Beirut', 166–7.

[55] See n. 33 above.

[56] Nickerson, 'The seigneury of Beirut', 169; LaMonte, 'Lords of Caesarea', 151–4.

[57] See n. 26 above.

[58] See n. 38 above.

[59] H. E. Mayer, 'Carving up crusaders: the early Ibelins and Ramla', in *Outremer*, 108, 117–18.

[60] Russel, 'Population', 296.

11

'Sont çou ore les fems que jo voi la venir?' Women in the *Chanson d'Antioche*

SUSAN B. EDGINGTON

The *Chanson d'Antioche* is a long, epic poem, written in Old French, which incorporates apparently authentic material about the First Crusade.[1] It survives as the first part of a three-poem cycle written in the last quarter of the twelfth century, probably by Graindor de Douai.[2] It seems most likely that Graindor reworked three independently circulating poems to give them elements of dramatic unity. The *Chanson d'Antioche* had its origins among the first crusaders themselves; it was developed by Richard the Pilgrim – possibly a participant – and further rewritten by Graindor. The *Chanson des Chétifs* told the story of those remnants of Peter the Hermit's armies who were taken captive, and Graindor concentrated on their fictional adventures as a bridge between the sieges of Antioch and Jerusalem. The *Chanson de Jérusalem* recounted the capture of Jerusalem in 1099, but any historical content bears little resemblance to the chronicles and other sources.[3] So, of the three, only the *Chanson d'Antioche* may offer us useful information about the part played by women in the First Crusade.

Near the beginning of the *chanson* we learn the reaction of the women to Pope Urban's preaching:

> They soon found out and started to weep about their misfortune: 'Alas,' they said to one another, 'what a sad fate is ours! The assembly of the barons has turned out badly for us! Tomorrow the walls of our chambers will not be decked with tapestries, there will be no more songs or celebrations. Even the most powerful lady will find herself deserted.' They kept saying they had been born under an evil star. The young girls lamented, while the ladies called on their husbands: 'Seigneurs, God witnessed our weddings, we have vowed to be faithful to you. When you have conquered

the lands where He lived and you have seen the city where He suffered, may it remind you of us – make sure you don't forget us!' God, the tears that were shed! Many ladies took the cross themselves and many noble young girls whom God loved departed with their fathers. (828–49)[4]

These nameless women who participated in the expedition are mentioned later by the poet in contexts which seem not at all unlikely. There is a harrowing account of women in the camp being taken captive by the Turks after the crusaders left Nicaea:

> The infidels swooped down on the women's quarter: they carried off on their horses those they fancied, they tore the breasts from the old women. As the women died their babies nuzzled their chests, looking for their breasts and suckling on the dead women. What grief! They should be in heaven with the holy Innocents. (2033–40)[5]

Some women survived, however, and were able to assist the crusaders in the battle of Dorylaeum:

> The sun came up and it was fine weather; at noon the heat was overpowering; thirst began to overwhelm the barons: Tancred's knights could think of nothing save getting something to drink. The ladies and young girls of their country who were there in great numbers did them a great service. They rolled up their sleeves and took off their long cloaks, they brought drink to the exhausted knights in jars, in bowls and in gilded goblets. (2147–51)[6]

Afterwards, as the army crossed the Anatolian plateau, 'A thousand people died of thirst alone, as many ladies and young girls as serjeants and squires' (2203–4).[7] And at Antioch we hear of the famine, when 'even the mother could do nothing for her child', and the appalling weather which made 'young people and serjeants and maidens with fair faces rend their clothing and wail to God for succour' (3424–5). Later, nursing mothers are again the subject: their milk dries up and they die (6992–4).

These passing references are mundane enough, and casual enough, to seem entirely authentic. But should we believe the author when he tells us that a battalion of women took part in the battle of Antioch? The context is important. This is the final and climactic scene of the poem. In each *laisse* a leader is described, at the head of his battalion, and as they ride out the Turkish general Corbaran (Kerbogha) turns to his spy Amédélis and interrogates him about the leader's reputation. So, in some order of precedence, he sees Hugh of France ride out, Robert of Flanders, Robert of Normandy, Godfrey, Tancred and Bohemond. They are followed by a battalion of veterans, which provokes laughter from Corbaran, but Amédélis warns him that they have proved themselves in the conquest of Spain and have killed more pagans than are in Corbaran's army. The next battalion is led by four barons; then Adhémar rides into battle for the very first time; the clergy, who have formed their own division, are gently mocked, while the Tafurs, with their formidable king and Peter the Hermit, elicit much more dread. And then:

> Now see, seigneurs, a battalion which is really worth talking about: it is the battalion of women who left home to serve Our Lord. They took counsel in Antioch, and one said to another that their husbands were preparing to attack the Turks, but, if God let them die, 'these scum will seize us and dishonour us. But it is better to go together and to become martyrs. So be it, by God's grace,' they shouted unanimously. They ran to their quarters to grab their staffs, and fixed their wimples high on their heads to protect them from the wind. Some of them collected stones in their sleeves, others filled bottles with water: the thirsty would have something to refresh them. Then they went out of the gate to join their husbands. When he saw this, Corbaran asked Amédélis who was sitting next to him if these really were women whom he saw advancing. 'Yes, lord, on my faith, I can tell you that that will be some battle: think of the blows you will deal out!' – 'I no longer know which way to turn,' said Corbaran to himself, sighing. 'I am overcome,' said Rouge-Lion [one of Corbaran's generals, or 'kings']: 'but I'm so afraid I shan't get to enjoy them.' When the husbands saw their wives gathered in the field, such was their love and pity for them that they changed colour. Then they closed the visors of their helms and tested the edge of their swords which they brandished at arms length. And in their rancour they swore that before they would lose their wives they would make these treacherous pagans pay dearly ... Corbaran had watched the women closely from his tent: 'They will be given to me, Amédélis,' he said, 'and I shall take them with me on well saddled mules to marry them to my nobles.' – 'You have seen them, but you don't understand their husbands. Before letting them fall into your hands they will endure great blows and they will shave the beard of many a Saracen. If you want to have them, you will pay dearly.' (8296–8349)

This battalion is the last. As they ⌐ ⌐ Antioch the bishop of Le Puy addresses them: 'You are all ⌐ and sons of the same lineage, because you are all descended ⌐ am' (8357–8). The battle takes place, but the role of the women is as before: 'As for the ladies, they used lumpy stones as missiles and took water to the thirsty' (8936–7).

Unsurprisingly, there is no chronicle source which corroborates the *Chanson*'s claim that a women's battalion participated in the battle of Antioch. They are not even credited by other historians with assisting the men to the extent that they had at Dorylaeum. The poem's account must therefore be examined as a fiction and for the light it throws on its writer and intended audience. The women's motivation appears rooted in the notion that their husbands would be defeated and that the fate which then befell them if they stayed in the camp really would be 'worse than death'. Their husbands, however, were put on their mettle when they saw the battalion. The idea of emasculating the Saracens by shaving off their beards is put into the mouth of Amédélis, but it represents the husbands' intent. The supposed Turkish reaction is laden with sexual innuendo: 'the blows you will deal out' (*or pensés del ferir*), and Rouge-Lion's more explicit, 'I shan't get to enjoy them' (*ne me puis esbaudir*). Corbaran's supposed intention to marry the women off to his nobles is another motif in the mythology of the enemy as sexual predator.[8]

The battalion of women is pure fantasy, but it is echoed in the *Chanson de Jérusalem* where the women form their own division for the second assault on the walls. This is the tenth division and 'is not destined to shoot arrows or launch javelins', but to throw stones and carry water. The form of the episode is very similar to the *Chanson d'Antioche*. This time the king of Jerusalem, Corbadas, discusses what he sees from the tower of David with his aged brother Lucabel. He boasts that he will capture the women and send them to the sultan, who will in turn bestow each woman on a prince or emir to help repopulate the devastated lands.[9] The attack fails, and there is no mention of women in the later successful assault,[10] while they are explicitly left in Jerusalem for the battle of Ascalon.[11] As in the *Chanson d'Antioche*, the scenes of the battalions under observation were intended humorously; the point being the pagan leader's boasting and his subsequent defeat – the well-loved story of 'nemesis clobbers hubris'. The suspicion that both scenes – in the *Antioche* and in the *Jérusalem* – were the work of Graindor is supported by the fact that the *Antioche* one does not appear in the Provençal fragment analysed by Duparc-Quioc.[12] Thus the battalions of women may be summarily dismissed as historical evidence, which perhaps makes them even more pertinent as evidence for male attitudes to women at the time Graindor was writing: he invented scenes which would amuse, entertain and perhaps inspire his audience.

Pagan, or 'Saracen', women in the *Chanson* are interesting, because they achieve more individuality than the crusaders' own women. Corbaran's mother is a case in point. Her portrait is sexist, ageist and far from flattering, but it is vivid. These scenes with Corbaran's mother are ascribed by Duparc-Quioc to the primitive *chanson* of 'Richard the Pilgrim', on the basis of the Provençal fragment. This would tally with their inclusion in the *Gesta Francorum*. However, the editor also points out that Graindor drew on Robert the Monk in preference to an earlier *chanson*.[13] The early diffusion of the tale as well and its enthusiastic elaboration by Graindor attest its potency. In fact, it was such an achievement that Graindor used it twice: in the *Antioche* and in the *Chétifs*.[14] As with the women's battalion, he is saying, surely, 'This made them laugh the first time, so let's do it again.'[15]

Another striking vignette is the wife of the traitor of Antioch, the Emir Dacien. The emir has entered into negotiations to regain his son, who has been taken hostage by Bohemond. He returns home to his palace, where he meets his wife. She accuses him of plotting treason, even of planning to become a Christian; he offers to show her their son in the Christians' camp from the walls of their tower. When she discovers that he is indeed set on her conversion and the betrayal of Antioch, she resists, at which he seizes her and hurls her from the tower (5885–5919). Devils take her soul; her body is found by the barons when they come to climb the ladder into the city (5976). It is a morally ambivalent story. The emir is said to have loved his wife (5735), but apparently he loved his son more. She threatens to betray him, but he is already engaged in an act of betrayal, and the two are deliberately juxtaposed. Only his readiness to adopt Christianity distinguishes him. This strange and tragic episode, on the evidence of the Provençal chanson, was appropriated by Graindor from an earlier version, and he does not seem to have known quite what to make of it. Certainly he assumed, as has frequently been observed, that a pagan noble would have the same values and motivations as a Christian one, but he does not enter into the dilemma of the wife in any way.

Other references to pagan women are fleeting and conventional: fathers, mothers, sisters and sweethearts reacted with horror and grief when they recognized the severed heads of their men (3335–7); they crowded on the walls to see the Tafurs eating the Turkish dead (4081); when Antioch was captured and the garrison took refuge in the citadel, husbands abandoned wives, and lovers deserted lovers, without a farewell, such was their fear, 'If only you could have seen these beautiful pagans wringing their hands and tearing out their hair!' (6433). There is no love interest between Christian and Saracen, as so often portrayed in later poems in the genre, and very little intra-faith romance either. The marriage of Baldwin to the daughter of the Old Man of the Mountains is shown as an exotic and somewhat barbaric ceremony, but the poet stresses the political advantages of the alliance, while saying nothing at all about the attributes of the bride (2423–8; 2470–80).

Examination of the *Chanson d'Antioche* is complicated by the fact that nineteenth-century editors did not differentiate between the testimony of different manuscripts of the *Chanson*. In the oldest surviving manuscripts, the first redaction, it is thought that we have the crusade cycle as brought together by Graindor of Douai in the 1180s or 1190s. In this version, as shown above, we do not meet the Christian women as individuals, but only as undifferentiated groups. However, a manuscript of the later half of the thirteenth century (the second or transitional redaction) incorporates two accounts of a more romantic nature. In the first, Robert of Flanders is shown going home from Clermont to Arras and telling his wife that he is going on crusade. Both weep as he tells her about the expedition and he promises to hurry back to her once he has prayed at the Holy Sepulchre.[16] The passage may have been interpolated to create a link with a later passage in the first redaction where Robert (one of its heroes) took inspiration from reminding himself of his sacrifice in leaving Flanders and his fiefs and his wife Clemence who loved him so much, and his two sons, to claim the honour of leading the escalade into Antioch (6053–5).

Another of the heroes of the *Chanson* is Reynaud Porquet, who was captured by the Turks and tortured. He refused to convert, and after praying he turned his thoughts directly to his sweetheart: 'Alas, sweetheart, we shall never see each other again, that is what hurts me most. When we parted and when I returned to you, you would give me four kisses as a sign of your great love for me.' And he hopes that someone will be good to her. His capture and torture and death are in the first redaction of the *Chanson* (and in Tudebode),[17] but the girlfriend only in a later interpolation.[18] The process of 'romanti-cization' represented in these two interpolations culminated in the absurd and formulaic love stories of the late medieval crusade cycle. These later poems grafted the romantic conventions exemplified in the Arthurian cycles onto the epic traditions of the *chansons de geste*. Graindor cannot have been unaware of the new and fashion-able genre – Chrétien de Troyes and Béroul were writing in the second half of the twelfth century – but he chose to write in the older style.

Useful comparison may be made with the *Chanson de Roland*, which has no Christian women characters save Alde. Her role is to drop dead when she hears that Roland has been killed, which speaks volumes for the poet's views on women.[19] The *Roland* is, however, at a polar extreme in its lack of interest in Christian heroines, and the author made the Saracen Bramimonde, like the pagan women in the *Chanson d'Antioche*, a much more interesting character: a queen and a prophetess whose bitter predictions may have influenced the pic-ture of Kerbogha's mother.[20] The more matter-of-fact portrayal of Christian women in the *Chanson d'Antioche* is closer to the chronicle accounts, while their humorous depiction is matched in contempo-rary *chansons* such as the *Chanson d'Aspremont* or the *Voyage de Charlemagne*. *Aspremont*'s editor has observed: 'Paynim . . . soldiers, women and the clergy constitute three major groups whose appear-ance in the *chansons de geste* frequently cause laughter.'[21] All three groups are used to comic effect in the *Chanson d'Antioche*. Of the women, there are some mentions which seem to reflect their actual presence on the first crusade, usually in ancillary or passive roles, while at other times the poet introduces women deliberately for their entertainment value. In the latter case we do see women going against the stereotypes, but only as a way of evoking laughter. We should not expect anything else.

At least Graindor's attitude to women is largely affectionate: it may be contrasted with the only slightly later, and thoroughly mis-ogynistic, account of the Third Crusade, written in verse by Ambroise, and presented here in verse translation.[22] The poet blamed the women for the men's behaviour in Acre: 'And with the wines and women they / Caroused in vile and shameful way' (5680–2), and famously Ambroise went on to say, '. . . in Acre they remained, / Save for the good old dames who toiled, / And dames who washed the linen soiled / And laved the heads of pilgrims – these

/ Were good as apes for picking fleas' (5693–8). Later, in Jaffa, the women 'plied the trade of lust and shame' (7041). Notably, Ambroise's only anecdote which records an act of self-sacrifice by a woman is sandwiched between two scatological tales, and so was probably not intended to be taken seriously. Thus the poet devoted some forty lines to the tale of a knight who was attacked 'while attending to the needs of nature' and successfully defended himself by throwing stones: 'It was most cowardly and base / To take a knight thus unaware / While occupied in such affair . . . He scarcely had the time to rise / But managed to get to his feet / And left his duty incomplete' (3583–3624). In the following lines stones were being brought to fill the moat at Acre: 'And many women bore their share, / Taking delight the load to bear.' One in particular – we are not told her name – was mortally wounded, and when her husband came to her she prayed that her body be used to fill the moat (3625–60). In the anecdote immediately following, a Turkish emir made a sortie to set fire to the Christian siege engines, but he was struck down and the greek fire he was carrying was poured on his genitals as he lay on the ground (3661–3700).[23]

Returning to the gentler style of the *Chanson d'Antioche*: it has embedded within it a few precious scraps of evidence that females of all ages – almost invisible in the chronicles – shared in the sufferings of the First Crusade. We know little about them, but their contribution was deliberately exaggerated by Graindor at the time of the Third Crusade as one element in the entertainment he devised to dress up the tale of heroic deeds to inspire his audience to emulate them. His women are viewed indulgently – but always through the eyes of men.

NOTES

[1] The most recent and best edn. is: S. Duparc-Quioc (ed.), *La Chanson d'Antioche* (2 vols., Paris, 1977). References are to the text (vol. 1) unless otherwise stated.

[2] Many aspects of the origins and authorship of the cycle are disputed, but it is convenient to refer to the poet as Graindor. See S. B. Edgington, 'Albert of Aachen and the *chansons de geste*', in *Crusades Sources*, 23–37, at 23–9; M. Bennett, 'First Crusaders' images of Muslims: the influence of vernacular poetry?', *Forum for Modern Language Studies* 22 (1986), 101–22, at 106–8.

[3] Vols. 5 and 6 of *The Old French Crusade Cycle: Les Chétifs*, ed. G. M. Myers (Tuscaloosa, AL, 1981) and *La Chanson de Jérusalem*, ed. N. R. Thorp (Tuscaloosa, AL, 1992).

[4] Line numbers refer to the Duparc-Quioc edn. All translations by the present writer.

[5] Cf. Albert of Aachen 2: 39 (edn. and trans. forthcoming (S. B. Edgington, Oxford Medieval Texts); references here are to book and chapter).

[6] Cf. *Gesta Francorum*, ed. R. Hill (Edinburgh, 1962), 19.

[7] Cf. Albert of Aachen 3: 1–2.

[8] N. Daniel, *Heroes and Saracens: A Re-interpretation of the Chansons de Geste* (Edinburgh, 1984), 76–7.

[9] *Chanson de Jérusalem*, laisse 105, pp. 108–9.

[10] It should perhaps be noted that there is evidence for women participating in the final assault on Jerusalem in a liturgical fragment: see J. France (ed.), 'The text of the account of the capture of Jerusalem in the Ripoll manuscript, Bibliothèque Nationale (latin) 5132', *EHR* 103 (1988), 640–57, at 645.

[11] *Chanson de Jérusalem*, laisse 223, vers 8118, p. 215.

[12] *Chanson d'Antioche*, vol. 2, p. 184.

[13] *Chanson d'Antioche*, notes on pp. 268 and 344.

[14] *Chanson d'Antioche,* laisse 218, pp. 268–9; *Les Chétifs*, laisses 10–11, pp. 9–10 *et passim.*

[15] See Bennett, 'First crusaders' images', 110–11; N. Hodgson, Chapter 12, below.

[16] *Chanson d'Antioche*, interpolation 3b, p. 519.

[17] *Chanson d'Antioche*, pp. 212–36; Peter Tudebode, *Historia de Hierosolymitano Itinere*, ed. J. H. and L. L. Hill (Paris, 1977), 79–80.

[18] *Chanson d'Antioche*, interpolation 7, pp. 528–9.

[19] G. J. Brault (ed.), *The Song of Roland: An Analytical Edition* (2 vols., London, 1978), vol. 2, laisses 268–9, pp. 226–7.

[20] *Song of Roland*, vol. 2, laisses 188 and 195, pp. 158–9 and 164–7.

[21] *The Song of Aspremont*, ed. M. A. Newth (New York, 1989), p. xviii.

[22] Ambroise, *The Crusade of Richard Lion-heart*, tr. and ed. M. J. Hubert and J. L. LaMonte (New York, 1941), 233, 277–8, 162–3.

[23] Cf. H. J. Nicholson, *Chronicle of the Third Crusade: A Translation of the Itinerarium Peregrinorum et Gesta Regis Ricardi* (Aldershot, 1997): the *Itinerarium* has versions of the same episodes on pp. 105–9. A new edn. of Ambroise by M. Ailes is forthcoming.

12

The Role of Kerbogha's Mother in the *Gesta Francorum* and Selected Chronicles of the First Crusade

NATASHA HODGSON

The conversation between Kerbogha and his mother in the *Gesta Francorum* stands out quite dramatically from the rest of the text both in style and content. Rosalind Hill refers to it as 'the curious tale of Karbuqa's second-sighted and rapacious mother'.[1] The conversation appears in several other chronicles of the First Crusade, including the works of Robert the Monk, Guibert of Nogent, Peter Tudebode and Baldric of Dol.[2] While the character of Kerbogha's mother is most probably a creation of the author, the unusual nature of her inclusion has in the past caused speculation that the passage was written by a collaborator on the *Gesta* rather than the same person.[3] Whether from a literary precedent or a factual basis, the origins of this story are probably not determinable; therefore this chapter will rather question the purpose of this passage, its inclusion in the *Gesta* and in related sources. Kerbogha's mother occupies a significant amount of the text in those chronicles in which she appears; therefore why, as a woman and a non-Christian, is she given such attention? Her appearance in the sources has largely been dismissed by historians as 'camp gossip', an interesting anomaly with little or no historical value.[4] The conversation of Kerbogha and his mother requires re-examination to determine how it fits into the *Gesta* and other crusade chronicles, and what it can tell us about contemporary attitudes to women, motherhood and non-Christians. In order to achieve such a re-examination, it is worth considering briefly how mothers and women in general are portrayed by the authors of narrative sources of the crusades.

Women are usually defined by their familial roles, most often with regards to their relationship to men in the narrative sources of the crusade, and indeed in the wider sphere of medieval literature: as mothers, wives, daughters, aunts and sisters. In describing a woman, great store is set by marital status: if not a wife, then a widow, a chaste woman religious or saint, or an unmarried prostitute or virginal daughter. These classifications transcend social boundaries in terms of wealth or nobility, although these factors are also used to describe women. By looking at the narrative sources of the crusade as separate from other contemporary literature, it is possible to add to current work on 'gendering' crusade history, and to bring as yet unused evidence to the field of medieval gender history in general.

The traditional form of women's history tries to evaluate and reconstruct women's experience, but medieval chronicles are often mistrusted as source material.[5] If we presume that the character of Kerbogha's mother is a work of fiction, her personality can only be accurately compared with the imagined attributes of femininity created by male and predominantly ecclesiastic authors. In medieval literature, such gender stereotypes describing the attributes of 'woman' were common. Whilst 'misogyny' implies a negative view of women, the school of feminist scholarship has tended to mistrust even so-called positive images of womanhood as misogynistic.[6] Alcuin Blamires considers it anachronistic to call authors who provide positive images of women 'pro-feminist', or even 'proto-feminist', in terms of medieval society, choosing instead the word 'profeminine' to describe them.[7] Both misogynistic and 'profeminine' arguments appear in the narrative sources of the crusade and they are subject to the bias and opinions of individual chroniclers. As Pauline Stafford points out, the 'palette of images' available to describe women was mostly Biblical and ranged from Mary to Jezebel, but their meanings could be 'contradictory and ambiguous' and so, in some circumstances, 'powerful women became images in themselves, dynastic saints – and sinners'.[8] Examples of both types appear in the crusader chronicles.

In assessing the portrayal of Kerbogha's mother, it is worth considering what kind of general roles mothers were given by authors of crusade chronicles. Those mothers who feature prominently include the Virgin Mother, queens as mothers, noble mothers and some common mothers. There is also a considerable amount of imagery concerning childbirth and motherhood, and some evidence about non-Western mothers, of which Kerbogha's mother is a foremost example. As for all women, there were positive and negative images of motherhood available to the authors of the narrative sources of the crusades, but attitudes to mothers appear to have been largely favourable. According to Blamires, one of the cornerstones of the so-called 'case for women' was the honour due to one's mother, featured in one of the Ten Commandments.[9] Joinville records how, on his deathbed, Louis IX instructed his son Philippe to 'honour and respect your father and mother, and obey their commands'.[10] To medieval authors, it was to a certain extent the capacity for mother-hood that justified women having any authority. In medieval society, and particularly in a frontier society like the Latin kingdom of Jerusalem, the status of a noble woman hinged upon her lineage, what birthright she inherited and was thus able to pass on to her children through motherhood.

In crusade chronicles, mothers most often appear sorrowing on the departure of their sons on crusade. As a result of such descriptions, Jonathan Riley-Smith argues that 'one of the most clear and straightforward messages of the sources for crusading' was that 'women were inhibitors', although he agrees that in practice women may well have been encouraging the crusade effort, and were in fact influential in spreading the crusade idea across areas of France through intermarriage.[11] However, such a portrayal of women could also be seen as a recognition by the authors of crusade chronicles of the sacrifice made by both crusaders and their womenfolk, in order to follow God's command. It does seem that mothers in particular were used by crusade authors to evoke sympathy in the reader at various points in the texts, a mother's love for a child perhaps being considered less suspect than a wife's for her husband.[12] In general, however, motherhood is not a topic with which crusade chroniclers are naturally concerned, and therefore those passages that mention mothers can take on added significance.

It is not insignificant that Kerbogha's mother is a non-Christian. A most interesting aspect of crusader texts as a source for women is the portrayal of women from foreign cultures and religions. Such women are in some respects treated differently from Western European women, but the characteristics of women were generally assumed to be the same across cultural boundaries. Specific examples of non-Western women as mothers are rare, but they do exist. Maria Comnena, the mother of Isabella of Jerusalem, was criticized for her political machinations surrounding the succession of her daughter to the kingdom of Jerusalem. Maria's foreign birth became a tool for discrediting her. The author of the *Itinerarium Peregrinorum et Gesta Regis Ricardi* described Maria as 'steeped in Greek filth from the cradle'.[13] Blanche of Castille faced similar problems during her regency in France: Joinville tells us that she was viewed as 'a foreigner'.[14] In the cases of both women their authority as mothers is not so much disputed as their 'otherness', suggesting a usurpation of rightful power.

Of course, Maria was still a Christian and an extremely important noblewoman, who married into and adapted to a new society, as did many. Inter-religious marriage in Spain and the Latin East was extremely limited, engendering a lack of sanctioned familiarity with Muslim women. There are a few examples of Christians marrying Muslims in the Latin East, but these were usually with the precondition of conversion to Latin Christianity.[15] These are seldom mentioned in the crusade chronicles, save for rumours of the proposed marriage between Joanna of Sicily and the brother of Saladin.[16] Perhaps other marriages were simply not high profile enough to attract the attention of chroniclers, although in truth they would probably also have been at odds with the rest of their subject-matter.

Despite this general lack of familiarity, women of different cultural backgrounds were again ascribed similar characteristics. Jacqueline de Weever explores the problems that ensue when the heroine of a *chanson de geste* is a Saracen woman. She asserts that because of the lack of language available to portray a black heroine as beautiful, 'the poets invariably fall back on the literary tradition of the ideal heroine in its appropriate rhetorical and linguistic rigidities', thus 'whitening' her.[17] This may also have had the effect of playing down the differences between European and Saracen women. Daniel argues that the Franks were able to share some courtly ideals with the Arabs in the Latin East.[18] William of Tyre recounts how Baldwin I, after capturing the pregnant wife of a powerful Saracen noble, treated her courteously, leaving her to be found by her husband with food and water, a maid to assist her, two camels and his own cloak. A universal respect for motherhood in this case transcends the boundaries of religion – however, it is not insignificant that this is 'a woman of high rank'.[19] No such mercy seems to have been extended to the numerous non-Christian mothers and their children who are recorded time and time again being slaughtered by crusaders in captured cities.

The appearance of Kerbogha's mother in the chronicles of the First Crusade provides an intriguing portrayal of a Saracen mother. Kerbogha of Mosul was the Turkish general who besieged the First Crusaders inside the city of Antioch. It is possible that the conversation between Kerbogha and his mother recorded in the *Gesta Francorum* is its earliest version. All versions of the conversation share key elements. Kerbogha's mother, on hearing that her son is besieging Antioch, comes to visit him from Aleppo, begging him not to undertake battle with the Christians. While she does not doubt the prowess of her son, nor is she a Christian herself, she fears the God who fights on behalf of the Christians. Kerbogha's first reaction is to tell her that she must be 'mad' or 'possessed by furies', for his forces outnumber the Franks'.[20] She uses biblical quotations from David and the prophets to prove her case. Kerbogha then asks who has told her about the Christian people and their God, wanting to know the origins of her fears. She replies that, through her study of astronomy and arcane knowledge, her 'observations and careful calculations', she has predicted the defeat and death of her son.[21] Kerbogha refuses her advice and she returns to Aleppo 'taking with her everything on which she could lay her hands'.[22] Whether this is included to add to the finality of her words or simply to demonstrate the general 'rapaciousness' of the enemy is open to interpretation.

Prevailing opinion of the conversation remains that of Hagenmeyer and Hill, that it is a recounting of a tale told around the camp.[23] If so, the story may have been concocted to rally the Frankish troops before the battle.[24] However, in many respects this fails to recognize the importance of the speech to the author. That is not to suggest that the dialogue had a basis in fact. It is possible that Kerbogha's mother did indeed visit and then leave with some booty, fuelling rumours that she believed her son would be defeated, but even so it is unlikely that there would be any fixed idea of what was said between them. It seems more credible that she is purely fictional, developed from some literary precedent of a mother dissuading her son from fighting. Sarah Lambert is currently working on the possibility of a tenth-century precedent, but even if one can be found, the fact that Kerbogha's mother is also a non-Christian arguing in defence of Christianity still lends a unique quality to the conversation.

Susan Edgington includes the dialogue between Kerbogha and his mother among other conversations between the Turks in the *Gesta*, 'they must be dismissed as historical evidence, but ... they make interesting historiographical evidence'.[25] Therefore, the conversation can still retain a certain historical value. The author must have had a genuine purpose for including the dialogue; as it occupies a significant amount of the text, and quite obviously stands out as different in style. Rather than dismissing the episode as gossip it is likely that the author of the *Gesta* seized the opportunity to use Kerbogha's mother as a mouthpiece for his own justifications of the crusade, championing the Christian cause. The conversation is interpreted differently by its various authors, but looking at any of these versions can give important insights into how the crusade message was received and understood. It can also shed more light on contemporary attitudes to mothers and motherhood in general.

Kerbogha's mother demonstrates many values attributed to Western mothers in the course of her speech. Within Western medieval society, mothers, especially noble mothers, played a key role in the religious education of their children. A 'good mother' was to demonstrate piety, honesty and moral character. Joinville said that he trusted his own mother's word 'without question'.[26] Mothers are also portrayed as protective.[27] Kerbogha's mother is concerned for her son's welfare but careful not to offend his pride. She tries to instruct him on religious matters, and although she is a so-called 'pagan' she is given the characteristics of a Christian mother. The relationship between Kerbogha and his mother is demonstrated through the use of endearments. In the version of Robert the Monk, his mother refers to him as 'My son, the solace of my old age and the only token I have of all my love.'[28] This maternal affection is reciprocated by Kerbogha in most versions: he and his mother refer to each other as beloved.

It might be expected that Kerbogha's mother was included in order to ridicule the Turkish general for listening to the advice of a woman, but in fact almost the opposite is the case. Kerbogha is a fool for not paying attention to his mother's wisdom, as it ultimately leads to his downfall. Nor is Kerbogha's mother unique in her role as an adviser. Western mothers often appear in such a capacity, justified in their authority by a desire to act in the best interests of their children. Those mothers who act on their own behalf are severely criticized.[29] Like a Western woman, Kerbogha's mother can only achieve her aim through intercession with her male relative, she cannot command him. In the *Chanson d'Antioche* she is personified when she is named as Calabre, but the fact that she is not named in the other sources implies that it was not her as a person, but her words that were of consequence to these authors.[30] It also shows that her authority was considered to come only from the relationship with her son. Ultimately she is unable to enforce her opinion when her son chooses to ignore it, and must leave him to his fate.

The biblical quotations in the *Gesta* version are often slightly incorrect. Hill asserts that 'The use of texts suggests that the Author was a devout layman, quoting familiar scriptural passages from a good but not completely accurate memory.'[31] Colin Morris has suggested that the author of the *Gesta* was in fact a cleric from an alternative academic tradition, and that the conversation follows the form of a set-piece, not dissimilar from those used in *chansons*.[32] Either way, the words of Kerbogha's mother justifying the superiority of Christianity can be used as further evidence to support the idea that the crusade message was well disseminated. There are textual variations between the versions of the conversation, and, if it was indeed intended as a vehicle for the opinions of the author, it is natural that the dialogue should change as different authors added their own embellishments. Peter Tudebode adds yet more biblical references to the speech, as does Robert the Monk, elaborating it into a rhetorical exercise justifying Christian supremacy.[33] Perhaps their efforts were genuinely a result of their wanting to correct and improve the *Gesta* version. This was often cited as a reason for chroniclers wishing to produce a history of the First Crusade, although the appearance of such texts has also been argued to be linked to the propaganda drive for Bohemond in 1105.[34]

The character and opinions of Kerbogha's mother also change under the influence of different authors. In the version of Baldric of Dol, Kerbogha's mother employs arguments similar to profeminine ones about the duty due to mothers; she criticizes her son for entering into combat with the Franks '*me inconsulta*', and appears far more authoritative.[35] Guibert of Nogent portrays Kerbogha's mother as more critical of the Christians, calling them weak and ignorant. In his *Dei Gesta per Francos*, Kerbogha's treatment of his mother is less affectionate; he does not refer to her as beloved and when she returns to Aleppo she has been spurned by her son.[36] Robert the Monk's embellishments take the form of more colourful descriptions and he plays on the emotions of mother and son. He gives more detail about the sources of Kerbogha's mother's knowledge.[37] He also omits the rumour of Bohemond and Tancred eating 2,000 cows and 4,000 horses in one meal. Perhaps he feared its levity was not in keeping with the dramatic atmosphere he was trying to create.

Kerbogha's mother differs significantly from a Western, Christian woman in her power of prophecy and knowledge of the arcane. There are other accounts of Saracen women with supernatural powers, but these are more often accused of witchcraft. The *Eracles* chronicle tells of a Saracen sorceress who, captured and tortured by soldiers, admitted to casting spells 'by the devil' on their camp. She then supposedly prophesied correctly that few of them would escape capture or death.[38] Her power is attributed to the devil, and is different in nature from that of Kerbogha's mother. Interestingly, although Raymond of Aguilers does not include the episode concerning Kerbogha's mother, he includes an incident of Saracen 'witchcraft'. On the day of the conquest of Jerusalem, Raymond writes:

> I cannot pass by this interesting incident. When two women tried to cast a spell over one of our *petrariae*, one of the stones from the same machine hurtled whistling through the air and smashed the lives out of the two witches as well as the lives of the three nearby small girls, and thus broke the spell.[39]

Given these examples, one might expect that such extraordinary powers would be limited to so-called 'pagan' women. However, there are Christian women in the crusade chronicles who are portrayed as prophetic. Walter the Chancellor relates how a 'moon struck' woman made a prophecy of doom on the eve of the Field of Blood, but his description of her suggests that her predictions were not derived from books or other specialist knowledge.[40] Mothers were sometimes portrayed with distinct powers of prophecy with regard to their own offspring. Guibert of Nogent refers to the mother of the Byzantine Emperor Alexius as a 'sorceress' who predicted that a man of Frankish origin (whom Guibert considered to be Bohemond) would take her son's life and empire.[41] The Minstrel of Reims suggests that Blanche of Castile knew on the departure of Louis IX for crusade that she would never see him again.[42]

Kerbogha's mother differs from these in that her prophecy does not come from a diabolic or instinctive source but through her own learning and that of her soothsayers. Some of the chroniclers were aware that they were portraying something considered to be out of the ordinary. Guibert of Nogent reports that Kerbogha is stunned by the miraculous eloquence of his mother.[43] Robert the Monk remarks that 'No one should be surprised at what she said, for she was well versed in the books of Moses and the prophets', implying that there were those who would be surprised.[44] He also recounts that Kerbogha grew angry after his mother's prediction of his death and her son tries to discredit her by criticizing her inane ideas and untrained rhetoric.[45]

Kerbogha's mother does not appear in the chronicles of Fulcher of Chartres or Raymond of Aguilers.[46] Fulcher of Chartres, absent from Antioch at the time, probably used Raymond of Aguilers's work to fill in the details about this part of the crusade, which may explain her absence from his chronicle.[47] It seems odd that Raymond with his obvious enthusiasm for recording visions and portents saw fit to exclude the episode, even though he probably had access to the *Gesta*. John France suggests this is because of the different 'preoccupations' and background of Raymond.[48] It is possible that Raymond may have considered the story to be camp gossip not worth repeating. Certainly, in chronicling the events at Antioch, he was more concerned with justifying the story of the Holy Lance. However, he may also have balked at ascribing Christian values to a woman and a Saracen, preferring only to give evidence of supernatural power on the side of the Christians.

There are a certain number of questions raised by the very appearance of the conversation in the *Gesta*. Kerbogha's mother not only predicts her son's defeat, but also that her son will die within a year.[49] Hill argues that 'the confidence of the prophecy suggests that the Author wrote it in the summer of 1098, after the Great Battle of Antioch'.[50] However, the date cited most often by historians for Kerbogha's death is 1102.[51] If the speech of Kerbogha's mother was filled with the confidence of hindsight, why not simply be content with a prediction of Kerbogha's defeat? Why would the author put such a stricture on Kerbogha's forthcoming death? If the *Gesta* was completed in 1101 as is commonly believed, or possibly earlier as Colin Morris suggests, when Kerbogha was still alive, why include a prophecy that appears to be wrong?[52] Could it be possible that the author was writing later with the benefit of hindsight, confident that Kerbogha was already dead? Obviously, this is not conclusive proof that the *Gesta* was written later than thought. Even if the author was writing in 1102, Kerbogha's mother's prediction of her son dying within a year of the battle in 1098 would still be wrong, yet the prediction is reiterated in all versions of the speech. Hill asserts that Kerbogha may have died as early as 26 October 1101; but would the *Gesta*, or at least this part of it, have been complete in time to be used as the original source for Raymond of Aguilers and Fulcher of Chartres in that same year?[53] The Hills suggest that the '*libellus*' seen by Ekkehard of Aura in Jerusalem in 1101 was not in fact the *Gesta*, but may have been an earlier common source used by the *Gesta*, Raymond and Fulcher.[54] According to them, 'a cursory study of the speech reveals a great number of ecclesiastical terms as well as ecclesiastical dramatic writing'.[55] Could a common source account for the absence of Kerbogha's mother from the accounts of Raymond and Fulcher? The prediction may simply be a literary device derived from an undiscovered precedent, but at present there are no obvious solutions to such questions. However, it is clear that the speech of Kerbogha's mother deserves more than the cursory attention it has attracted so far in the debate surrounding the primacy of the *Gesta* as the original source for many chronicles of the First Crusade.

In conclusion, Kerbogha's mother is unique in crusade literature, a knowledgeable non-Christian woman arguing in defence of Christianity.[56] While her character is largely fictional, it seems that historians have been unjustified in dismissing the conversation as without historical importance, 'highly fanciful' and 'camp gossip'.[57] The conversation is valuable in two ways: first, the author is primarily concerned with using Kerbogha's mother as a mouthpiece for his propaganda on crusading, and secondly, she herself can still provide an interesting study for views on both women and motherhood. Perhaps it is by virtue of Kerbogha's mother's very 'otherness', as a woman and a Saracen, that the audience would have found it acceptable for her to be well educated, conversant with the Christian faith as well as her own, and deciphering prophecies from the stars. On the other hand, she may provide a mirror for the experience of Christian mothers, providing wise and devout advice to her son, in his best interests, but ultimately unable to protect him from his fate. The speech itself raises yet more questions about the relationship between the sources of the First Crusade, and as such could benefit from a more far-reaching analysis. Ultimately, the conversation of Kerbogha and his mother provides a foremost example of how a re-examination of crusader sources focusing on aspects of gender can provide new and relevant insights into the history of the crusades.

NOTES

[1] Rosalind Hill (ed. and trans.), *Gesta Francorum et aliorum Hierosolimitanorum* (Nelsons Medieval Texts; Edinburgh, 1962), xv.

[2] Ibid., 53–6; Robert the Monk *Historia Iherosolimitana* in *RHC Oc* 3, 811–14; R. B. C. Huygens, *Guibert de Nogent Gesta Dei Per Francos et cinq autres textes* (Turnholt, 1996), 212–16; John Hugh Hill and Laurita L. Hill (trans.), *Peter Tudebode, Historia de Hierosolimitano Itinere* (Philadelphia, 1974), 69–72; Baldric of Dol, *Historia Jerosolimitana* in *RHC Oc* 4. Kerbogha's mother appears as 'Calabre' periodically in the *Chanson d'Antioche*, see Suzanne Duparc-Quioc, *La Chanson d'Antioche*, 1 (Paris, 1976), 51–2, 268–9, 523–4. The speech does not appear in the version of Fulcher of Chartres or Raymond d'Aguilers.

[3] Bréhier includes the speech of Kerbogha's mother in a list of suspect passages which he suggests could have been added to the original text. Louis Bréhier (ed.), *Histoire Anonyme de la Première Croisade* (Paris, 1924), vi.

[4] See Hill, *Gesta*, xvi and August C. Krey 'A neglected passage in the *Gesta* and its bearing on the literature of the First Crusade', in Louis J. Paetow (ed.), *The Crusades and Other Historical Essays presented to Dana C. Munro* (Freeport, NY, 1928), 78, n. 47.

[5] Helen Jewell asserts that chronicles 'were mainly the product of religious houses, and of authors who had little personal experience of women and much exposure to antifeminist texts'. Helen Jewell, *Women in Medieval England* (Manchester, 1996), 130.

[6] According to R. Howard Bloch, 'any essentialist definition of woman, whether negative or positive, whether made by a man or a woman, is the fundamental definition of misogyny'. *Medieval Misogyny and the Invention of Western Romantic Love* (Chicago and London, 1991), 6.

[7] Alcuin Blamires, *The Case for Women in Medieval Culture* (Oxford, 1997), 12.

[8] Pauline Stafford, 'The portrayal of royal women in England, mid-tenth to mid-twelfth centuries', in John Carmi Parsons (ed.), *Medieval Queenship* (Stroud, 1994), 144.

[9] Blamires, *Case for Women*, see Chapter 3, 'Honouring Mothers', 70–95.

[10] M. R. B. Shaw (trans.), *Joinville and Villehardouin; Chronicles of the Crusades* (London, 1963), 348.

[11] Jonathan Riley-Smith, *The First Crusaders (1095–1131)* (Cambridge, 1997), 97–98, and idem, 'Family traditions and participation in the second crusade', in Michael Gervers (ed.), *The Second Crusade and the Cistercians* (New York, 1992), 101–8.

[12] John Carmi Parsons, 'Family, sex, and power: the rhythms of medieval queenship', in John Carmi Parsons (ed.), *Medieval Queenship* (Stroud, 1994), 6.

[13] Helen J. Nicholson (trans.), *Itinerarium Peregrinorum et Gesta Regis Ricardi* (Aldershot and Vermont, 1997), 123.

[14] Shaw, *Joinville,* 182.

[15] Norman Daniel, *The Arabs and Mediaeval Europe* (London and Beirut, 1975), 195.

[16] Nicholson, *Itinerarium,* 120.

[17] Jacqueline de Weever, *Sheba's Daughters: Whitening and Demonising the Saracen Woman in Medieval French Epic* (New York and London, 1998), xii.

[18] Daniel, *Arabs,* 167.

[19] 'Quaedam illustris femina', WT 464.

[20] Hill, *Gesta,* 53.

[21] Ibid., 55.

[22] Ibid., 56.

[23] Ibid., xvi.

[24] My thanks to Professor P. M. Holt for this suggestion.

[25] Susan Edgington, 'Romance and reality in the sources for the sieges of Antioch, 1097–8', forthcoming in Charalambos Dendrinos, Jonathan Harris, Eirene Harvalia-Crook and Judith Herrin (eds.), *Porphyrogenita: Essays in Honour of Julian Chrysostomides* (Aldershot, 2003).

[26] Shaw, *Joinville,* 173.

[27] For example, Isaac Angelus is portrayed as being protected by his mother in the *Itinerarium*. Nicholson, *Itinerarium,* 21.

[28] Robert, *RHC Oc* 3, 812.

[29] For instance, Alice of Antioch, who became regent for her daughter Constance on the death of her husband Bohemond II of Antioch. She was condemned by William of Tyre for acting in her own interests. WT 623.

[30] See n. 2.

[31] Hill, *Gesta,* 54.

[32] Colin Morris, 'The Gesta Francorum as narrative history', *Reading Medieval Studies* 19 (1993), 55–71.

[33] 'Fili, Pharaonem, regem Aegyph, quis submersit in mori Rubro, cum omni exercitu suo? Quis exhaereditavit Seon, regem Amorreorum, et Og, regem Basan, et omnia regna Cha naam, et dedit suis in haaredidatem?' *RHC Oc* 3, 812.

[34] Guibert of Nogent states that he took up the project to correct a previous work in his introduction. Huygens, *Guibert,* 80. Robert the Monk asserts that he undertook his history at the request of the Abbot Bernard, because he had been present at the Council of Clermont, and in order to compose the history in a more careful style. Robert, RHC *Oc* 3, 721. For propaganda drive see A. C. Krey, 'A neglected passage', 68–76.

[35] Baldric *RHC Oc* 4, 62.

[36] '*de filio suo nimium suspecta*', Huygens, *Guibert,* 216.

[37] Including soothsayers, magi and prophets, oracles, entrails and animal limbs. Robert, *RHC Oc* 3, 813–14.

[38] Peter W. Edbury (ed.), *The Conquest of Jerusalem and the Third Crusade* (Aldershot, 1996), 40.

[39] John Hugh Hill and Laurita L. Hill (trans.), *Raymond d'Aguilers, Historia Francorum Qui Ceperunt Iherusalem* (Philadelphia, 1968), 126.

[40] Thomas S. Asbridge and Susan B. Edgington, *Walter the Chancellor's The Antiochene Wars* (Aldershot, 1999), 120.

[41] Huygens, *Guibert*, 105–6.

[42] Natalis de Wailly (ed.), *Récits d'un ménéstral de Riems au troisième siècle* (Paris, 1876), 192.

[43] '*Ad haec Curbaran ex materni miraculo serminos redditur hebes*'. Huygens, *Guibert*, 215.

[44] Robert, *RHC Oc* 3, 811.

[45] Ibid., 813.

[46] See n. 2.

[47] John France, 'The Anonymous Gesta Francorum and the Historia Francorum qui ceperunt Iherusalem of Raymond of Aguilers and the Historia de Hierosolymitano itinere of Peter Tudebode: an analysis of the textual relationship between primary sources for the First Crusade', in *Crusades Sources*, 42.

[48] 'The Anonymous enjoyed retailing fabulous stories and what was probably camp gossip about, for example, Kerbogha's mother or Emperor Alexius, while the story of Mirdalin and Kerbogha playing chess as the crusaders sallied out from Antioch is the only example in the *Historia*.' Ibid., 56–7.

[49] '*Tu autem in hoc bello non morieris modo, sed tamen in hoc anno*'. Hill, *Gesta*, 54.

[50] Ibid., 54, n. 7.

[51] In Ibn Al-Athir's *Histoire des Atabecs de Mosul* Kerbogha's death is cited as 494 (1100–1101) *RHC Or* 2: 31. In *Extraid Du Kamel-Altevarykh* under the year 495 of Hegira (AD 1101 and 1102) is the following quote 'Kerbouca, whose surname was Kivan-ed Daule (according to the empire) died this year in the month of Doulcada (September 1102)'. *RHC Hist. Or.* 1: 208. The *Annales D'Aboulfeda* also has Kerbogha dying in 495 (Paris, 1872) *RHC Hist. Or.* 1: 6. For the date of Kerbogha's death as 1102, see Baldric of Dol, *Historia*, 63 [n. a]; Hill and Hill, *Peter Tudebode* 70, n. 12; W. B. Stevenson, *The Crusaders in the East* (Cambridge, 1958), 121, on 121, n. 3; S. Runciman, *A History of the Crusades: The Kingdom of Jerusalem* (Cambridge, 1952), 41; and C. Cahen, *La Syrie du Nord à l'époque des croisades et la principauté d'Antioche* (Paris, 1940), 237. Rosalind Hill asserts that Kerbogha died sometime between 26 October 1101 and 14 October 1102, but does not refer to a source. Hill, *Gesta*, 54.

[52] Morris, *Gesta*, 66.

[53] France, 'The Anonymous Gesta', 58. Fink asserts that Fulcher of Chartres was writing before the death of Stephen of Blois in 1102, using the *Gesta* and Raymond which were finished 'between late 1100 and late 1101'. Fink, *Fulcher*, 20. Also see Susan Edgington, 'The First Crusade: reviewing the evidence', in Jonathan Phillips (ed.), *The First Crusade Origins and Impact* (Manchester, 1997), 55–77.

[54] Hill and Hill, *Peter Tudebode*, 10. See Ekkehard of Aura, *Hierosolymitana, RHC Oc* 5, 21.

[55] Hill and Hill, *Peter Tudebode*, 69, n. 1.

[56] Possible parallels could be drawn with Saracen heroines of the *chansons de gestes*, although these are normally required to betray their own kin to the Christians. See De Weever, *Sheba's Daughters,* xii.

[57] See Hill, *Gesta* , xvi, and Krey, 'A neglected passage', 78, n. 47.

13

The Crusader's Departure and Return: A Much Later Perspective

ELIZABETH SIBERRY

Medieval poets and chroniclers wrote of the sacrifice made by the crusader as he left his home, wife and family for an uncertain future, and of the legal and personal consequences of long absences and uncertainty for the womenfolk left behind. This theme was picked up by much later writers.[1] As I have discussed elsewhere,[2] the crusades as a subject appealed to the nineteenth-century romantic artist, poet, novelist and composer, and one of the standard themes and images was the impact upon the crusader's wife, sister or daughter of his departure, lengthy absence and then sometimes unexpected return. This offered plenty of scope for individual artistic interpretation and became an important strand in the development of the popular image of the crusades and crusaders, inspiring works of variable quality.

One nineteenth-century artist who seems to have been particularly interested in the image of the departing and returned crusader was the Pre-Raphaelite John Everett Millais. There are two pen and ink drawings dated 1846, entitled *The Crusader's Departure* and *The Crusader's Return*, which depict the family assembling to mark the crusader's departure and a more sombre gathering around a warrior's tomb, which seems to indicate that the returning crusader had been given up for dead by his unhappy family.[3] The list of Millais's works compiled by his son John Guille Millais includes other crusader sketches and a drawing of *The Crusader's Bride* (1863),[4] and there is also an oil entitled *The Departure of the Crusaders* in the collection of the Art Gallery at Oldham, which dates from 1857–8.[5] It was apparently a sketch intended for a larger work entitled *The Crusader's Return* which Millais commenced in 1857, after discussions with his fellow artist Holman Hunt. The larger work was, however, never completed and the frustrations associated with it were recorded in a notebook kept by Millais's wife in 1858:

> Mr Millais began a last picture of a crusader's return and stuck, after 5 months' hard labour. I was much averse to his painting every Sunday, and thought no good would come of it, as he took no rest, and hardly proper time for his meals. He made no progress, only getting into a greater mess, so when spring came, we were thankful to pack up the picture and go to Scotland.[6]

The uncertainty of life for the absent crusader's wife was the subject of a pencil drawing by the artist James Joseph Tissot, inspired by a medieval Breton ballad collected and published by Vicomte Hersart de la Villemarque, with an English translation in 1865 by the playwright and editor of *Punch*, Tom Taylor.[7] Tissot illustrated the scene as the lord of Le Faouet, near Quimperlé in Brittany, returns from a long crusade to find that his wife, having refused his brother's attempts to seduce her, has been left to tend the sheep:

> For a space of seven long years she wept, a mournful thing,
> At the end of seven long years she set herself to sing,
> When a young knight, from the Holy War that homeward chanced to ride,
> He heard a sweet voice singing on the mountain side . . .
>
> 'But tell me, tell me, pretty one, where now thy lord may be,
> For methinks upon thy finger a wedding ring I see.'
> 'Unto the Holy War, sweet sir, went this dear lord of mine,
> Oh! long and fair his golden hair hung down, as fair as thine.'
>
> 'If long and fair hung down his hair like mine, look well on me,
> If I am not thy very lord, that went away from thee.'
> 'Oh, yes!, oh yes! and I'm your love, your wedded wife am I,
> The lady of Faouet I was called in days gone by.'
>
> 'Now leave thy sheep, my gentle love, upon the hills to stray,
> And ride we to the manor; my wrath brooks no delay.'

The lord of Faouet duly challenges and rebukes his brother for the way in which he has abused his trust.[8] The origins of the story or ballad are more difficult to establish. In his notes, Villemarque states that it was probably the First Crusade and there were certainly Breton crusaders in the army of Robert of Normandy. Their involvement is, for example, mentioned in the *Historia Jherosolimitana* by Baldric, archbishop of Dol,[9] but I have not been able to identify any reference to a lord of Le Faouet.

Another painter who seems to have been attracted by the idea of the departing, absent and returning crusader and his family was William Bell Scott, a close associate of Rossetti. Bell Scott produced at least three works entitled *Return (or Returned) from the Long Crusade*. The first, a study which was exhibited at the Dudley Gallery in 1865, depicts a rather wild-looking crusader, in pilgrim's garb, who receives a wary welcome from his wife and son, who hides behind his mother, dubious about this apparent stranger. *The Illustrated London News* described the work as a 'representation of the return, after long absence, of a crusader, who, half knight, half palmer, presents an appearance so grotesque as to be scarcely recognised by his astonished wife'.[10] A second smaller study varied this scene but with the same three characters, and in a work dated 1886 the returning crusader is met by a larger family, but with similar caution.[11]

A very different crusade reunion scene was the subject of a bronze *Wilhelm and Lenore* by the eminent Victorian sculptor, Sir Joseph Boehm. Drawing on the 1796 translation by Sir Walter Scott of Gottfried August Bürger's romance *Lenore*, the sculpture shows Lenore being carried away at dead of night by the spectre of her dead crusader lover to his open grave. To add atmosphere, the details on the tombstone include a lizard and skull. A terracotta of the sculpture was exhibited at the Royal Academy in 1867 and the bronze version was purchased by the then Prince of Wales and is still in the Royal Collection.[12]

In similarly macabre vein, the poem *Châtivel or The Lay of Love's Unfortunate*, by Arthur O'Shaughnessy, another friend of Rossetti, recounts how the spectre of Lady Sarrazine's beloved returns from his tomb in the East to challenge a rival for her love; a fight which lasts till doom.[13] And a writer who styled himself QED wrote of a squire who returned from crusade with the embalmed heart of his lord. He is intercepted by a jealous husband who tricks his wife into eating her lover's heart. When she discovers what has happened, she starves herself to death. The British Library copy of this work bears an inscription stating that it was presented by the author to Gladstone as 'an authentic episode from the holy wars'.[14] The

William Bell Scott's Return from the Crusade *(watercolour),*
reproduced by permission of Elizabeth Siberry.

painter George Cattermole depicted a scene in which a crusader's wife attempted to prevent his departure. In *The Warning*, dated *c.*1868, the prospective crusader is shown in his armoury preparing for departure. Unbeknown to him, his wife has persuaded a retainer to hide in a suit of armour and warn him against the perils of crusading. The baron, thinking the warning comes from the spirits of his ancestors, abandons his design.[15]

Not surprisingly, the idea of the departing and returning crusader appealed to the early nineteenth-century Romantic novelist and poet. For example, it provided the inspiration for Sir Walter Scott's novel, *The Betrothed*, published, along with *The Talisman*, as one of the *Tales of the Crusaders* in 1825. In his Introduction, Scott wrote:

> It was no unusual thing for a crusader, returning from his long toils of war and pilgrimage, to find his family augmented by some young offshoot, of whom the deserted matron could give no very accurate account, or perhaps to find his marriage-bed filled, and that, instead of becoming nurse to an old man, his household dame had preferred being the lady love of a young one. Numerous are the stories of this kind told in different parts of Europe; and the returned knight or baron, according to his temper, sat down good-naturedly, contented with the account which his lady gave of a doubtful matter, or called in blood and fire to vindicate his honour, which, after all, had been endangered chiefly by his forsaking his household gods to seek adventures in Palestine.

The plot of *The Betrothed*, which was apparently inspired by conversations about Welsh history and antiquities between Scott and his friend Archdeacon Williams,[16] concerned the Norman constable of Chester, Hugo de Lacy, and his affianced, Eveline de Berenger. In his absence on the Third Crusade, Eveline becomes attached to his much younger nephew Damian, who has been appointed by his uncle to look after her. On his return, the constable has to accept his fate and the couple are duly married.[17]

The subject of the absent and returning crusader also provided inspiration for two female writers: Felicia Hemans (née Browne) and Letitia Landon. Both are relatively unknown today, but in their own time they were very popular and their works went through numerous editions. Felicia Dorothea Hemans was born in Liverpool in 1793, the daughter of a merchant and banker. Her marriage to Captain Hemans, who had fought in the Peninsular War, was short and unsuccessful and she turned her attention to poetry, spending most of her life near St Asaph in north Wales until her early death in 1835. She corresponded with contemporary writers such as Wordsworth and Shelley and her publishing record is illustrated by the 144 entries in the British Library catalogue. Her collected poems, for example, went through six editions between 1836 and 1872.[18] I have written elsewhere about the range of Mrs Hemans's works on the subject of the crusades,[19] but there is one particular poem of interest in the context of this chapter, 'The Crusader's Return', which seems to have been inspired by a scene from Scott's *Marmion* (Canto 1: xxiii–xxviii). It begins thus:

> Rest pilgrim, rest-thou'rt from the Syrian land,
> Thou'rt from the wild and wondrous east, I know,
> By the long withered palm-branch in thy hand,
> And by the darkness of thy sunburnt brow.
> Alas, the bright, the beautiful, who part,
> So full of hope, for that far country's bourne
> Alas, the weary and the changed in heart,
> And dimmed in aspect, who like thee return.

The onlooker proceeds to lament the absence of her only son, 'who heard the trumpet of the Red Cross blow', and ponders his fate. Then with joy she recognizes his features in the sunburnt pilgrim.

Letitia Elizabeth Landon, known as LEL, was born in 1802 and was a regular contributor to publications as diverse as the *Literary Gazette* and *The Drawing Room Scrap Book* by the age of twenty. She, again, had a short and unhappy married life with a Captain Maclean and died in Africa in 1838.[20] Her *Collected Poems* went through six editions between 1827 and 1850 and a few deal with the crusades. In 'The Crusader' the knight returns full of expectation:

> He is come from the land of the sword and shrine,
> From the sainted battles of Palestine;
> The snow plumes wave o'er his victor crest,
> Like a glory the red cross hangs at his breast;
> His courser is as black as black can be,
> Save the brow star white as the foam of the sea,
> And he wears a scarf of broidery rare,
> The last love gift of his lady fair.

The news which greets him is, however, that his family is no more, his castle fallen to ruin and his beloved in her grave:

> They pointed him to a barren plain
> Where his father, his brothers, his kinsmen were slain;
> They showed him the lowly grave, where slept
> The maiden whose scarf he so truly had kept;
> But they could not show him one living thing
> To which his withered heart could cling.

The crusades also formed the background to one of Landon's longer works, *The Troubadour*, published in three cantos in 1825. The story is woven around the crusader Raymond and his love Eva, who has a tragic family history also linked with the crusades. Whilst on crusade, Raymond's life is saved by Amirald, who turns out to be Eva's father in exile. After a spell in Muslim captivity, Raymond returns home. He exchanges his helm and sword for 'the lute and one sweet song to urge his suit' and they are happily reunited. And in the anonymous poem 'The Last Crusader' (1867), the Norman knight Menteeth returns from the crusade just in time to save his beloved Lurline from a forced marriage.

A further variation on this theme was the wife who, anxious not to be parted from her husband, accompanies him on crusade, but in disguise so that he is not aware of her identity. This is, for example, the subject of 'The Romaunt of the Page' by Elizabeth Barrett Browning, published in 1844, and apparently one of her husband Robert Browning's favourites. The poem ends tragically. Having saved her husband's life in battle on several occasions, the page dies without revealing her identity.[21]

One of the familiar troubadour themes was the departure scene as the crusader left his beloved for the uncertainties of war, and a nineteenth-century version of this can be found in 'The Crusader's Farewell' by the Scottish poet William Motherwell, which appeared in his popular *Minstrelsy Ancient and Modern* published in 1827.

> The banners rustle in the breeze,
> The angry trumpets swell;
> They call me, lady, from thy arms,
> They bid me sigh farewell!
>
> They call me to a distant land,
> To quell a paynim foe;
> To leave the blandishments of love
> For danger, strife and woe.

> Yet deem not, lady, though afar
> It be my hap to roam,
> That e'er my constant heart shall stray
> From love, from thee, and home.
>
> No! in the tumult of the fight,
> Midst Salem's chivalrie,
> The thought that arms this hand with death
> Shall be the thought of thee.

Motherwell was another enthusiast for the Middle Ages and a memoir of his life by James McConechy, published as an Introduction to the 1846 edition, recalled how at school he would keep his fellow classmates amused with stories about castles and exotic adventures and sketched figures of mailed knights.[22] 'The Crusader's Farewell' was subsequently set to music and published as a song[23] and similar farewell poems provided the lyrics of a number of Victorian parlour songs, of which more later.

A satirical perspective on the implications of the crusader's departure and return can be found in a collection of stories entitled *The Ingoldsby Legends* by Richard Harris Barham, a minor canon of St Paul's Cathedral in London. The individual stories were first published in *Bentley's Miscellany*, but the collected *Legends* appeared in 1840 and proved an instant success. In fact, between 1857 and 1864 over 55,000 copies of the *Legends* were printed in twenty-three different editions and an 1881 edition sold over 60,000 copies on the first day. Allegedly based on extracts from the Ingoldsby family history deposited in an old oak chest at the family home, Tappington Hall, the *Legends* drew loosely on Kentish legend. However fanciful, they appealed to a wide audience, from, as one commentator noted, fervent high churchmen to devotees of romance.[24]

Given Barham's knowledge of and passion for the Middle Ages, it is not surprising that several of the *Legends* make reference to the crusades. 'The Ingoldsby Penance' tells the story of Sir Ingoldsby Bray, a member of the Third Crusade, who in a jealous rage murders his wife Dame Alice, whom he suspects of having been unfaithful during his absence, and who founds Ingoldsby Abbey as a penance. In the 'Lay of St Gengulphus', Gengulphus returns from the East and is greeted joyfully by his wife who claims that she has barely slept with worry over his fate. However, in the night, she and her lover, a 'learned clerk', kill and dismember Gengulphus. They are found out when Gengulphus's head is drawn up with water from the well. The body then gradually reassembles in front of the guests and Gengulphus subsequently performs a number of miracles. The legend concludes with a moral for those who return unexpectedly from a long absence in the Holy Land:

> Now you grave married pilgrims who wander away,
> Like Ulysees of old (vide Homer and Naso),
> Don't lengthen your stay to three years and a day,
> And when you are coming home, just write and say so.

> And you, learned Clerks, who're not given to roam,
> Stick close to your books, nor lose sight of decorum;
> Don't visit a house when the master's from home:
> Shun drinking – and study the *Vitae sanctorum*.

> Above all, you gay ladies, who fancy neglect
> In your spouses, allow not your patience to fall;
> But remember Gengulphus's wife – and reflect
> On the moral enforced by her terrible tale.[25]

One of the Breton ballads collected by Villemarque, 'The Clerk of Rohan', also told the story of Mathieu de Beauvais, a member of the crusade of 1239/41, whose wife, Jeanne de Rohan, and son fall victim during his absence to the wicked clerk of Rohan. He writes to the crusader suggesting that his wife has been unfaithful and announcing the death (in fact murder) of his baby son. Beauvais returns and kills his innocent wife. Her spectre then haunts the churchyard.[26]

The fate of the crusader's wife or sister was also the subject of at least three operas – Verdi's *Aroldo* (1857); Rossini's *Count Ory* (1828) and Schubert's *Der häusliche Krieg* (1823) – and Glazunov's ballet *Raymonda* (1898).[27] Verdi's *Aroldo* was a reworking of his *Stiffelio* and told the story of Mina, who has been unfaithful to her husband Aroldo during his absence on the Third Crusade. Her father Egberto kills her lover Godvino and the couple part. In the end, however, they are reunited, rather strangely for an Italian opera, on the shores of Loch Lomond in Scotland. Rossini's *Count Ory* was much more frivolous. His Ory attempts to infiltrate himself, disguised first as a hermit and then as a nun, into the castle of the count of Fourmoutiers and the affections of his sister Adele and her female

retinue, while the count is away on crusade, possibly the Fourth
Crusade. In the nick of time, the victorious crusaders return and Ory
is forced to flee. In a different vein, *Der häusliche Krieg* (Domestic
Warfare) tells the story of wives who object to their husbands'
absence on crusade and eventually persuade them to abandon their
weapons of war for 'weapons of love and tenderness'.[28] And in
Raymonda, John of Brienne arrives home from crusade just in time
to save his fiancée from being abducted by the Saracen
Abderakhman.

There were also a number of songs on the theme of the departing
crusader by composers and lyricists who were popular in their own
day but are now long forgotten. For example 'The Crusader', published by Chappells in 1829 and priced 2*s.*, with words by Frederick
Fox Cooper and music by Augustus Meves, runs as follows:

> The warrior sprang on his jet black steed,
> his plume on his helmet waving,
> as onto battle he hied with speed,
> each hour of danger braving.
> Twas then to the mouldering battlements flew
> the lovely Isabel,
> who with tears on her cheek like pearly dew,
> was sighing oh my true love farewell.
>
> Sweet Isabel said Sir knight,
> go win thee a wreath of glory.
> The minstrel shall sing of the glorious day,
> when telling his eastern story,
> the chords of the harp shall strike to thy praise.
> Your fame in the Holy Land dwell,
> when the sun o'er blest victory darts his rays,
> till then O my true love farewell.

The title-page depicted a crusader on horseback riding away as his
lady waves a handkerchief from a castle tower. In a later song ('The
Crusader', 1892), with words and music by Henry St Clair and
Valentine Hemery respectively, the departing knight takes with him
as a token a lock of his beloved's golden hair: 'thy gage shall be my
flowing crest in distant Palestine'. And there were other songs
recounting the crusader's return. For example, the opening verse of
'The Crusader's Return' (1850) by Miss Lydia Smith, with words
from Scott, runs as follows:

The title page of the song 'The Crusader', composed by Augustus Meres, with words by Frederick Fox Cooper, published in 1829.

> High deeds achiev'd of knightly fame,
> from Palestine the Champion came,
> The Cross upon his shoulders borne
> battle and blast had dimm'd and torn,
> Each dint upon his batter'd shield
> was token of a foughten field,
> And thus beneath his lady's bow'r
> he sung as fell the twilight hour.[29]

The full sequence of events is covered in 'The Crusader', composed by Theo Bonheur and with words by Samuel Cowan and published in 1886. It begins, in *tempo di marcia*, with the crusader taking leave of his beloved with the vow that he will remain true to his love and honour. The next verse is an *andante religioso*, as the lady prays in the cloister that her knight will return unharmed. Returning to the original tempo, the war is done, the knight returns and 'beauty weds with chivalry'.[30]

Such songs are long and probably best forgotten, but at the time they would have been available individually and in published collections for home entertainment. And, together with poems, novels and paintings, either seen at first hand or as illustrations in journals and books, they would have played their part in creating a popular romantic nineteenth-century image of the crusader, his departure and his return.

NOTES

[1] For this theme in medieval poetry, see M. Routledge, 'Songs', in J. S. C. Riley-Smith (ed.), *The Oxford Illustrated History of the Crusades* (Oxford, 1995), 91–111 and J. E. Siberry, 'Troubadours, trouvères and minnesingers and the crusades', *Studi Medievali,* 3rd series, 29/1 (1988), 19–43. In his *England and the Crusades* (Chicago, 1988), 208–15, 417–18, C. Tyerman also writes of the domestic repercussions such as legal suits and challenges to the legality of marriages of long-absent crusaders. See also Riley-Smith, 'The state of mind of crusaders to the East 1095–1300', in idem (ed.), *Oxford Illustrated History*, 73–4.

[2] J. E. Siberry, *The New Crusaders: Images of the Crusades in the Nineteenth and Early Twentieth Centuries* (Aldershot, 2000).

[3] *The Crusader's Departure* now seems to be in a private collection; its pair is in the Ashmolean Museum, Oxford.

⁴ J. G. Millais *The Life and Letters of John Everett Millais* (London, 1899), vol. 2.

⁵ Illustrated in P. Bate, *The English Pre Raphaelite Painters, their Associates and Successors* (London, 1901), 34. The oil formed part of a collection assembled by the prominent Oldham industrialist Charles E. Lees, who was involved in the establishment of the Oldham Art Gallery in 1883 and was a founder governor of the Whitworth Institute in Manchester in 1889. See T. Coombs, *Watercolours: The Charles Lees Collection at Oldham Art Gallery* (Oldham, 1993).

⁶ Quoted in Millais, *The Life and Letters of John Everett Millais*, 1, p. 311.

⁷ 'The Crusader's Wife', in T. Taylor (ed.), *Ballads and Songs of Brittany* (London, 1865), 71–7. The original was in La Villemarque's *Barzaz Breiz: Chants populaires de la Bretagne* (4th edn., Paris, 1846), 146–50.

⁸ Tissot's drawing was much admired by Rossetti, who wrote to the publishers asking for a copy. See L. M. Packer (ed.), *The Rossetti–Macmillan Letters* (Cambridge, 1963), 41. It also inspired a wood engraving by Millais. In 1810 the popular Astley's amphitheatre had also staged a hippodrama, entitled *The Blood Red Knight,* about an attempt to seduce the virtuous wife of an absent crusader.

⁹ See Baldric of Dol, *Historia Jherosolimitana*, in *RHC Oc* 4: 18–27. For Breton crusaders in general, see J. Riley-Smith, *The First Crusade and the Idea of Crusading* (London, 1986), 77, 136, and idem, *The First Crusaders (1095–1131)* (Cambridge, 1997). There is no reference to a lord of Faouet in the list of crusaders published by M. Pitre-Chevalier, *La Bretagne ancienne* (Paris, 1859), 144–9.

¹⁰ *The Illustrated London News* (25 February 1865), 190.

¹¹ I am grateful to Sotheby's for these references from their sales catalogues.

¹² Illustrated in *Princes as Patrons: The Art Collections of the Princes of Wales from the Renaissance to the Present Day, an Exhibition from the Royal Collection at the Museum of Wales* (London, 1998), 139. See also M. Stocker, *Royalist and Realist: The Life and Work of Sir Joseph Edgar Boehm* (London, 1988), 310–11.

¹³ *Châtivel* was published in *The Lays of France* (1872). O'Shaughnessy's career provides an interesting example of Victorian eclecticism. He worked in the printed books and natural history department of the British Museum and, as well as publishing volumes of poetry, became an acknowledged expert on fish and reptiles. See C. W. Reilly, *Mid-Victorian Poetry 1860–79: An Annotated Bibliography* (London, 1999).

¹⁴ See QED, *The Knight's Heart* (Belfast, 1875).

¹⁵ The story is explained in Cattermole's hand on the wooden backing of the painting, but without any indication of sourcing.

[16] See J. Lockhart, *Memoirs of the Life of Sir Walter Scott* (Edinburgh, 1878), 2: 549.

[17] Scott was also inspired by a story of a returning crusader, Sir William Bradshaigh of Haigh Hall, near Wigan, Lancs, who, finding that his wife Mabel had remarried, killed her new husband, a Welsh knight. The couple then did penance for their actions and were buried in the church of All Saints' Wigan. See Siberry, *New Crusaders*, 43–4.

[18] See P. W. Trinder, *Mrs Hemans* (Cardiff, 1984); *Dictionary of National Biography (DNB)* (1908 edn.), 9: 382–3. Her sister Mrs Hughes also wrote a biographical memoir published in 1839.

[19] See Siberry, *New Crusaders*, 131–3.

[20] See *DNB*, 9: 493–4; Landon, *Poetical Works*, 1 (London, 1853), pp. ix–xix.

[21] M. Forster, *Elizabeth Barrett Browning* (London, 1988), 130, 144. See also Nicolas Michell, *The Saxon's Daughter: A Tale of the Crusades* (London, 1835).

[22] W. Motherwell, *Poems* (Paisley, 1881), pp. vi, xiv. *DNB* 13: 1090–1.

[23] 'The Crusader's Farewell', music by Frederick Westlake, 1881.

[24] W. G. Lane, *Richard Harris Barham* (Columbia, MO, 1967), 214–17; *Cambridge History of English Literature* (Cambridge, 1915), 123.

[25] *The Ingoldsby Legends*, 'A Lay of St Gengulphus', 67–78; 'The Ingoldsby Penance', 205–21.

[26] See 'The Clerk of Rohan', in *Ballads and Songs of Brittany*, 79–92; Villemarque, *Barzaz Breiz*, 260–3.

[27] Siberry, *New Crusaders*, 181–3.

[28] The title of Schubert's opera was originally *Die Verschwörenen* (The Conspirators), but this was considered dangerous by the censors, who preferred *Domestic Warfare*. Not performed until 1861, well after Schubert's death, the libretto by the Austrian playwright Ignaz Castelli inspired the British composer Henry Hiles to write an operetta with the same title in 1884.

[29] See also 'The Crusader's Bride' (1830 – music by G. A. Hodson and words by J. O'Donoghue) and 'The Crusader's Farewell' (1835 – music by Mrs Richard Groom, née Wilkinson, and words by Miss Fanny Kemble).

[30] Two dramatic cantatas – *Y Croesgadwr* by Benjamin Parsons (1889) and *The Crusader* by Thomas Facer (1893) – also feature the crusader's beloved who is left at home whilst he goes to Jerusalem. In both cases, after various trials and tribulations, the story ends happily. See Siberry, *New Crusaders*, 184–6.

Bibliography

MANUSCRIPTS

Cambridge University Library: Geniza collection: CUL add. 3388; ENA
2808; TS 16.250; TS 20.138; TS NS 176, 2–3; TS NS J 270.
Wiesbaden, Hessische Landesbibliothek 2, fo. 341r-v.

PRIMARY SOURCES

Note: Victorian primary sources, for E. Siberry's chapter, are listed as
secondary.

Abou'l-feda, *Annales*, in *RHC Or* 1: 1–165.
*Acta sanctorum quotquot toto orbe coluntur: Vel a catholicis scriptoribus cele-
brantur quæ ex latinis & græcis, aliarumque gentium antiquis monumentis*,
ed. Joannes Bollandus and Godefridus Henschenius, 2nd edn., ed. Joanne
Carnandet, 70 vols. and supplement (Brussels, Paris and Rome, 1863–75).
Albert of Aachen, *Liber christianae expeditionis pro ereptione, emundatione
et restitutione sanctae Hierosolymitanae ecclesiae*, in *RHC Oc* 4: 269–713.
Ambroise, *Estoire de la Guerre Sainte: Histoire en vers de la Troisième
Croisade*, ed. Gaston Paris (Paris, 1897).
——, *The Crusade of Richard Lion-heart*, trans. and ed. M. J. Hubert and J.
L. LaMonte (New York, 1941).
Analecta S. Hildegardis, in *Analecta Sacra* 8, ed. J.-B. Pitra (Monte Cassino,
1882).
Anna Comnena, *Alexiade*, ed. B. Leib (3 vols., Paris, 1937–45).
——, *The Alexiad*, ed. and trans. E. R. A. Sewter (Harmondsworth, 1969).
Annales Londonienses, in *Chronicles of the Reigns of Edward I and Edward II*,
ed. William Stubbs, RS 76 (London, 1882).
Arnoldi, *Chronica Slavorum*, ed. G. Pertz, *MGH Scriptores rerum
Germanicarum* 21 (Hanover, 1859).

Baldric of Bourgueil, *Historia Jherosolimitana*, in *RHC Oc* 4: 1–111.

Beha Ed-din, *The Life of Saladin 1137–1193*, trans. C. W. Wilson, *PPTS* 13 (London, 1897).

Bernard of Clairvaux, *Epistola ad Eugenium*, in *RHGF* 15, 603.

——, *Liber ad milites Templi de laude novae militiae*, in *S. Bernardi opera*, ed. Jean Leclercq, C. H. Talbot and H. M. Rochais (8 vols., Rome, 1957–77), 3: 213–39.

Cartulaire de S. Lazare, ed. A. de Marsy, *AOL* 2 (1884).

Cartulaire général de l'ordre des hospitaliers de S. Jean de Jérusalem, 1130–1310, ed. J. Joseph Delaville Le Roulx (4 vols., Paris, 1894–1906).

Cartulaire du chapitre de Saint-Sépulcre de Jérusalem, ed. G. Bresc-Bautier (Paris, 1984).

Cartulaires des abbayes d'Aniane et de Gellone (Montpellier, 1898–1900).

Chanson d'Antioche, ed. S. Duparc-Quioc (2 vols., Paris, 1977).

Chartes inédites concernant les comtes de Hainaut, ed. C. Duvivier (Brussels, 1904).

Clef des Assises de la Haute Cour, in *RHC Lois* 1: 573–600.

Conquête de Jerusalem faisant suite à la Chanson d'Antioche composée par le pelerin Richard, ed. C. Hippeau (Paris, 1868).

Continuation de Guillaume de Tyr (1184–1197), ed. M. R. Morgan (Paris, 1982).

Continuation of William of Tyre, trans. P. W. Edbury as *The Conquest of Jerusalem and the Third Crusade* (Aldershot, 1996).

Corpus juris canonici, ed. P. Lancelot (Lugduni, 1591).

Councils of Urban II. 1. Decreta Claromontensia, ed. Robert Somerville (*Annuarium Historiae Conciliorum Supplementum, 1*; Amsterdam, 1972).

Coutumiers de Normandie, ed. E. Tardif (Paris and Rouen, 1896).

Decrees of the Ecumenical Councils I: Nicea to Lateran V, ed. G. Alberigo and N. P. Tanner (Washington, DC, 1990).

Documents relatifs à la successibilité, in *RHC Lois* 2: 393–422.

Du Bon William Longespee, ed. Simon Lloyd, in 'William Longespee II: the making of an English crusading hero', *Nottingham Medieval Studies* 36 (1992), 110–21.

Ekkehard of Aura, *Hierosolymitana*, in *RHC Oc* 5: 11–40.

Ennodius of Arles, *Carmina*, in *PL* 63, cols. 309–62.

Epistulae et chartae ad historiam primi belli sacri spectantes: Die Kreuzzugsbriefe aus den Jahren 1088–1100, ed. H. Hagenmeyer (Innsbruck, 1901).

Ernoul, *Chronique d'Ernoul et de Bernard Le Tresorier*, ed. M. L. de Mas Latrie (Paris, 1871).

Estoire d'Eracles Empereur et de la Conqueste de la Terre d'Outremer, in *RHC Oc* 2.

Estoires d'Outremer et de la naissance Salehadin, ed. Margaret A. Jubb (Westfield Publications in Medieval Studies, 4; London, 1990).

Établissements de St. Louis, ed. Paul Violet (Paris, 1881).

France, J. (ed.), 'The text of the account of the capture of Jerusalem in the Ripoll manuscript, Bibliothèque Nationale (latin) 5132', *EHR* 103 (1988), 640–57.

Fulcher of Chartres, *Historia Hierosolymitana (1095–1127)*, ed. Heinrich Hagenmeyer (Heidelberg, 1913).

——, *A History of the Expedition to Jerusalem 1095–1127*, ed. H. Fink and trans. F. R. Ryan (Knoxville, TN, 1969).

Gabrieli, F. (trans.), *Arab Historians of the Crusades* (Berkeley, CA, 1969).

Gautier, P. (ed.), 'Le Typikon de la Théotokos Kécharitôménè', *Revue des Études Byzantines* 43 (1985), 5–165.

Gesta Francorum et aliorum Hierosolimitanorum, ed. and trans. Rosalind Hill (Edinburgh, 1962).

Gesta Francorum Hierusalem expugnantium, in *RHC Oc* 3: 491–543.

Gesta Regis Henrici Secundi, ed. W. Stubbs, RS 49 (2 vols., London, 1867).

Gestes des Chiprois, Recueil des chroniques françaises écrites en orient, ed. Gaston Raynaud (Publications de la Societé de l'Orient Latin, 5; Geneva, 1887).

Gislebert de Mons, *Chronique*, ed. L. Vanderkindere (Brussels, 1904).

Guibert de Nogent, *Dei gesta per Francos et cinq autres textes*, ed. R. B. C. Huygens, CCCM 127A (Turnhout, 1996).

Guibert of Nogent, *Gesta Dei per Francos*, in *RHC Oc* 4: 117–263.

——, *The Deeds of God through the Franks,* trans. R. Levine (Woodbridge, 1997).

Hildegard of Bingen, *Epistolarium*, ed. L. van Acker, *Pars prima I–XC*, CCCM 91; *Pars secunda XCL–CCLR*, CCCM 91A.

——, *Liber divinorum operum*, ed. A. Derolez and P. Dronke, CCCM 92.

——, *Liber vitae meritorum*, ed. A. Carlevaris, CCCM 90.

——, *Opera omnia, PL* 197.

——, *Scivias*, ed. A. Führkötter, CCCM 43–43A.

Histoire Anonyme de la Première Croisade, ed. Louis Bréhier (Paris, 1924).

Historia de expeditione Friderici imperatoris, ed. A. Chroust, MGH, new series, 5 (Berlin, 1928).

Historia Nicaena, in *RHC Oc* 5: 133–85.

Humbertus Romanus, *Opus tripartitum*, in *Concilia*, 24, ed. Mansi.

Ibn al-Athir, *Extrait du Kamel-Altevarykh*, in *RHC Or* 1: 189–744, and 2: 3–180.

——, *Histoire des Atabecs de Mosul*, in *RHC Or* 2, ii, 5–375.

Ibn al-Furat, *Ayyubids, Mamlukes and Crusaders: Selections from the Tarikh al-Duwal wa'l-Muluk of Ibn al-Furat*, ed. and trans. U. and M. C. Lyons (2 vols., Cambridge, 1971).

Ibn al-Qalanisi, *The Damascus Chronicle of the Crusades,* ed. H. A. R. Gibb (London, 1932).

Ibn Hijja al-Hamawi (Abu Bakr ibn Ali), *Thamarat al-awraq* (Cairo, 1971).

'Imad ad-Din al-Isfahani, *Kitab al-fath al qussi fi'l-fath al-qudsi,* trans. H. Masse as *La Conquête de la Syrie et de la Palestine par Saladin* (Paris, 1972).

Innocentius III, *Opera Omnia, PL* 214–17.

Itinerarium peregrinorum et gesta regis Ricardi, ed. William Stubbs, in *Chronicles and Memorials of the Reign of Richard I,* RS 38/1 (London, 1864).

Itinerarium Peregrinorum et Gesta Regis Ricardi, trans. H. J. Nicholson as *Chronicle of the Third Crusade* (Aldershot, 1997).

Itinerarium Peregrinorum: Eine zeitgenössische englische Chronik zum dritten Kreuzzug in ursprünglicher Gestalt, ed. Hans E. Mayer (Stuttgart, 1962).

Ivo Carnotensis, *Opera, PL* 162, cols. 9–616.

Jacobus de Voragine, *The Golden Legend: Readings on the Saints,* trans. William Granger Ryan (2 vols., Princeton, 1992).

Jacques de Vitry, *Lettres,* ed. R. B. C. Huygens (Leiden, 1960).

——, *Sermones,* in *Analecta novissima spicilegii solesmensis: altera continuatio,* 2: *Tusculana,* ed. J. P. Pitra (Paris, 1888).

James of Vitry, *Exempla,* ed. F. Crane (London, 1890).

Jean, sire de Joinville, *Histoire de Saint Louis,* ed. and trans. Natalis de Wailly (Paris, 1874).

——, *The History of St. Louis,* trans. Joan Evans (Oxford, 1938).

John of Salisbury, *Letters,* ed. W. J. Millor and C. N. L. Brooke (Oxford, 1979).

John Zonaras, *Epitome Historiarum,* ed. B. G. Nieburg (2 vols., Bonn, 1841–5).

Joinville and Villehardouin, *Chronicles of the Crusades,* trans. M. R. B. Shaw (Harmondsworth, 1963).

Krey, August C. (ed.), *The First Crusade: The Accounts of Eye-Witnesses and Participants* (Gloucester, MA, 1958).

Life of St Thaïs, ed. R. C. D. Perman, in 'Henri d'Arci: the shorter works', in E. A. Francis (ed.), *Studies in Medieval French Presented to Alfred Ewert in Honour of his Seventieth Birthday* (Oxford, 1961), 279–321.

Livre au Roi, ed. Myriam Greilsammer (Paris, 1995).

Livre au Roi, in *RHC Lois* 1: 601–44.

Livre de Geoffroy le Tort, in *RHC Lois* 1: 433–50.

Livre de Jacques d'Ibelin, in *RHC Lois* 1: 451–68.

Livre de Jean d'Ibelin, in *RHC Lois* 1: 1–430.

Livre de Philippe de Navarre, in *RHC Lois* 1: 469–571.

Livre des Assises de la Cour des Bourgeois, in *RHC Lois* 2: 5–226.

Livre des Juges: Les Cinq Textes de la version française faite au XII siècle pour les chevaliers du Temple, ed. le Marquis d'Albon (Lyons, 1913).

Michaelis Glycae Annales, ed. I. Bekker (Bonn, 1836).

Monumenta iuris canonici, ed. J. J. Ryan, ser. C, vol. 1 (Vatican City, 1965).

Niketas Choniates, *Annals*, ed. and trans. H. J. Magoulis as *'O City of Byzantium', Annals of Niketas Choniates* (Detroit, 1984).

Old French Crusade Cycle, 5: *Les Chétifs*, ed. G. M. Myers (Tuscaloosa, AL, 1981).

Old French Crusade Cycle, 6: *La Chanson de Jérusalem*, ed. N. R. Thorp (Tuscaloosa, AL, 1992).

Old French Crusade Cycle, 8: *The Jérusalem Continuations: The London–Turin Version*, ed. Peter R. Grillo (Tuscaloosa, AL, 1994).

Oliver of Paderborn, *The Capture of Damietta*, trans. J. J. Gavigan (New York, 1948).

Orderic Vitalis, *The Ecclesiastical History*, ed. and trans. Marjorie Chibnall (6 vols., Oxford, 1969–80).

Papsttum und Untergang des Templerordens, ed. Heinrich Finke (2 vols., Münster, 1907).

Papsturkunden für Templer und Johanniter: Vorarbeiten für den Oriens pontificus, 1, ed. Rudolf Hiestand (Göttingen, 1972).

Papsturkunden in Frankreich, 2: *Normandie*, ed. Johannes Ramackers (Göttingen, 1937).

Peter Tudebode, *Historia de Hierosolimitano Itinere*, trans. John Hugh and Laurita L. Hill (Philadelphia, 1974).

Peter von Dusburg, *Chronik des Preussenlandes*, ed. Klaus Scholz and Dieter Wojtecki (Darmstadt, 1984).

Philippe de Beaumanoir, *Coutumes de Beauvaisis*, trans. F. R. P. Akehurst (Philadelphia, 1992).

Philippi de Harveng, *Epistolae*, PL 203, cols. 1–180.

Philippi, *Descriptio Terrae Sanctae*, ed. W. A. Neumann, in 'Drei mittelalterliche Pilgerschriften III', *Oesterreichische Vierteljahresschrift für katholische Theologie* 9 (1872), 1–78.

Pierre Dubois, *De recuperatione Terre Sancte. Dalla Respublica Christiana ai primi nazionalismi e alla politica anti-mediterranea*, ed. A. Diotti (Florence, 1997).

Procès des Templiers, ed. Jules Michelet (2 vols., Paris, 1841–51).

Prutz, Hans (ed.), 'Ein zeitgenössisches Gedicht auf die Belagerung Accons', *Forschungen zur deutschen Geschichte* 21 (1889), 449–94.

Quinti belli sacri scriptores minores, ed. Reinhold Röhricht (Geneva, 1879).

Radulfi de Diceto, *Ymagines historiarum*, ed. William Stubbs, RS 68 (London, 1876).

Ramon Muntaner, *The Chronicle of Muntaner*, trans. Lady Goodenough (2 vols., London, 1920).

Rassow, Peter (ed.), 'Der Text der Krezzugsbulle Eugens III, vom 1. März 1146, Trastevere', *Neues Archiv* 45 (1924), 300–5.

Raymond of Aguilers, *Historia Francorum qui ceperunt Jerusalem*, in *RHC Oc* 3, 231–309.

——, *Historia Francorum qui ceperunt Iherusalem*, trans. John Hugh and Laurita L. Hill (Philadelphia, 1968).

Récits d'un ménéstrel de Reims au troisième siècle, ed. Natalis de Wailly (Paris, 1876).

Regesta Honorii Papae III, ed. Petrus Pressutti, 1 (Rome, 1888).

Regesta Pontificum Romanorum, ed. P. Jaffe (Leipzig, 1898).

'Régeste de Philippe d'Alsace, comte de Flandre', ed. H. Coppieters-Stochove, *Annales de la Société d'Histoire et Archéologie de Gand* 7 (1906), 1–177.

Register Gregors VII, ed. Erich Caspar, 1 (Berlin, 1967).

Register Innocenz' III, ed. O. Hageneder, A. Haidacher and H. Eberstaller, 1 (Graz, 1964).

Règle du Temple, ed. Henri de Curzon (Paris, 1886).

Reineri, *Annales, 1066–1230*, ed. G. Pertz (*MGH Scriptores rerum Germanicarum* 16; Hanover, 1859).

Robert the Monk, *Historia Ihierosolimitana*, in *RHC Oc* 3: 721–882.

Ruperti Tuitiensis, *De sancta Trinitate*, ed. Hr. Haacke, CCCM 23.

Sigeberti, *Continuatio aquicinctina (a.1149–1237)*, ed. G. H. Pertz, MGH SS 6: 405–38.

Song of Aspremont, ed. M. A. Newth (New York, 1989).

Song of Roland: An Analytical Edition, ed. G. J. Brault (2 vols., London, 1978).

Tabari, *Kitab al-Jihad*, ed. J. Schacht (Cairo, 1933).

Theodore Skutariotes, *Mesaionike Bibliotheke*, ed. K. Sathas (7 vols., Biblioteca Graeca Medii Aevii, 7; Paris, 1872–94).

Thomas of Froidmont, edn. in P. G. Schmidt, 'Peregrinatio Periculosa. Thomas von Froidmont über die Jerusalem-fahrten seiner Schwester Margareta', in U. Justus Stache, W. Maaz and F. Wagner (eds.), *Kontinuität und Wandel: Lateinische Poesie von Naevius bis Baudelaire: Franco Munari zum 65. Geburtstag* (Hildesheim, 1986), 461–85 (at 472–85).

Thousand Nights and a Night, ed. R. F. Burton (London, 1885).

Untergang des Templerordens mit urkundlichen und kritischen Beiträgen, ed. Konrad Schottmüller (2 vols., Berlin, 1887).

Usamah ibn-Munqidh, *An Arab-Syrian Gentleman and Warrior in the Period of the Crusades*, ed. and trans. P. K. Hitti (New York, 1929).

Villehardouin and De Joinville, *Memoirs of the Crusades*, trans. F. Marzials (London, 1908).

Vita Sanctae Hildegardis, ed. M. Klaes, CCCM 126.

Walter the Chancellor, *The Antiochene Wars*, ed. and trans. T. S. Asbridge and Susan B. Edgington (Aldershot, 1999).

William of Tyre, *A History of Deeds Done beyond the Sea*, trans. and ed. E. A. Babcock and A. C. Krey (2 vols., New York, 1943).

——, *Historia rerum in partibus transmarinis*, ed. R. B. C. Huygens, CCCM (Turnhout, 1986).

SECONDARY SOURCES

Acker, L. van, 'Der Briefwechsel der heiligen Hildegard von Bingen: Vorbemerkung zu einer kritischen Edition', *Revue Bénédictine* 98 (1988), 141–68; 99 (1989), 118–54.

Albu, E., 'Bohemond and the rooster: Byzantines, Normans and the artful ruse', in T. Gouma-Peterson (ed.), *Anna Komnene and her Times* (New York, 2000), 157–68.

Andressohn, John C., *The Ancestry and Life of Godfrey of Bouillon* (Bloomington, IN, 1947).

Arjava, A., 'Women and Roman Law in Late Antiquity', doctoral thesis (Helsinki, 1994).

Baker, Derek (ed.), *Medieval Women* (Oxford, 1978).

Balard, Michel (ed.), *Autour de la première croisade* (Paris, 1996).

Barber, Malcolm, *The New Knighthood: A History of the Order of the Temple* (Cambridge, 1994).

Barham, T., *The Ingoldsby Legends* (London, 1840).

Barker, R., 'When is a knight not a knight?', in S. Church and R. Harvey (eds.), *Medieval Knighthood* 5 (Woodbridge, 1995), 1–17.

Bate, P., *The English Pre Raphaelite Painters, their Associates and Successors* (London, 1901).

Bennett, M., 'First Crusaders' images of Muslims: the influence of vernacular poetry?', *Forum for Modern Language Studies* 22 (1986), 101–22.

——, '*La Règle du Temple* as a military manual *or* How to deliver a cavalry charge', in C. Harper-Bill, C. J. Holdsworth and J. L. Nelson (eds.), *Studies in Medieval History for R. Allen Brown* (Woodbridge, 1987), 7–19.

Berges, W., *Die Fürstenspiegel des hohen und späten Mittelalters* (Leipzig, 1938).

Blamires, Alcuin, *The Case for Women in Medieval Culture* (Oxford, 1997).

Bloch, R. Howard, *Medieval Misogyny and the Invention of Western Romantic Love* (Chicago and London, 1991).

Bloss, Celestia Angenette, *Heroines of the Crusades* (Auburn, NY, 1853).

Bolton, B., '*Paupertas Christi*: old wealth and new poverty in the twelfth century', in D. Baker (ed.), *Renaissance and Renewal in Christian History* (Oxford, 1977), 95–103.

Bouhier, B., *Observation sur la coutume de Bourgogne* (Dijon, 1787).

Bradbury, J., *The Medieval Siege* (Woodbridge, 1992).

Brady, L. A., 'Essential and despised: images of women in the First and Second Crusades: 1095–1148', MA thesis (Windsor, Ontario, 1992).

Brandt, W. J., 'Pierre Dubois: modern or medieval?', *AHR* 35 (1929/30), 507–21.

Bridrey, R., *Le Statut juridique des croisés* (Paris, 1901).

Brodman, J., *Ransoming Captives in Crusader Spain: The Order of Merced on the Christian–Islamic Frontier* (Philadelphia, 1986).

Brown, R., *The Normans* (London, 1984).

Brundage, J., 'An errant crusader: Stephen of Blois', *Traditio* 21 (1960), 380–95.

——, 'Prostitution, miscegenation and sexual purity in the First Crusade', in *CS* 57–64.

——, 'The crusader's wife: a canonistic quandary', *Studia Gratiana* 12 (1967), 425–41.

——, 'The marriage law in the Latin kingdom of Jerusalem', in *Outremer*, 258–71.

——, 'The votive obligations of crusaders: the development of a canonistic doctrine', in idem (ed.), *The Crusades, Holy War and Canon War* (Aldershot, 1991), 77–118.

Buckler, G., *Anna Comnena* (Oxford, 1929).

Büttner, H., 'Die Beziehungen der heiligen Hildegard von Bingen zu Kurie, Erzbischof und Kaiser', in *Universitas: Festschrift A. Stohr* (Mainz, 1960), 2: 60–8.

Bynum, Caroline Walker, *Jesus as Mother: Studies in the Spirituality of the High Middle Ages* (Berkeley, CA, 1982).

——, '. . . And woman his humanity', in eadem (ed.), *Fragmentation and Redemption: Essays on Gender and the Human Body in Medieval Religion* (New York, 1992), 151–79.

Caenegem, R. C. van, *Criminal Law in England and Flanders under King Henry II and Count Philip of Alsace* (Gent, 1982).

Cahen, C., *La Syrie du Nord à l'époque des croisades et la principauté d'Antioche* (Paris, 1940).

Caille, J., 'Les Seigneurs de Narbonne dans le conflit Toulouse–Barcelone au xiie siècle', *Annales du Midi* 97 (1985), 227–44.

Cambridge History of English Literature (Cambridge, 1915).

Carlson, C. L., and A. J. Weir, *Constructions of Widowhood and Virginity in the Middle Ages* (Basingstoke, 1999).

Chalandon, F., *Essai sur le règne d'Alexis I Comnène* (Paris, 1900).

Charanis, P., 'Byzantium, the West, and the origin of the First Crusade', *Byzantion* 19 (1949), 17–36.

Cheynet, J-C., *Pouvoir et contestations à Byzance (963–1210)* (Paris, 1990).

Ciggaar, K. N., 'Flemish counts and emperors: friends and foreigners in Byzantium', in V. D. van Aalst and K. N. Ciggaar (eds.), *The Latin Empire: Some Contributions* (Hernen, 1994), 33–62.

Cipollone, Giulio, *Christianità–Islam: Cattività e liberazione in nome di Dio. Il tempo di Innocenzo III dopo 'il 1187'* (Rome, 1992).

Clarke, G., *'This Female Man of God': Women and Spiritual Power in the Patristic Age AD 350–450* (London, 1995).

Cole, Penny, '"O, God, the Heathen have come into Your Inheritance" (Ps. 78.1): the theme of religious pollution in crusade documents, 1095–1188', in Maya Schatzmiller (ed.), *Crusaders and Muslims in Twelfth-Century Syria* (Leiden, 1993), 84–111.

Contamine, P., *War in the Middle Ages* (Cambridge, 1994).

Coombs, T., *Watercolours: The Charles Lees Collection at Oldham Art Gallery* (Oldham, 1993).

Cowdrey, H. E. J., *Pope Gregory VII* (Oxford, 1998).

Curtius, R., 'Der Kreuzzugsgedanke und das Altfranzösische Epos', in idem (ed.), *Gesammelte Aufsätze zur romanischen Philologie* (Bern and Munich, 1960), 98–105.

Daniel, N., *The Arabs and Mediaeval Europe* (London, 1975).

——, *Heroes and Saracens: A Re-interpretation of the Chansons de Geste* (Edinburgh, 1984).

Delaruelle, É., 'L'Idée de croisade chez Saint Bernard', in *Mélanges Saint Bernard* (Dijon, 1953), 53–67.

Derolez, A., 'The manuscript transmission of Hildegard of Bingen's writings: the state of the problem', in C. Burnett and P. Dronke (eds.), *Hildegard of Bingen: The Context of her Thought and Art* (London, 1998), 17–28.

Deschamps, Paul, and Marc Thibaut, *La Peinture murale en France: Le Haut Moyen Age et l'époque romane* (Paris, 1951).

Diaconu, P., *Les Pétchénègues au Bas-Danube* (Bucharest, 1970).

Dictionary of National Biography (London, 1908 edn.).

Dillard, H., *Daughters of the Reconquest: Women in Castilian Town Society* (Cambridge, 1984).

Dinzelbacher, P., 'Pour une histoire de l'amour au moyen âge', *Le Moyen Age*, 5th series, 1 (1987), 228–41.

Dronke, P., *Women Writers in the Middle Ages* (Cambridge, 1984).

Drory, Joseph, 'New data on Muslims in Palestine under the crusades' (17th International Conference of CISH, Madrid 1990: unpublished).

Duby, G., *The Three Orders: Feudal Society Imagined* (London, 1980).

——, *Le Chevalier, la dame et le prêtre* (Paris, 1981).

—— and M. Perrot (eds.), *A History of Women*, 2: *Silences of the Middle Ages* (Cambridge, MA, 1992).

Dunbabin, J., 'William of Tyre and Philip of Alsace', *Academiae Analecta* 48 (1986), 109–17.

Edbury, P. W., 'Feudal obligations in the Latin East', *Byzantion* 47 (1977), 345–7.

——, and J. G. Rowe, *William of Tyre: Historian of the Latin East* (Cambridge, 1988).

Edgington, Susan B., 'The First Crusade: reviewing the evidence', in Jonathan Phillips (ed.), *The First Crusade: Origins and Impact* (Manchester, 1997), 55–77.

——, 'Albert of Aachen and the *chansons de geste*', in *Crusades Sources*, 23–37.

——, 'Romance and reality in the sources for the sieges of Antioch, 1097–8', forthcoming in Charalambos Dendrinos, Jonathan Harris, Eirene Harvalia-Crook and Judith Herrin (eds.), *Porphyrogenita: Studies in Honour of Julian Chrysostomides* (Aldershot, 2003).

Engels, O., 'Die Zeit der hl. Hildegard', in A. Ph. Brück (ed.), *Hildegard von Bingen 1179–1979: Festschrift zum 800. Todestag der Heiligen* (Mainz, 1979), 1–29.

Erdmann, C., *Die Entstehung der Kreuzzugsgedanke* (Stuttgart, 1935).

——, *The Origin of the Idea of Crusade* (Princeton, 1977).

Farmer, Sharon, 'Persuasive voices: clerical images of medieval wives', *Speculum* 61 (1986), 517–43.

Ferrante, Joan, *Woman as Image in Medieval Literature: From the Twelfth Century to Dante* (New York, 1975).

Finucane, R., *Soldiers of the Faith: Crusaders and Moslems at War* (London, 1977).

Flanagan, S., *Hildegard of Bingen 1098–1179: A Visionary Life* (London, 1989).

Flandrin, J., *Families in Former Times: Kinship, Household and Sexuality* (Cambridge, 1979).

Flood, B., 'St Bernard's view of crusade', *The Australasian Catholic Record* 47 (1970), 130–43.

Flori, J., 'De la chevalerie féodale à la chevalerie chrétienne? La notion de service chevalereque dans les très anciennes chansons de geste françaises', '*Militia Christi' e crociata nei secoli XI–XIII: Miscellanea del Centro di studi medioevali* 13 (Milan, 1992), 67–101.

——, 'Pur eshalcier sainte crestiënté: croisade, guerre sainte et guerre juste dans les anciennes chansons de geste françaises', *Le Moyen Age* 97 (1997), 171–87.

——, 'Réforme, reconquista, croisade (l'idée de reconquête dans la correspondance pontificale d'Alexandre II à Urbain II)', in idem (ed.), *Croisade et chevalerie, XIe–XIIe siècles* (Brussels, 1998), 51–80.

Forey, Alan, *The Templars in the Corona de Aragón* (London, 1973).

——, 'Literacy and learning in the military orders during the twelfth and thirteenth centuries', in Helen Nicholson (ed.), *The Military Orders*, 2: *Welfare and Warfare* (Aldershot, 1998), 185–206.

Forster, E. (ed.), *Hildegard von Bingen: Prophetin durch die Zeiten: Zum 900. Geburtstag* (Freiburg, 1998).

Forster, M., *Elizabeth Barrett Browning* (London, 1988).

France, J., 'The departure of Tatikios from the crusader army', *BIHR* 44 (1971), 137–47.

——, 'Anna Comnena, the *Alexiad* and the First Crusade', *Reading Medieval Studies* 10 (1984), 20–38.

——, *Victory in the East* (Cambridge, 1994).

——, 'The Anonymous *Gesta Francorum* and the *Historia Francorum qui ceperunt Iherusalem* of Raymond of Aguilers and the *Historia de Hierosolymitano itinere* of Peter Tudebode: an analysis of the textual relationship between primary sources for the First Crusade', in *Crusades Sources*, 39–70.

Frappell, L. O. (ed.), *Principalities, Powers and Estates: Studies in Medieval and Early Modern Government and Society* (Adelaide, 1979).

Friedman, M. A., 'New sources from the Geniza for the crusader period and for Maimonides and his descendants' (Hebrew), *Cathedra* 40 (1986), 63–82.

Führkötter, A., *Hildegard von Bingen* (Salzburg, 1972).

Gervers, Michael (ed.), *The Second Crusade and the Cistercians* (New York, 1992).

Gibbon, E., *The History of the Decline and Fall of the Roman Empire* (London, 1776–88), and ed. D. Womersley (3 vols., London, 1994).

Goitein, S. D., 'Geniza sources for the crusader period: a survey', *Outremer*, 306–22.

Gravdal, Kathryn, *Ravishing Maidens: Writing Rape in Medieval French Literature and Law* (Philadelphia, 1991).

Hagenmeyer, H., *La Chronologie de la première croisade* (Paris, 1902).

Hamilton, B., 'Women in the crusader states: the queens of Jerusalem (1100–1190)', in Derek Baker (ed.), *Medieval Women* (Oxford, 1975), 143–74.

——, 'The titular nobility of the Latin East: the case of Agnes of Courtenay', in *CS* 197–201.

——, 'Miles of Plancy and the fief of Beirut', in *Horns*, 136–46.

——, *The Leper King and his Heirs: Baldwin IV and the Crusader Kingdom of Jerusalem* (Cambridge, 2000).

Harper-Bill, C., C. J. Holdsworth and J. L. Nelson (eds.), *Studies in Medieval History for R. Allen Brown* (Woodbridge, 1987).

He Agia Endoxos Megalomartus kai Paneuphemos Euphemia (Kateríni, 1997).

Hemptinne, Th. de and M. Parisse, 'Thierry d'Alsace, comte de Flandre: biographie et actes', *Annales de l'Est* 43 (1991), 83–108.

——, 'Les Épouses des croisés et pèlerins flamands au XIe et XIIe siècles: l'exemple des comtesses de Flandre Clémence et Sybille', in *Autour*, 83–95.

Herlihy, D., *Opera Muliebra: Women and Work in Medieval Europe* (Philadelphia, 1990).

Hill, B., 'Imperial women and the ideology of womanhood in the eleventh and twelfth centuries', in L. James (ed.), *Women, Men and Eunuchs: Gender in Byzantium* (London, 1997), 76–99.

——, *Imperial Women in Byzantium 1025–1204: Power, Patronage and Ideology* (Harlow, 1999).

Hill, J. H. and L. L., 'The convention of Alexius Comnenus and Raymond of St. Gilles', *AHR* 58 (1953), 322–7.

Holt, James C., *Magna Carta* (Cambridge, 1965).

Holum, K. and R. L. Hohlfelder (eds.), *King Herod's Dream: Cesarea on the Sea* (New York, 1988).

Honeycutt, L. L., 'Female succession and the language of power in the writings of twelfth-century churchmen', in J. C. Parsons (ed.), *Medieval Queenship* (Stroud, 1994), 189–201.

Hönmann, M.-A., 'Die Morgenröte (aurora) bei Hildegard von Bingen: Symbol für die "andere", die göttliche Dimension', *Erbe und Auftrag: Benediktinische Zeitschrift* 71 (1995), 486–95.

Howard-Johnston, J., 'Anna Komnene and the *Alexiad*', in M. Mullett and D. Smythe (eds.), *Alexios I Komnenos* (Belfast, 1996).

——, 'Gibbon and the middle period of the Byzantine Empire', in R. McKitterick and R. Quinault (eds.), *Edward Gibbon and Empire* (Cambridge, 1997), 53–77.

Huyghebaert, N., 'Une comtesse de Flandre à Béthanie', *Les Cahiers de Saint-André* 21 (1964), 1–13.

Irwin, Robert, 'Usamah ibn Munqidh: an Arab–Syrian gentleman at the time of the crusades reconsidered', in *Crusades Sources*, 71–88.

Iversen, G., 'Tradition och förnyelse i Hildegards vision om dygderna', in M. Asztalos and C. Gejrot (eds.), *Symbolae Septentrionales in honorem J. Öberg* (Stockholm, 1995), 73–102.

James, C., 'Women, death and the law', in D. Wood (ed.), *Martyrs and Martyrologies* (Studies in Church History, 30; Oxford 1993).

Jewell, Helen, *Women in Medieval England* (Manchester, 1996).

Johnen, J., 'Philipp von Elsass, Graf von Flandern, 1157 (1163)-1191', *Bulletin de la commission royale d'histoire* 79 (1910), 341–469.

Kaeuper, R. W., *Chivalry and Violence in Medieval Europe* (Oxford, 1999).

Kagay, D. J., and L. J. A. Villalon (eds.), *The Circle of War in the Middle Ages* (Woodbridge, 1999).

Kambylis A., 'Zum "Programm" der byzantinischen Historikerin Anna Komnene', in K. Vourveris and A. Skiadas (eds.), *Dorema: Hans Diller zum 70. Geburtstag* (Athens, 1975), 127–46.

Kazhdan A., 'Die Liste der Kinder des Alexios I in einer Moskauer Handschrift (GIM 53/147)', in R. Stiehl and H. Stier (eds.), *Beiträge zur alten Geschichte und deren Nachleben: Festschrift für F. Altheim* (2 vols., Berlin, 1969–70), 1: 233–7.

——, and G. Constable, *People and Power in Byzantium* (Washington, DC, 1982).

Kedar, B. Z., 'Palmarée Abbaye Clunisienne du XIIe siècle en Galilée', *Revue Bénédictine* 93 (1983), 260–9.

——, *Crusade and Mission* (Princeton, NJ, 1984).

——, 'The subjected Muslims of the Frankish Levant', in J. M. Powell (ed.), *Muslims under Latin Rule 1100–1300* (Princeton, NJ, 1990), 135–74.

—— (ed.), *The Horns of Hattin, Proceedings of the Second Conference of the Society for the Study of the Crusades and the Latin East* (Jerusalem, 1992).

Kelly, A., *Eleanor of Aquitaine and the Four Kings* (Cambridge, 1950).

Kelly, K. C., *Performing Virginity and Testing Chastity in the Middle Ages* (London, 2000).

Khadduri, M., *War and Peace in the Law of Islam* (Baltimore, 1955).

Klaes, M., 'Von einer Briefsammlung zum literarischen Briefbuch: Anmerkungen zur Überlieferung der Briefe Hildegards von Bingen', in E. Forster (ed.), *Hildegard von Bingen: Prophetin durch die Zeiten: Zum 900. Geburtstag* (Freiburg, 1998), 153–70.

Kleinbaum, A. W., *The War against the Amazons* (New York, 1983).

Kraus, Henry, 'Eve and Mary: conflicting images of medieval woman', in idem (ed.), *The Living Theatre of Medieval Art* (Bloomington, IN, 1967), 41–62.

Krey, A. C., 'A neglected passage in the *Gesta* and its bearing on the literature of the First Crusade', in Louis J. Paetow (ed.), *The Crusades and Other Historical Essays presented to Dana C. Munro* (Freeport, NY, 1928), 57–78.

Laarhoven, J. van, 'Chrétienté et croisade: une tentative terminologique', *Cristianesimo nella storia* 6 (1985), 27–43.

Laiou, A., 'The role of women in Byzantine society', *Jahrbuch der Österreichischen Byzantinistik* 31 (1981), 233–60.

——, 'Observations on the life and ideology of Byzantine women', *Byzantinische Forschungen* 9 (1985), 59–102.

Lambert, S., 'Heroines and Saracens', *Medieval World* 1 (1991), 3–9.

——, 'Queen or consort: rulership and politics in the Latin East, 1118–1228', in Anne J. Duggan (ed.), *Queen and Queenship in Medieval Europe: Proceedings of a Conference Held at King's College, London, April 1995* (Woodbridge, 1997), 153–69.

LaMonte, J. L., 'The lords of Caesarea in the period of the crusades', *Speculum* 22 (1947), 152–4.

Landon, L. E., *Poetical Works*, 4 vols. (London, 1853).

Lane, W. G., *Richard Harris Barham* (Columbia, MO, 1967).

La Villemarque, H. de, *Barzaz Breiz: Chants populaires de la Bretagne* (4th edn., Paris, 1846).

Leclercq, J., 'L'Attitude spirituelle de S. Bernard devant la guerre', *Collectanea Cisterciensia* 36 (1974), 195–225.

——, 'L'Encyclique de saint Bernard en faveur de la croisade', in idem, *Recueil d'études sur Saint Bernard et ses écrits*, 4 (Rome, 1987), 227–46.

——, *La donna e le donne nel pensiero di San Bernardo* (Milan, 1997).

Leyser, Henrietta, *Medieval Women: A Social History of Women in England 450–1500* (London, 1995).

Lilie, R.-J., *Byzantium and the Crusader States* (Oxford, 1993).

Lindeman, H., 'S. Hildegard en hare Nederlandische vrienden', *Ons Geestlijk Erf* 2 (1928), 128–60.

Liubarskii, Ia., 'Zamechaniya k khronologii XI knigi "Aleksiada" Annyi Komninoi', *Vizantiiskii Vremmenik* 24 (1963), 47–56.

——, *Aleksiada* (Moscow, 1965).

Lockhart, J., *Memoirs of the Life of Sir Walter Scott* (5 vols., Edinburgh, 1878).

Loengard, Janet Senderowitz, '*Of the Gift of her Husband:* English dower and its consequences in the year 1200', in Julius Kirshner and Suzanne F. Wemple (eds.), *Women of the Medieval World: Essays in Honor of John H. Mundy* (Oxford, 1985), 215–55.

Lozar, A., 'Hildegard von Bingen und Bernard von Clairvaux', *Unsere Liebe Frau von Himmerod* 68 (1998), 8–18.

McLaughlin, Megan, 'The woman warrior: gender, warfare and society in medieval Europe', *Women's Studies* 17 (1990), 193–209.

Macrides, R., 'The historian in the history', in C. Constantinides, N. Panagiotakes, E. Jeffreys and A. Angelou (eds.), *Filellen: Studies in Honour of Robert Browning* (Venice, 1996), 205–24.

Magdalino, P., 'The pen of the aunt: echoes of the mid-twelfth century in the *Alexiad*', in T. Gouma-Peterson (ed.), *Anna Komnene and her Times* (New York, 2000), 15–43.

Maier, C., 'Crisis, liturgy and the crusade in the twelfth and thirteenth centuries', *JEH* 48 (1997), 628–57.

——, 'Mass, the Eucharist and the Cross: Innocent III and the relocation of the crusade', in John C. Moore (ed.), *Pope Innocent III and his World* (Aldershot, 1999), 351–60.

Maier, Christel, 'Die Bedeutung der Farben im Werk Hildegardis von Bingen', *Frühmittelalterliche Studien* 6 (1972), 245–355.

——, 'Ildegarde di Bingen: profezia ed esistenza letteraria', *Cristianesimo nella storia* 17 (1996), 271–303.

Marshall, C., *Warfare in the Latin East 1192–1291* (Cambridge, 1994).

Mayer, H. E., 'Studies in the history of Queen Melisende of Jerusalem', *Dumbarton Oaks Papers* 26 (1972), 93–189.

——, *Das Siegelwesen in den Kreuzfahrerstaaten* (Abhandlungen der Bayrischen Akademie der Wissenschaften. Phil.-Hist. Klasse, Neue Folge 83; Munich, 1978).

——, 'Carving up crusaders: the early Ibelins and Ramla', in *Outremer*, 107–29.

——, 'Henry II of England and the Holy Land', *EHR* 97 (1982), 721–39.

——, 'Études sur l'histoire de Baudouin Ier roi de Jérusalem', in idem, *Mélanges sur l'histoire du royaume latin de Jérusalem* (Paris, 1983), 73–91.

——, 'The double county of Jaffa and Ascalon: one fief or two?', in *CS* 181–90.

Mazeika, R., '"Nowhere was the fragility of their sex apparent": women warriors in the Baltic crusade chronicles', in A. V. Murray (ed.), *From Clermont to Jerusalem: The Crusades and Crusader Societies* (Turnhout, 1998), 229–48.

Meschini, M., *San Bernardo e la seconda crociata* (Milan, 1998).

Metz, Renée, 'Le Statut de la femme en droit canonique médiéval', in eadem, *La Femme et l'enfant dans le droit canonique médiéval* (London, 1985), 59–113.

Michell, N., *The Saxon's Daughter: A Tale of the Crusades* (London, 1835).

'Militia Christi' e crociata nei secoli XI–XII: Atti della undecima Settimana internazionale di studi medioevali, Mendola, 28 agosto–1 settembre 1989 (Milan, 1992).

Millais, J. G., *The Life and Letters of J. E. Millais* (2 vols., London, 1899).

Morris, Colin, 'The Gesta Francorum as narrative history', *Reading Medieval Studies* 19 (1993), 55–71.

Morrison, K. F., *History as Visual Art* (Princeton, 1990).

Motherwell, W., *Poems* (Paisley, 1881).

Murray, A. V., 'The origins of the Frankish nobility of the kingdom of Jerusalem, 1100–1118', *Mediterranean Historical Review* 4 (1989), 281–300.

——, 'Baldwin II and his nobles: factionalism and dissent in the kingdom of Jerusalem, 1118–1134', *Nottingham Medieval Studies* 38 (1994), 60–85.

——, 'Ethnic identity in the crusader states: the Franks and the settlement of Outremer', in S. Forde, L. Johnson and A. Murray (eds.), *Concepts of National Identity in the Middle Ages* (Leeds, 1995), 59–73.

Newman, B., *Sister of Wisdom: St Hildegard's Theology of the Feminine* (Berkeley, CA, 1987).

Nicholson, H. J., *Templars, Hospitallers and Teutonic Knights: Images of the Military Orders, 1128–1291* (Leicester, 1993).

——, 'Women on the Third Crusade', *JMH* 23 (1997), 335–49.

Nickerson, M. E., 'The seigneury of Beirut in the twelfth century and the Brisebarre family of Beirut-Blanchegarde', *Byzantion* 19 (1949), 141–85.

Nicolle, D., *Medieval Warfare Source Book* (2 vols., New York, 1996).

Noonan, J., *Contraception: A History of its Treatment by Catholic Theologians and Canonists* (Cambridge, MA, 1966).

Onclin, W., 'L'Age requis pour le mariage dans la doctrine canonique médiévale', in Stephan Kuttner and J. J. Ryan (eds.), *Proceedings of the Second*

International Congress of Medieval Canon Law: Monumenta iuris canonici, ser. C, vol. 1 (Vatican City, 1965), 237–47.

Oroz Reta, J., 'La Sibila del Rhin: misión profética de sancta Hildegarda de Bingen', *Latomus* 53 (1994), 608–34.

O'Shaughnessy, A., *The Lays of France* (London, 1872).

Owen, D. D. R., *Eleanor of Aquitaine: Queen and Legend* (Oxford, 1993).

Packer, L. M. (ed.), *The Rossetti–Macmillan Letters* (Cambridge, 1963).

Parsons, John Carmi, 'Family, sex, and power: the rhythms of medieval queenship', in idem (ed.), *Medieval Queenship* (Stroud, 1994), 1–11.

Paterson, Linda, 'Knights and the concept of knighthood in the twelfth-century Occitan epic', in W. H. Jackson (ed.), *Knighthood in Medieval Literature* (Woodbridge, 1981), 23–38.

Pellegrini, M., 'L'idea di Christianitas nei cronisti latini della prima crociata', *Rivista di Bizantinistica* 1 (1991), 69–99.

Pernoud, R., *Storia e visioni di sant'Ildegarda* (Casale Monferrato, 1996).

Phillips, J., *Defenders of the Holy Land: Relations between the Latin East and West, 1119–1187* (Oxford, 1996).

——, 'Saint Bernard of Clairvaux, the Low Countries and the Lisbon Letter of the Second Crusade', *JEH* 48 (1997), 485–97.

——, 'The murder of Charles the Good and the Second Crusade: household, nobility, and traditions of crusading in medieval Flanders', *Medieval Prosopography* 19 (1998), 55–76.

Pitre-Chevalier, M., *La Bretagne ancienne* (Paris, 1859).

Polemis, D., *The Doukai* (London, 1968).

Porges, W., 'The clergy, the poor and the non-combatants on the First Crusade', *Speculum* 21 (1946), 1–23.

Powell, James M., *Anatomy of a Crusade, 1213–1221* (Philadelphia, 1986).

——, 'The role of women in the Fifth Crusade', in *Horns*, 294–301.

Power, Eileen, *Medieval Women,* ed. M. M. Postan (Cambridge, 1975).

Prawer, J., *Histoire du Royaume Latin de Jérusalem* (2 vols., Paris, 1969); English trans., *A History of the Latin Kingdom of Jerusalem* (London, 1972).

——, *The Latin Kingdom of Jerusalem: European Colonialism in the Middle Ages* (London, 1972).

——, *Crusader Institutions* (Oxford, 1980).

Princes as Patrons: The Art Collections of the Princes of Wales from the Renaissance to the Present Day: An Exhibition from the Royal Collection (London, 1998).

Pringle, Denys, 'Reconstructing the castle of Safad', *Palestine Exploration Quarterly* 117 (1985), 139–48.

Purcell, M., 'Women crusaders: a temporary canonical aberration?', in L. O. Frappell (ed.), *Principalities, Powers and Estates: Studies in Medieval and Early Modern Government and Society* (Adelaide, 1979), 57–67.

QED, *The Knight's Heart* (Belfast, 1875).

Raedts, P., 'The Children's Crusade of 1212', *JMH* 3 (1977), 279–324.

Randall, L. M. C., *Images in the Margins of Gothic Manuscripts* (Berkeley and Los Angeles, CA, 1966).

Ranff, V., 'Durch Mitwirken antworten: "Iustitia" und "Misericordia" als Ausdruck der interpersonalen Konstitution des Menschen', in E. Forster (ed.), *Hildegard von Bingen: Prophetin durch die Zeiten: Zum 900. Geburtstag* (Freiburg, 1998), 249–61.

Reilly, C. W., *Mid-Victorian Poetry 1860–79: An Annotated Bibliography* (London, 1999).

Rey, E., 'Les Seigneurs de Mont-Réal et de la Terre d'outre le Jourdain', *ROL* 4 (1896), 19–24.

Richard, J., 'Le Statut de la femme dans l'Orient Latin', *La Femme, 2: Recueils de la Société Jean Bodin pour l'Histoire Comparative des Institutions* 12 (Brussels, 1962), 377–87.

——, 'Urbain II, la prédication de la croisade et la définition d'indulgence', in E.-D. Hehl, H. Seibert and F. Staub (eds.), *Deus qui mutat tempora: Menschen und Institutionen im Wandel des Mittelalters. Festschrift für Alfons Becker* (Sigmaringen, 1987), 129–35.

Riley-Smith, J. S. C., *The Feudal Nobility and the Kingdom of Jerusalem, 1174–1277* (London, 1973).

——, *The First Crusade and the Idea of Crusading* (London, 1986).

——, *The Crusades: A Short History* (London, 1987).

——, 'Family traditions and participation in the Second Crusade', in Michael Gervers (ed.), *The Second Crusade and the Cistercians* (New York, 1992), 101–8.

——, 'The state of mind of crusaders to the East 1095–1300', in idem (ed.), *The Oxford Illustrated History of the Crusades* (Oxford, 1995), 66–91.

——, *The First Crusaders (1095–1131)* (Cambridge 1997).

—— (ed.), *The Oxford Illustrated History of the Crusades* (Oxford, 1995).

Rogers, R., *Latin Siege Warfare in the Twelfth Century* (Oxford, 1992).

Roscher, Helmut, *Papst Innocenz III und die Kreuzzüge* (Göttingen, 1969).

Rousset, P., *Les Origines et les caractères de la première croisade* (Geneva, 1945).

——, 'Etienne de Blois, croisé fuyard et martyr', *Genava*, NS 11 (1963), 183–95.

——, 'La Notion de Chrétienté aux XIe et XIIe siècles', *Le Moyen Age* 58 (1963), 191–203.

Routledge, M., 'Songs', in J. S. C. Riley-Smith (ed.), *The Oxford Illustrated History of the Crusades* (Oxford, 1995), 91–111.

Runciman, S., *History of the Crusades* (3 vols., Cambridge, 1952–5).

Russel, E., 'Bernard et les dames de son temps', in Commission d'Histoire de l'Ordre de Citeaux (ed.), *Bernard de Clairvaux* (Paris, 1953), 411–25.

Saint-Hilaire, Paul de, *Les Sceaux des Templiers et leurs symboles* (Puiseaux, 1991).

Schein, Sylvia, 'The future *regnum Hierusalem*: a chapter in medieval state planning', *JMH* 10 (1984), 101–3.

——, 'Bridget of Sweden, Margery Kempe, and women's Jerusalem pilgrimages in the middle ages', *Mediterranean History Review* 14 (1999), 44–58.

Schmeidler, B., 'Bemerkungen zum Korpus der Briefe der hl. Hildegard von Bingen', in E. E. Stengel (ed.), *Corona Quernea: Festgabe K. Strecker* (Leipzig, 1941), 335–66.

Schrader, M., and A. Führkötter, *Die Echtheit des Schrifttums der heiligen Hildegard von Bingen: Quellenkritische Untersuchungen* (Cologne and Graz, 1956).

Schulenburg, J. T., *Forgetful of their Sex* (Chicago, 1998).

Scott, L., 'Marriage, class and royal lordship in England under Henry III', *Viator* 16 (1985), 181–207.

Scott, R., 'The classical tradition in Byzantine historiography', in M. Mullett and R. Scott (eds.), *Byzantium and the Classical Tradition* (Birmingham, 1991), 61–74.

Searle, Eleanor, 'Seigneurial control of women's marriage: the antecedents and function of merchet in England', *Past and Present* 82 (1979), 3–14.

Sejourné, P., 'Les Correspondants de Sainte Hildegarde à Utrecht', *Nederlandsch archief voor kerkgeschiedenis*, NS 16 (1921), 144–62.

Selwood, Dominic, *Knights of the Cloister: Templars and Hospitallers in Central-Southern Occitania 1100–1300* (Woodbridge, 1999).

Setton, K. M. (ed.), *A History of the Crusades*, vol. 6 (Madison, WI, 1989).

Shahar, Shulamith, *The Fourth Estate: A History of Women in the Middle Ages* (London and New York, 1983).

Shepard, J., 'Aspects of Byzantine attitudes and policy towards the West in the 10th and 11th centuries', *Byzantinische Forschungen* 13 (1988), 67–118.

——, 'When Greek meets Greek: Alexius Comnenus and Bohemund in 1097–8', *Byzantine and Modern Greek Studies* 12 (1988), 185–277.

Shlosser, F., 'The *Alexiad* of Anna Comnena as a source for the crusades', *Byzantinische Forschungen* 15 (1990), 397–406.

Siberry, E., *Criticism of Crusading 1095–1274* (Oxford, 1985).

Siberry, J. E., 'Troubadours, trouvères and minnesingers and the crusades', in *Studi Medievali*, 3rd series, 29 (1988), 19–43.

——, *The New Crusaders: Images of the Crusades in the Nineteenth and Early Twentieth Centuries* (Aldershot, 2000).

Skoulatos, B., *Les Personnages byzantins de l'Alexiade: Analyse prosopographique et synthèse* (Louvain, 1980).

Smail, R. C., *Crusading Warfare 1097–1193* (Cambridge, 1956).

Solterer, H., 'Figures of female militancy in medieval France', *Signs* 16 (1991), 522–49.

Southern, R.W., 'Aspects of the European tradition of historical writing, 3: history as prophecy', *TRHS* 22 (1972), 159–80.

Stafford, P., *Unification and Conquest: A Political and Social History of England in the Tenth and Eleventh Century* (London, 1989).

——, 'The portrayal of royal women in England, mid-tenth to mid-twelfth centuries', in John Carmi Parsons (ed.), *Medieval Queenship* (Stroud, 1994), 143–67.

——, *Queen Emma and Queen Edith: Queenship and Women's Power in Eleventh-Century England* (Oxford, 1997).

Stevenson, W. B., *The Crusaders in the East* (Cambridge, 1907).

Stock, L. K., '"Arms and the (wo)man in medieval romance: the gendered arming of female warriors in the *Roman d'Eneas* and Heldris's *Roman de Silence*', *Arthuriana* 5 (1995), 56–83.

Stocker, M., *Royalist and Realist: The Life and Work of Sir Joseph Edgar Boehm* (London, 1988).

Strickland, A., *Lives of the Queens of England* (12 vols., London, 1840–7).

Strobel, Margaret, *European Women and the Second British Empire* (Bloomington, IN, 1991).

Tangl, G. (ed.), *Studien zum Register Innocenz' III* (Weimar, 1929).

Taylor, T. (ed.), *Ballads and Songs of Brittany* (London, 1865).

'The crusading kingdom of Jerusalem: the first European colonial society?' A symposium, in *Horns*, 341–66.

Thomas, R., 'Anna Comnena's account of the First Crusade: history and politics in the reign of the emperors Alexius I and Manuel I Comnenus', *Byzantine and Modern Greek Studies* 15 (1991), 269–312.

Thompson, Roger, *Women in Stuart England and America: A Comparative Study* (London and Boston, 1974).

Throop, Palmer A., *Criticism of the Crusade: A Study of Public Opinion and Crusade Propaganda* (Amsterdam, 1940).

Tibble, Steven, *Monarchy and Lordship in the Latin Kingdom of Jerusalem 1099–1291* (Oxford, 1989).

Tommasi, Francesco, 'I Templari e il culto delle reliquie', in G. Minucci and F. Sardi (eds.), *I Templari: mito e storia. Atti del convegno internazionale di studi alla magione Templare di Poggibonsi–Siena* (Siena, 1989), 191–210.

Topping, Peter W., *Feudal Institutions as Revealed in the Assises of Romania: The Law Code of Frankish Greece* (Philadelphia, 1949).

Traux, Jean A., 'Anglo-Norman women at war: valiant soldiers, prudent strategists or charismatic leaders?', in D. J. Kagay and L. J. A. Villalon (eds.), *The Circle of War in the Middle Ages* (Woodbridge, 1999), 111–25.

Trinder, P. W., *Mrs Hemans* (Cardiff, 1984).

Tyerman, C., *England and the Crusades* (Chicago, 1988).

——, 'Who went on crusades to the Holy Land?' in *Horns*, 13–26.

Varzos, K., *He Genealogia tôn Komnenôn* (2 vols., Thessalonica, 1984).

Verbruggen, J. F., *The Art of Warfare in Western Europe during the Middle Ages from the Eighth Century to 1340*, 2nd edn. by S. Willard and R. W. Southern (Woodbridge, 1997).

Vogel, C., 'Le Pèlerinage pénitentiel', in A. Faivre (ed.), *En rémission des pechés: Recherches sur les systèmes pénitentiels dans l'Église latine* (Aldershot, 1994), paper VII, pp. 113–53.

Webb, D., *Pilgrims and Pilgrimage in the Medieval West* (London, 2000).

Weever, Jacqueline de, *Sheba's Daughters: Whitening and Demonising the Saracen Woman in Medieval French Epic* (New York and London, 1998).

Werveke, H. van, 'Filips van de Elzas en Willelm von Tyrus: een episode uit de geschiedenis van de kruistochten', *Mededelingen van de koninklijke Vlaamse Academie voor Wetenschappen, Letteren en Schone Kunsten van België, Klasse der Letteren* 33 (1971), 3–36.

——, *Een Vlaamse graaf van Europees formaat: Filips van de Elzas* (Haarlem, 1976).

Wheelwright, J., *Amazons and Military Maids: Women who Dressed as Men in Pursuit of Life, Liberty and Happiness* (London, 1989).

Widmer, B., *Heilsordnung und Zeitgeschehen in der Mystik Hildegards von Bingen* (Basel and Stuttgart, 1955).

Index